Kishwaukee College Library
21193 Malta Road
Malta, IL 60150-06
D0213902

America's War on Sex

Kishwaukee College Library
21193 Malta Road
Malta, IL 60150-9699

America's War on Sex

The Attack on Law, Lust and Liberty

Marty Klein, Ph.D

Foreword by Nadine Strossen

Sex, Love, and Psychology
Judy Kuriansky, Series Editor

Westport, Connecticut
London

Library of Congress has catalogued the hard cover edition as follows:

Klein, Marty.
    America's war on sex: the attack on lust, law and liberty. / Marty Klein ; foreword by
Nadine Strossen.

        p.   cm.—(Sex, love, and psychology, ISSN 1554–222X)
    Includes bibliographical references (p.   ) and index.
    ISBN 0–275–98785–X
    1. Sex—United States—History—20th century.   2. Sexual ethics—
United States—History—20th century.   3. Sex and law—United States—
History—20th century.   I. Title.   II. Series.
    HQ18.U5K645 2006
    306.70973—dc22   2006015708

British Library Cataloguing in Publication Data is available.

Copyright © 2006, 2008 by Marty Klein

All rights reserved. No portion of this book may be
reproduced, by any process or technique, without the
express written consent of the publisher.

Library of Congress Catalog Card Number: 2006015708
ISBN: 978-0-313-36320-7
ISSN: 1554–222X

First published in 2006

Praeger Publishers, 88 Post Road West, Westport, CT 06881
An imprint of Greenwood Publishing Group, Inc.
www.praeger.com

Printed in the United States of America

The paper used in this book complies with the
Permanent Paper Standard issued by the National
Information Standards Organization (Z39.48–1984).

10 9 8 7 6 5 4 3 2 1

*To the members of the First Amendment Lawyers Association:
Who, to protect you and your family, have pledged
their Lives, their Fortunes and their sacred Honor.*

Contents

Acknowledgments

I am a fortunate fellow. Standing at the nexus of several dynamic, creative professions, I have met many extraordinary people. I am privileged to present a work that is liberally seasoned with their ideas. It is a pleasure to publicly thank them.

My sincere thanks go to Debra Haffner, Bennett Hasselton, Kat Sunlove, Bill Taverner and Larry Walters for reading and commenting on various chapters—frequently on airplanes or while writing their own books and columns, often on tight deadlines. Each of these incredibly accomplished people took the time to challenge me to write better, and to lavish praise on me when I did. Larry also gave me a crash course in First Amendment law, for which I will always be grateful. And I'll never tell another lawyer joke again.

Many others contributed comments and answered my endless questions. I am touched to have received wise and timely help from Barry Boss, Bob Corn-Revere, Clyde DeWitt, Milo Fencl, Nancy Fencl, Rebecca Fox, Judy Hanna, Phil Harvey, Marjorie Heins, Mitchell Katine, Mark Kerns, Doug Kirby, Raymond Lawrence, Judith Levine, Ricci Levy, Donell McDonell, Robert McGinley, James Morone, Candida Royalle, Bill Smith, and Jen Heitel Yakush, very busy people all. Without them this would have been a less compelling book.

Nadine Strossen has honored me by taking this book seriously. Her energy, commitment, courage, and clarity have inspired me from the minute I discovered her many years ago.

"Intellectual posse" may sound pretentious, but it captures the respect and affection I have for the world-class thinkers who supported me before and throughout this process: Stan Dale, Larry Hedges, Peter Lehman, Janet Lever, Jack Morin, Lillian Rubin, Michael Sand, and Pepper Schwartz.

I am pleased to thank Michael Carrera, who defines the word "mensch;" Sandra Cole, whose affection is like a purifying flame; and Jim Petersen, whose lessons about combining social science, artistic writing, show business, and a wicked sense of humor I still value and turn to.

I told Cynde Moya month after month that I would need her research skills "very soon." When I finally gave her an entire manuscript to format, and asked for it back within a week, she dropped everything else in her life and prepared a handsome, very useful stack of pages.

I do not toil alone. I am heartened by the powerful and important work of many colleagues in AASECT (American Association of Sexuality Educators, Counselors and Therapists), SSSS (Society for the Scientific Study of Sexuality), and SIECUS (Sexuality Information and Education Council of the United States). Without them I would have died a thousand deaths of scholarly loneliness.

I proposed writing this book over a decade ago, but agents and publishers assured me there was no market for it. Over the years I burned to write it, but often became frustrated and considered giving up. My friends Michael Castleman and Vena Blanchard never let me forget how much I needed to complete this book, and urged me to persist. They were right. I am grateful to each of them.

Thanks to Judy Kuriansky for bringing me to the attention of Debbie Carvalko at Praeger, and thanks to Debbie for recognizing the value of my work.

My wise and dear friend Veronica Randall read every sentence of every chapter (except this one) at least once, alternately massaging and wrestling with many of them. As a result this book is easier to read, and so you and I are both very much in her debt.

Finally, I thank my wife Randi—who, just by being herself, did everything a partner could possibly do to help me write this. I may be the one who writes about the human race, but she is the one who understands it. Like I said, I'm a fortunate fellow.

Foreword

I am honored to write a Foreword to this important book by my longtime colleague in the civil liberties movement, Dr. Marty Klein.

The reasons why I consider this book so central to core civil liberties concerns can be graphically illustrated through my own family history. My beloved father was born a so-called "half-Jew" in Germany in 1922, and therefore suffered horrific human rights abuses under Hitler, including in the sexual realm. Until the day he died, my father was eternally grateful to the young woman who had been his first love, when he was a young man living in Berlin as the Nazis were rising to power. The Nazis had classified her as an "Aryan," so she was risking her own safety when she defied Hitler's strict anti-miscegenation laws and continued her relationship with my father. Meaningful as her love and loyalty were to my father, they couldn't protect him from being deported to the Buchenwald concentration camp. Ultimately, though, my father was liberated from that death camp by the American troops who saved him—literally one day before he was slated to be sterilized.

In short, I have the most profound personal stake in preserving individual freedom in the sexual realm. I owe my very existence to my father's last-minute rescue from a regime that denied such freedom, as an essential element of its overall human rights abominations.

To be sure, it has been a while since we have faced such extreme discriminatory, coercive measures in this country as those that my father faced in Nazi Germany. Nonetheless, anti-miscegenation and forced sterilization measures did constitute official U.S. policy until shockingly recently—1967, in the case of miscegenation.[1] Moreover, had it not been for constant advocacy efforts by organizations such as the ACLU, and by individuals such as Marty Klein, we might well still be subject to such repressive measures.

We must have the historic humility to recognize that it is always far easier, with twenty-twenty hindsight, to criticize past abuses—especially if they occurred elsewhere—than it is to recognize their current counterparts in our own backyards. Accordingly, Marty Klein's book shines a welcome spotlight on the many public policies today that continue to stifle full and equal freedom of choice for all mature individuals in the essential arena of sexuality.

I hope that the next generation will look back on our laws that bar marriage between individuals of the same gender with the same incredulity and shame with which we now look back on the laws from two generations ago, barring marriage between individuals of different races.

In short, in the words of the ACLU's principal founder, Roger Baldwin, "No fight for civil liberties ever stays won."[2] That in turn means, to quote a statement that has been attributed to Thomas Jefferson, which is also an ACLU motto: "Eternal vigilance is the price of liberty."[3]

Marty Klein's book vigorously rises to the challenge posed by both of these rallying cries. He explains in vivid detail the ongoing struggles to maintain freedom and equality concerning the whole spectrum of rights in the sexual realm: from the right to convey and receive medically accurate information about sexual matters; to the right to make our own choices about such fundamental, personal matters as contraception, abortion, and our sexual partners and intimacies. By documenting the mounting assaults on these essential rights, Marty is not only maintaining "eternal vigilance" himself, but also galvanizing all of you readers to do likewise.

In recent years, we have made some great strides forward in securing some rights regarding sexuality. For example, the Supreme Court has issued two pathbreaking decisions protecting the rights of lesbians and gay men,[4] and the Court also has consistently protected freedom for sexually oriented expression in various "new media," including the Internet and cable television.[5] I note these positive developments not at all to suggest that we should rest on our laurels, content with the progress we have made. To the contrary, I note the progress we have made, through education and advocacy, in the hope of encouraging all readers to raise their valued voices to help further these ongoing efforts. Marty's book is itself a valuable contribution to the ongoing struggles, and I share his hope and belief that it will in turn spur others to make their own contributions.

From my dual perspectives as a constitutional law professor and civil liberties advocate, the most important recent positive development was the Supreme Court's landmark 2003 ruling in *Lawrence v. Texas*.[6] In that case, the Court not only struck down the statute that was directly at issue—Texas's discriminatory ban on "sodomy" (oral or anal sex) only when it took place between same-gender couples. Additionally, of even more enduring consequence, the Court based its holding on broad-ranging libertarian and egalitarian rationales, which should sound the death-knell for other laws that restrict other personal conduct by consenting adults in the privacy of their homes.

Significantly, the *Lawrence* Court reversed its infamous 1986 decision in *Bowers v. Hardwick*,[7] in which the ACLU had challenged Georgia's law that criminalized all "sodomy," or oral or anal sex, even between consenting adults in the privacy of their own homes. In *Bowers,* the Court had held that government may criminalize private, consensual adult conduct, which inflicts no harm on anyone, merely because the majority of the community disapproves of the conduct. This reminds me of H.L. Mencken's famous definition of Puritanism: "the haunting fear that someone, somewhere, may be happy"![8] Seriously, it is hard to think of any purported justification for criminal laws that is more antithetical to individual liberty.

Let me quote John Stuart Mill's classic 1859 essay, "On Liberty":

> Over himself, over his own body and mind, the individual is sovereign.... [T]he only purpose for which government may rightfully exercise power ... over anyone is to prevent harm to others. His own good, either physical or moral, is not a sufficient warrant.[9]

This famous statement well captures the bedrock civil libertarian premise that undergirds the ACLU's opposition to all laws that restrict the voluntary sexual choices of mature individuals. Indeed, this core concept of liberty is so fundamental that it also undergirds many other aspects of the ACLU's overall mission: to defend all fundamental freedoms for all people. One member of the ACLU's National Board put it very well, years ago, when we were reaffirming our opposition to criminalizing drug use by consenting adults. As he said, "When it comes to their own bodies, all adults have the right to imbibe, ingest, inhale, or insert whatever they want, wherever they want!"

The Supreme Court's opinion in *Lawrence v. Texas* contains language that celebrates a similarly broad concept of individual freedom of choice generally, and I find this especially exciting given that it was written by Justice Anthony Kennedy—a conservative, Republican, Catholic, who was appointed by a conservative, Republican President, Ronald Reagan.

At the outset of his *Lawrence* opinion, Justice Kennedy ringingly recognized that constitutionally protected "liberty" encompasses not only the freedom to choose the particular kinds of sexual intimacy that were at issue in the *Lawrence* case—oral or anal sex with a same-sex partner—but also sexual intimacy in general. As he declared: "Liberty presumes an autonomy of self that includes freedom of thought, belief, expression, and certain intimate conduct."[10] It is noteworthy that Justice Kennedy ranks this constitutionally protected sexual freedom along with the time-honored First Amendment freedoms of "thought, belief, and expression," which long have been deemed so signally important that some Justices and other legal experts have called them "preferred rights."[11]

Not only does Justice Kennedy's opinion for the Court begin with an encomium to sexual freedom that would be worthy of Marty Klein himself, but also, Justice Kennedy concludes his opinion by eloquently endorsing the concept of a living, evolving Constitution in words that are worthy of the most liberal judicial activists. He proclaimed:

> "Had those who drew and ratified the Due Process Clauses . . . known the components of liberty in its manifold possibilities, they might have been more specific. [But] [t]hey did not presume to have this insight. They knew times can blind us to certain truths, and later generations can see that laws once thought necessary and proper in fact serve only to oppress. As the Constitution endures, persons in every generation can invoke its principles in their own search for greater freedom."[12]

One aspect of the *Lawrence* decision is of special significance in our ongoing struggle for rights respecting sexuality, which Marty Klein so compellingly documents. In overturning *Bowers,* the Court expressly held that laws criminalizing sexual conduct or expression cannot constitutionally be based only on majoritarian views about morality. This holding provoked the fiercest tirade in Justice Scalia's strident dissent. He rightly recognized that this holding should doom a whole host of statutes that now outlaw certain sexual choices, far beyond the discriminatory anti-sodomy statutes that were at issue in *Lawrence* itself. While these sweeping implications of *Lawrence* were the cause of Justice Scalia's consternation, for civil libertarians they are cause for celebration! As Justice Scalia wrote:

> State laws [that are only based on moral choices include laws] against . . . bigamy, same-sex marriage, adult incest, prostitution, masturbation, . . . fornication, bestiality, and obscenity. . . . Every single one of these laws is called into question by today's decision. . . . This [decision] effectively decrees the end of all morals legislation.[13]

Make no mistake about it; it will take a long, hard struggle to realize fully the liberating, equalizing potential of the *Lawrence* decision, just as it has taken a long, hard—and still ongoing—struggle to realize fully the liberating, equalizing potential of the Constitution itself. But I always like to stress the positive. So although we are now facing increasingly strong assaults on our freedoms in the realm of sexuality—as *America's War on Sex* underscores—we must take heart from the fact that we also have increasingly strong tools to combat these assaults.

That said, it is always a struggle to persuade lower court judges and other government officials to actually enforce Supreme Court decisions upholding constitutional rights. Just as the Constitution itself is not self-executing, the same is true of Supreme Court decisions that enforce the Constitution. Often these are honored in the breach, and require much litigation, including more Supreme Court rulings, to translate them into real rights for everyone, all over the country.

Just think of the long struggle, still not over, to fulfill the promise of the Supreme Court's landmark ruling against "separate but equal" public education in *Brown v. Board of Education*,[14] issued more than half a century ago.

Likewise, in the almost three years since the Court issued its landmark ruling in *Lawrence v. Texas,* we have had many disappointments, when lower court judges have read that decision as if it had no implications for any factual situation other than the one that was directly at issue in that very case.

And so, as Marty Klein's powerful book reminds us, despite civil libertarians' winning of such key battles as the one that resulted in the high court victory in *Lawrence,* the larger war goes on. At stake are all civil liberties connected with sexuality, in contexts ranging from A to Z—or, to cite two specific examples from both ends of the alphabet, from "abstinence" to "zoning." In citing "abstinence," I am referring to the increasingly prevalent abstinence-only sex "education" programs in public schools, mandated by federal and state laws, which censor medically accurate information, thereby endangering the health and even lives of our nation's young people. In citing "zoning," I am referring to laws that discriminatorily exile from our communities any businesses that engage in sexual expression, including bookstores that specialize in materials for the LGBT community.

Yes, my view has been shifting back and forth between two equally plausible perspectives: one that sees the glass as half-empty, by focusing on the ongoing "War on Sex," and the other that sees the glass as half-full, by focusing on the defensive campaigns that have been successfully waged in that war, as well as the tools that these victories have provided to reinforce the continuing defense.

As an activist I am perforce an optimist, so I would like to close with the glass half-full perspective, quoting a key passage from a leading Supreme Court victory in this area.

The passage comes from the Court's 1992 ruling that reaffirmed a woman's constitutional right to choose whether or not to carry her pregnancy to term, *Planned Parenthood v. Casey*,[15] in which the ACLU represented Planned Parenthood.

This excerpt explains why decisions not only about childbearing, but also about other aspects of our sexual and family lives, should remain in the private realm, for all mature individuals to resolve on our own, free from the heavy hand of government.

Significantly, this passage appears in the opinion that was jointly authored by three Republican Justices who were appointed by conservative, Republican Presidents: Justices Sandra Day O'Connor and Anthony Kennedy, who were appointed by President Ronald Reagan, and Justice David Souter, appointed by the first President Bush. They declared:

> Our law affords constitutional protection to personal decisions relating
> to marriage, procreation, contraception, family relationships, childrear-
> ing, and education. . . . Our precedents 'have respected the private realm

of family life which the state cannot enter.' These matters, involving the most intimate and personal choices a person may make in a lifetime, choices central to personal dignity and autonomy, are [also] central to [constitutionally protected] liberty . . . At the heart of liberty is the right to define one's own concept of existence, of meaning, of the universe, and of the mystery of human life.[16]

All of us who share the inspiring vision of Justices O'Connor, Kennedy, and Souter about "the heart of liberty" should be heartened by Marty Klein's book. It should encourage us to do whatever we can, both as engaged citizens and in whatever walk of life we pursue, to help transform this vision into a reality that is equally enjoyed by everyone.

Nadine Strossen[17]
President, American Civil Liberties Union
Professor of Law, New York Law School
New York, New York
April 13, 2006

Chapter One

You're *the Target: Why a War on* Sex?

The familiar expression "culture war" is part of the problem.

It suggests two sides of equal strength lined up in a series of battles, honoring more or less the same rules of engagement, wanting to conquer each other.

But what we commonly call the "culture war" is not like this at all. Those who fear and hate sexuality (erotophobes) are attacking those who appreciate or tolerate sexuality (erotophiles). And while erotophiles are *not* attempting to force erotophobes to live more sexually adventurous lives, erotophobes insist that both sides—*everyone*—live according to their erotophobic values. Erotophiles say, "If you don't want to go to a nude beach, don't go, but don't shut it down to prevent me from going." Erotophobes say, "I don't want to go to a nude beach, and I don't want you to have the option of going either, so it must be closed."

While erotophobes acknowledge this recurring theme—that there's a huge range of opportunities for erotic stimulation, satisfaction, and imagination that they want to deny *everyone,* not just themselves—erotophobes also claim, paradoxically, that they are victims.

They say they are the ones who are tired of being attacked, their values and way of life undermined. Through so-called indecent entertainment, changing fashions, recent court decisions, easy Internet access, and a range of contraceptive technologies, they say they are being force-fed sex. They can't, they say, turn on a TV, go to a mall, boot up a computer, or even go to work without being assaulted by sexual images. And that when they aren't being confronted literally, they are still forced to abide others' private sexual activity next door and all over America—behavior that is immoral, disgusting, and sinful.

This is, undoubtedly, true for them—*but irrelevant to the governance of America.* Nowhere in our founding documents is there any mention of regulating anything considered immoral, disgusting, or sinful. In fact, the United States was founded on the idea that people could choose what to do and with whom to associate based on their *personal* values and ideals—not those of a king, feudal lord, or religious hierarchy. Nor even, as James Madison declared, a tyrannical majority in their own town, state, or country.

When our fellow citizens say they want to eliminate entertainment, fashion, medical technology, bedroom activity, and businesses that are "immoral" or "sinful," they are calling for a dramatic shift in American law. Such major changes in the rules of American life would bring us far closer to modern Saudi Arabia, the former Soviet Union, Taliban-era Afghanistan, and Nazi Germany.

Historically, American society has tried to balance the needs of individual freedom and community responsibility. And so you can't yell "fire" in a crowded theater. Another fundamental American principle is that the law should address actual crime and actual victims, and it should be drafted in ways that limit unwanted or unanticipated consequences when solving a problem.

Today's War on Sex seeks to change this balance, and it has already succeeded in many ways. Historically, it was against the law for someone to *actually* kill your cow; now it's as if there's also a law against someone *thinking* about killing your cow, or doing something that makes you *worried* about someone killing your cow. And so attempting to criminalize abortion, for example, isn't enough for conservatives; now they are trying to prevent over-the-counter availability of emergency contraception, saying wider distribution would "encourage promiscuity." Liberals rush in with scientific data that clearly shows it won't, and one more battle is joined. As is common, the erotophobes have no data with which to counter—but they do have "concerns" and "feelings," *which are now considered seriously in public policy debates.*

We must ask directly: So what if a medication does encourage promiscuity? In a country devoted to individual choice, this shouldn't be a problem. And yet sexual jihadists have actually made this a consideration in American policy debates. The latest example is their attempt to block preteen girls from getting the human papillomavirus (HPV) vaccine that would prevent cervical cancer. The Religious Right and "morality" groups don't claim the vaccine is dangerous, just that it will make sex less scary and thus promote "promiscuous" behavior.

Although our country makes cars safer in case of accidents, has school athletes wear helmets in case they fall awkwardly, and establishes poison centers in case toddlers get into cleaning supplies, erotophobes *don't* want to reduce the consequences of unauthorized, unprotected, or unlucky sex. They say that doing so encourages bad sexual choices. That's like saying seat belts encourage dangerous driving and poison centers encourage sloppy parenting.

The politically powerful in America know that if you can get people looking at the wrong questions, it doesn't matter *what* answers they come up with. And so those who are trying to "clean up" America say they're fighting for a number of critical reasons: children, the family, marriage, morals, education, community safety. But this isn't really true. *It's a war against sex:* sexual expression, sexual exploration, sexual arrangements, sexual privacy, sexual choice, sexual entertainment, sexual health, sexual imagination, sexual pleasure.

Most Americans care about their children, families, morals, and community safety. They are, understandably, easily drawn into a social conflict using terms like these, focused on the things that matter to them and about which they often feel powerless or confused. And so religious and other conservatives have Americans lined up behind them fighting a war that is not in their best interest. *The public is manipulated into fighting sexual expression, not sexual ignorance or poor sexual decision-making.* It then supports public policy that often defeats its own ostensible purpose. Kids who learn abstinence-only have just as much sex—only they use condoms less often. Limiting the availability of contraception doesn't reduce sexual activity—it just increases unwanted pregnancy. Closing swing clubs doesn't decrease swinging—it just destroys the ongoing community providing safety, supervision, and social norms.

Some people say that Americans are stupid, that we don't really care about the facts. I believe Americans do care about facts—but we need a context in which to understand these facts. When it becomes clear that the culture wars are not being fought on our behalf to preserve our families, but are being fought *against* us to undermine our expression, health, and choice, Americans will care about the facts.

Today's domestic conservative/fundamentalist political and social movements present a clear (though horrifically distorted) picture of sexuality. It's a narrative of danger and, therefore, of fear; a narrative of sin and, therefore, of self-destructiveness. Erotophobes typically describe their fear in socially acceptable terms: protecting children, supporting marriage, preventing disease, honoring women, sympathizing with the problematic "male sexual psyche."

But they really fear sexuality, *as they understand it*—its awesome power, the temptation to sin, the inevitable destructive decision-making surrounding it, the clear distinction between acceptable activities and unacceptable activities. So they have launched a War on Sex—not just against their own sexuality—against *everyone's*. Their goals are consistent, their strategy coherent. They can frame it in any civic language they want, but it's actually a War on Sex.

The goal of this war is to control sexual expression, colonize sexual imagination, and restrict sexual choices. It seeks to restrict our choices and shape the political/cultural/psychological environment in which we make those choices. It is, at this moment, changing our norms, culture, laws, vocabulary, and our very emotions.

In their never-ending quest to eliminate as much eroticism from American life as possible, erotophobes have enlisted the aid of the largest government in the history of humanity—contemporary American government. Their allies include school boards, zoning commissions, city councils, state legislatures, military leaders, the U.S. congress, and a series of American presidents. Our current President proudly aligns himself with this side against its enemy, and he prays—literally—for a day when those who want to mind their own business (and allow others the same privilege) are conquered by those who want to mind *everyone's* business, imposing their fears and values on the vanquished.

The outcome of these historic battles will determine how our children live—today, and for decades to come. It will determine what books they read in school, what they learn to fear, what private entertainment they're allowed to enjoy, what they know about their bodies, and how much they control their own fertility.

Millions of Americans are afraid of sex. Some admit it, some don't. Millions more hate sex. Again, some admit it, some don't. To deal with their fear and hate, some have declared a war on it. Some admit this, some don't.

If you're interested in sex, you're part of the war whether you like it or not. If you watch TV, use a sex toy, go to the movies, need an abortion, own a Web site, play sex games, use contraception, enjoy spicy online chat, want a physician trained in sexual medicine, or have a child in school, the cannons in the War on Sex are pointed at you.

This book is about that war.

America's pluralism is hated by fundamentalists around the world—including those right here in America. And sexuality is among the last human activities to enjoy the extraordinary, revolutionary promise of American pluralism. So this book is named *America's War on Sex*, not *Jerry Falwell's War on Sex* or *The Catholic War on Sex* or *Congress's War on Sex*. Because America's two centuries of history have been liberating more and more people to drink from the astounding well of democracy. Because it is imperative that we start asking the right questions, right now. And then the answers *will* matter.

And then we'll end the War on Sex.

And the American people will win.

Chapter Two

Battleground: *Sex Education—*
Where Children Come Second

For the children. For the children.

That's the refrain we hear—that their comprehensive efforts to destroy comprehensive sex education are ultimately designed to protect the children.

From sex.

The battle over sex education, however, isn't about what's safe and healthy for the children. It's about what's comfortable (and politically advantageous) for the adults. In the War on Sex, children are cannon fodder. The welfare of our children is being sacrificed so that adults can sleep better at night. It is, of course, supposed to work the other way around.

The battle over sex education comes down to a set of questions about values:

- Should public policy be shaped by science or by belief?
- Should private morality be allowed to shape public education policy? (And if so, what is "moral"?)
- Is childhood and adolescent sexuality a problem to be controlled and suppressed, or a healthy part of life to be celebrated, explored, and guided?
- Do only children who suppress, avoid, or hide sexual expression deserve protection?
- Do minors have rights to accurate information or health care services?

The battle over sex education is the battle over childhood and adolescent sexuality. The Right and government at all levels have set themselves a clear, if tragic (and ultimately dishonest) challenge: Preventing young people from having sexual experiences (and meticulously ignoring their health needs once they do).

They're asking kids to join them in an unholy alliance to deny sexuality—teaching kids to fear sexual feelings, while adults fear sexual information. They've put kids on the front lines of the War on Sex, demanding they patrol a minefield at a crossroads of cultural conflict.

These anti-sex educators are doing it with funding of more than $200 million in 2006 alone, in every state in the United States. Abstinence-only-until-marriage is taught in half of American public schools and most private schools. Probably in your kid's school.

Meanwhile, regardless of what their parents do or say, the overwhelming majority of today's kids pledging abstinence are going to have sex before they marry[1]—unless, of course, their parents can somehow drastically raise the age of puberty, drastically lower the age of marriage, dismantle MTV, disconnect the Internet, eliminate cell phones, take over the fashion industry, and reverse 40 years of kids having more privacy because both of their parents work outside the home.

It won't happen.

And so what we're left with is millions of kids being systematically prepared for what they *won't* experience: adolescence and young adulthood without sex. Of course, that means they're being systematically *un*prepared for what they *will* have: sex. Sexual feelings. Sexual relationships. Sexual decision-making.

THE "PROBLEM" OF CHILDHOOD SEXUALITY

Every culture has to deal with the sexuality of its young people. Around the world, throughout history, boys and girls would typically mate at or near puberty (e.g., Romeo and Juliet). In some cultures, girls and boys are introduced to sex at puberty by older teens, adults, or age peers. Today, the age of consent is 13, 14, or 15 in Japan and half of Europe. In Africa and elsewhere, clitoridectomy or penile subincision shape youthful sexuality. In some countries, schoolchildren are be-trothed to each other and marry in adolescence. In others, schoolgirls are married off as second or third wives to old men. Of course, prostitutes often provide the first sexual experiences for young males. (This was common in the United States prior to the 1960s). It's clear that most cultures around the world have assumed that young people will be sexual in their early teens, married or not.

For over a century, America's approach to youthful sexuality has been to minimize, distort, and control sexual knowledge, sexual health, sexual rights, and sexual activity of minors and unmarried young adults. (See, for example, the infamous career of Anthony Comstock.) Today this is achieved in a variety of ways, such as withholding contraceptive information, supplies, and services; criminalizing consensual teen-teen sex; removing books that mention sexual-ity from school libraries and school curricula; and forbidding teachers from answering certain questions about sex, and school counselors from discussing certain sexual issues.

But abstinence-only programs are the primary weapon. As America strug-gles to deal with non-adult sexuality, abstinence is its chosen way. Unlike other modern countries, America doesn't debate how young to begin teaching kids about contraception, or how to help kids accept their same-gender sexual curiosity, or how young is too young for genital sex, or how to enjoy sex with-out intercourse.

No, the main sex education debate in the United States is teaching abstinence versus teaching "abstinence plus." The latter is, "Abstinence is the best
and safest form of sexual behavior, but just in case you blow it, here are some
important facts you should know." It's as if medical debate were reduced to
leeches versus leeches-plus-bloodletting.

Whereas abstinence used to be an explicit goal of some individual families,
and an implicit goal of many others (mostly via a "don't ask, don't tell" understanding), it is now a public policy goal of the world's most technologically
advanced nation.

In a world where people are starving—in a country where people are
starving—America spends hundreds and hundreds of millions of dollars to
persuade kids to not "do it."

They still "do it."

They have relationships. They fall in love (regardless of our disdain for their
use of the word). They use sex for pleasure or rebellion or revenge. They also
use it to discover who they are, who their partner is, and what this amazing
thing is that everyone wants so much to keep them away from. Sometimes
they want babies. In other words, they use sex in many ways that adults do.

The original religious injunctions against premarital sex in Western culture
were developed when the age of puberty was much higher, and the age of
marriage much lower, than they are today (see Figure 2.1). Thus, it referred
to a much shorter period in a young male or female's life. And the injunction
was about property, not morals. A girl's virginity was considered patriarchal

Figure 2.1
Premarital Sexuality Zone

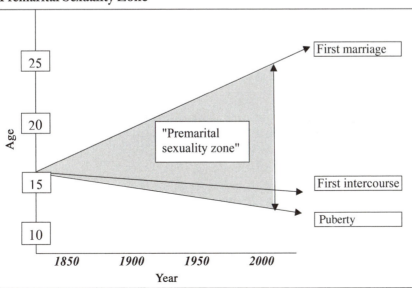

property. If you had sex with a virgin girl, you harmed her father, not her; if caught, you had to compensate him, not her.

With the age of puberty decreasing and the age of first marriage increasing, the average American now spends some ten years being sexually mature and unmarried.[2] This "premarital sexuality zone" is the largest in human history, and challenges the ideal of virginity-until-marriage in an entirely new way. There's never been a generation in human history from whom this many years of abstinence-until-marriage has been expected. (And we're not even discussing MTV, belly shirts, teen privacy, or other challenges to abstinence.)

While it's disingenuous to say that we are passive victims of human nature, it is important to know when social policy is attempting to rewrite human history and biology. When abstinence programs talk about traditional family or traditional values, they display their ignorance of how little today's lives have in common with those of even 100 years ago, much less 500 or 1000.

What are abstinence proponents trying to protect kids from?

- Being interested in sex
- Hearing about a variety of sex practices
- Having sex
- Having sex, resulting in emotional "devastation"
- Having sex, resulting in pregnancy or "devastating" sexually transmitted diseases (STDs)
- Going over to the other side: breaking God's laws, sinning, or leaving God
- Ruining (or even foreclosing!) future marriage
- Liking sex, or getting out of control during sex
- Breaking the female sex role of indifference to sex

Every one of these is a nightmare for those who war on sex. These fears explain why the premarital sexuality zone is a problem zone. At least in this regard, these people take sexuality seriously, although their perspective is distorted: they see sex as the ultimate gateway drug.

SOLUTION: WHAT IS "ABSTINENCE EDUCATION"?

In 1981, Senator Jeremiah Denton (R-AL) proposed to stop teen sex with the Adolescent Family Life Act. It would fund school and community programs "to promote self-discipline and other prudent approaches" to adolescent sex. It was dubbed chastity education.[3] A quarter-century later, it still operates—with a gigantic budget even Senator Denton couldn't have hoped for. It was, and is, the answer for everyone afraid of teen sexuality: abstinence until marriage. Twenty-three years later, Denton says America's "top priority should be to recover our most fundamental founding belief that our national objectives, policies, and laws should reflect obedience to the will of Almighty God."[4]

While much of the abstinence movement is sneaky, they are honest about one thing: their goal is to indoctrinate a whole generation (and, of course,

each succeeding gen-
eration). They want to
change the culture of
young people about
sexuality, away from it
being a means of self-
expression, a way to
get touching, a source
of personal power
(for better or worse,
of course), a form of
self-exploration and
relationship rehearsal,
and a vehicle for actual
intimacy. Instead, they
want kids to think of
sex as something dan-
gerous to fear, some-
thing seductive that
leads to shame, pain,
and a ruined future.
Somehow, this is all
supposed to change on
their wedding night.
Pioneer sex educator
Sol Gordon describes
this message as "sex
is dirty—save it for
someone you love."[5]
   The abstinence
project is no less than
transforming desire
and eroticism from a
semi-familiar, normal
part of life to a not-
understood, estranged
enemy.
   Different programs

THE FEDERAL DEFINITION FOR ABSTINENCE-ONLY PROGRAMS

The term "abstinence education" means an educational or motivational program which:

A. has as its exclusive purpose teaching the social, psychological, and health gains to be realized by abstaining from sexual activity;
B. teaches abstinence from sexual activity outside marriage as the expected standard for all school-age children;
C. teaches that abstinence from sexual activity is the only certain way to avoid out-of-wedlock pregnancy, sexually transmitted diseases, and other associated health problems;
D. teaches that a mutually faithful monogamous relationship in the context of marriage is the expected standard of sexual activity;
E. *teaches that sexual activity outside of the context of marriage is likely to have harmful psychological and physical effects;* [emphasis added]
F. teaches that bearing children out-of-wedlock is likely to have harmful consequences for the child, the child's parents, and society;
G. teaches young people how to reject sexual advances and how alcohol and drug use increase vulnerability to sexual advances, and
H. teaches the importance of attaining self-sufficiency before engaging in sexual activity.

Also, note that if any contraceptive method is discussed, its "failure rate" must be mentioned, *not* its "success rate." The only exception is the failure rate of abstinence, which is *never* discussed.

Section 510(b) of Title V of the Social Security Act, P.L. 104–193

define abstinence differently. While a few say that nonintercourse sex is OK, others exclude any non-genital sex, and some even exclude any activity (such as dancing or masturbating) that generates sexual thoughts or ideas. Regardless of definition, every abstinence program says it's for the children. No one admits it has anything to do with decreasing adult anxiety. No one admits it's part of a bigger War on Sex.

Abstinence education is the substitution of restriction for decision-making. It says that there's a flaw in every *other* form of sexuality education (of course there is), and it venally brags that it is unique in its protections of kids (of course it isn't). As shown in the figure below, it substitutes an abstinence zone for the premarital sex zone. It's a zone that has been getting bigger every decade for the past century. We may, in fact, have reached the climax of this zone's growth (puberty can't drop much earlier, and mean first marriage can't increase much later). Nevertheless, the dramatic social policy challenge is now established.

Abstinence education could be designed to be honest and dignified. (It could also be a lot more effective; see Taverner and Montfort, *Making Sense of Abstinence.*) But in today's America, abstinence is none of these. It is so wrapped up in lies, inaccuracies, and values presented as facts that it is hard to respect the message. And as presently designed, it is impossible for kids to get value from these programs without paying an enormous price.

Let's say society were to systematically withhold other vital information from kids—say, how to take care of their teeth. Toothpaste and floss would become illegal, the need to brush daily hushed up, the effectiveness of braces lied about, teens taught that gum disease can only be prevented by not eating sushi.

Or say that Congress decided it didn't want certain kids (maybe the children of immigrants, or New Yorkers, or Muslims) to do well in school. We'd see

Figure 2.2
Abstinence Expectation Zone

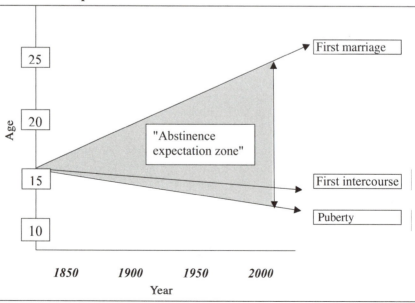

disinformation about study habits, libraries secretly relocated, card catalogs dismissed as unreliable, and kids told that completing their assignments on time might hurt their eyes.

How would America react? Wouldn't there be editorials and non-profit organizations standing up for those kids at risk for lifelong oral pain and school failure? How long could such policies endure?

BENEFITING ADULTS, NOT KIDS

The war on sex education pretends to be about kids. Adults say they want to protect kids from disease, pregnancy, and broken hearts. Some also say that God instructs everyone not to have premarital sex, even people who don't believe in God.

But abstinence programs don't protect kids from disease, pregnancy, or broken hearts. That's because they aren't effective at postponing sexual involvement or at making kids safer when they do have sex. For example, a Florida State University evaluation study found that, after taking an abstinence-only program, kids were more likely to agree that they *should not* have sex before marriage than before they began the program. But over the same period, their sexual behaviors *increased*.[6] And most abstinence programs assume kids aren't already having sex—which would be pretty funny if it weren't so dangerous.

So abstinence programs don't help kids. But they do benefit adults—both emotionally and financially. Abstinence programs help adults convince themselves that kids are less sexual than they really are. They get to maintain the illusion that kids aren't doing it, are going to stop doing it, or aren't going to start.

These programs also allow parents to believe that they don't have to have a long series of talks about sex over a period of years. If kids aren't doing it, and all they need is to be told, "Don't do it," there's no reason to talk about it more than once or twice. Abstinence programs encourage parents to evade one of their key responsibilities.

And abstinence programs allow adults to feel that their kids are safe from sin, hell, and religious error (and from unauthorized pleasure). For parents who are sincerely involved in that world, this concern is an enormous burden. Relief from this concern is worth almost any price to them. In this case, that price is hurting the kids about whom they're so concerned. Abstinence also relieves their anxiety about kids' autonomy and power in their own lives, a key religious concern.

At the very least, the clear message kids learn from abstinence programs is, "If you have sex, *do not tell us.*" "We will be disappointed in you, God will hate you, everything around here will change," the message says. Many adults crave the relief that their kids' deception provides. They make kids responsible for reducing adult anxiety about childhood sexuality.

A variety of studies definitively show that abstinence programs don't work. Thus, proponents can't still say that these programs are about kids' safety. Rather, abstinence programs are about morality—a vision of the values people should live by. This is fine for the home, but deadly for the public in a non-totalitarian, nontheocratic society. How can anyone think that teaching one set of personal values as *the* way to live can be OK in America? (Except, of course, the values that derive from nonsectarian, pluralist democracy: honesty, responsibility, and consent.)

In fact, the ubiquity of the abstinence goal and its programs is a turning point in the War on Sex, both financially and politically. Abstinence has brought the War on Sex into everyone's living room. Even if you're not kinky, don't want to go to a swing club, don't want an abortion, don't even have cable TV, if you have kids, abstinence brings the War on Sex into your home. It is, arguably, the single biggest challenge to your values as an American and as a sexual person.

Abstinence programs are also a forum for an explicit antigay agenda, although that can hardly be part of helping heterosexual kids be abstinent. (As a bonus, they also terrify the millions of heterosexual kids who think about, or experiment with, same-gender sex.) They validate adult delusions about human nature—that fear is the best motivator of behavior, that sexual decision-making is simple, that young adults can routinely abstain from sex into their mid-twenties (when most Americans marry).

The other major impact of abstinence is its economic windfall for (already tax-exempt) churches and faith-based organizations. Through it, individual churches, after-school programs, and so-called pregnancy crisis centers (actually antiabortion centers) have received hundreds of millions of dollars—more support than received by all the people displaced by Hurricane Katrina or all the handicapped people in the United States.

As Leslie Unruh, founder of the National Abstinence Clearinghouse, has noted, "Abstinence has become a business," one which Unruh estimates has increased by more than 900 programs in recent years.[7] Abstinence is a monster growth industry.

The abstinence industry is a huge federal and state gravy train, but only for a narrow segment of Americans. Because nonabstinence sexuality programs—programs that counsel kids to make good sexual decisions, to use contraception when they decide to have intercourse, to appreciate nonintercourse sex, to discuss sex with their parents, to develop good communication skills, to learn more about their bodies—*are not eligible* for this money. This is government money strictly for ideologically correct groups. Groups, of course, that vote. Abstinence programs are a new and completely legal way that the federal and state governments funnel hundreds of millions of dollars to religious groups that support them politically.

Figure 2.3
U.S. Funding for Abstinence Programs

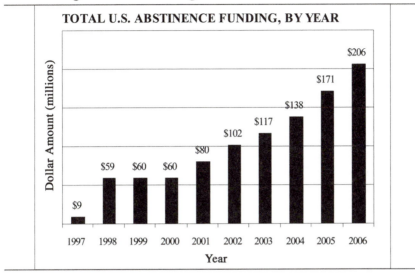

As the icing on the cake, recipients of these millions have never been required to prove that their efforts are effective. They resisted outside evaluation from the very start, in an age when the government demands that public schools and teachers prove their effectiveness. There are reasons abstinence leaders don't want programs evaluated: They believe so earnestly in the ideology of the programs that they don't care about the actual results; they value the anxiety reduction provided by the programs, and they don't want any negative data to jeopardize the wealth currently flowing their way.

Parents and abstinence leaders can say what they will—that they care about kids' values, physical health, mental health, preparation for monogamy, God's judgment, or whatever. Regardless, they are behaving selfishly, neglectfully, aggressively. These parents are so committed to reducing their own anxiety about their kids' well-being, and are so terrified about the threat of sex to their kids' health, that they will do anything, *anything,* to feel less frightened. They will even compromise their kids' well-being. Even pretend that their kid is an entirely different person.

THE STRUCTURE OF AMERICAN "ABSTINENCE"

In one sense, the policy goal of abstinence-only education is simple enough: Persuade young people to not have sex *before marriage,* no matter when that is (and if you're not legally allowed to marry, tough). To do this, their strategies include:

- Persuade young people that contraception and disease protection are so unreliable that they must not be trusted
- Persuade young people that premarital sex always has dreadful consequences
- Provide young people various forums for publicly committing to abstinence

The first strategy requires lying. Because condoms work, condoms work, condoms work. They work better today than they ever have. They work so well, hundreds of millions of people around the world use them to shape when and if they'll have children. They work so well, virtually every serodiscordant couple (one partner is HIV positive, the other HIV negative) who use condoms regularly prevent the HIV negative partner from contracting HIV.[8] They work so well, they help prevent herpes, chlamydia, and the newest STD demon of the Right, HPV. In the 1980s, they helped dramatically stem the tide of HIV among gay men.[9]

Contrast this with these lies told by the Abstinence Clearinghouse:

- "Condoms provide 0 percent protection against HPV."
- "Condoms do not protect against . . . genital herpes."
- "Trusting a condom to protect your health puts your future at risk."
- "Trusting condoms . . . is like playing with fire. Sooner or later you get burned."[10]

The second strategy relies on belief. To the extent that belief is presented as fact, it's a lie. A common lie of abstinence, for example, is that premarital sex ruins future marriage. But where's the data? Abstinence advocates trot out depressed Susie in Omaha and dysfunctional Pedro in Denver, and yes, of course those anecdotes are true. But they aren't representative. And what about kids who become terrified of sex by abstinence programs? Girls who learn that boys only want one thing? Boys who learn to feel guilty for masturbating? Abstinence programs have no data about any of this.

Abstinence programs should be honest: "We don't think anyone should have sex before marriage because it's wrong. Period." But they don't trust the power of their own values-laden message. They bolster their message by lying about the consequences of premarital sex.

Even if these two messages (condoms don't work, premarital sex is typically destructive) were accurate, these two strategies assume that kids, *unlike* millions of adults, make sexual decisions rationally. There is no data to suggest this is true. In fact, we know that many kids—like many adults—are willing to have sex despite virtually any consequences. And in general, attempting to shape kids' behavior by scaring them about what's going to happen in the future is futile. That's why kids smoke, don't exercise, refuse to study, and drink alcohol when the negative consequences are blindingly obvious.

Like many others, Secretary of Health and Human Services Michael Leavitt says that, with abstinence, teens don't have to worry about STDs and pregnancy. What he doesn't seem to understand is that *teens already don't worry—they're teens.* They certainly don't worry during moments of passion, love, or peer pressure—the same way many adults respond. So Leavitt apparently *wants* kids to worry, and like any good entrepreneur, he offers a product that solves their problem (their "worry"). In this case, the product is "abstinence." But since most teens, being teens, aren't worried, abstinence is a solution looking for a problem.

The third part of the abstinence strategy is providing forums for abstinence commitment. Public ceremonies, Ring Thing, virginity pledges, and so forth sound good, and it's easy to assume that kids are sincere when they do it. But the idea that 14-year-olds can make commitments that they will honor when they are 19 is ludicrous. Again, there's no data to support this theory of human development. In fact, 88 percent of teens pledging abstinence have sex before marriage—that is, abstinence *fails.* And it fails at a far, far higher rate than condoms or any other contraceptive method.[11]

Public virginity pledge forums are always religiously oriented. For example, the Silver Ring Thing's parent organization says it is an "evangelistic ministry" by which it is bringing "our world to Christ." Young people who attend and pledge virginity until marriage receive an "Abstinence Study Bible" and a silver ring inscribed with a reference to the Bible verse, "God wants you to be holy, so you should keep clear of all sexual sin." Participants are also encouraged to accept Christ as their savior.[12]

In response to an American Civil Liberties Union lawsuit, federal funding for the Silver Ring Thing was suspended in August 2005. Consequently, the Silver Ring Thing was required to restructure its program to be nonreligious in order to continue to receive federal funds. But its founder, Denny Pattyn, continues to see it as a religious program. As he told an audience of teens, "Unless you have God right here [patting his heart], at the center of this decision, I think you'll struggle keeping this decision [holding up his ring finger] of putting on a ring."[13]

As usual with sexuality, the Right wants it two ways. They want to claim sex is bad for kids and abstaining is good; when confronted with the data challenging this, they say, well, abstaining is good morality. OK, then it's a moral position—which people can differ over. Then they say, well, all our kids deserve protection.

IF IT DOESN'T WORK, WHY PROMOTE ABSTINENCE? FOLLOW THE MONEY

Abstinence is one of the more lucrative sources of nonmilitary, nonconstruction pork barrel funding in the history of America.

ABSTINENCE: HOW GOVERNMENT SUBSIDIZES RELIGION

Most of the $200,000,000 that goes to promote abstinence-only-before-marriage each year is awarded to agencies over which there is no oversight whatsoever. A huge amount of this taxpayer money goes to frankly religious organizations. Here are just a few examples:

Pennsylvania

Catholic Social Services	$46,000
Lutheran Social Ministries	$231,000
St. Luke's Health Network	$92,000
Shepherd's Maternity House	$50,000
Silver Ring Thing	$400,000

California

Catholic Charities of California	$361,605

New York

Catholic Charities of New York	$2,500,000

Illinois

Roseland Christian Ministries	$800,000
Lawndale Christian Health Center	$461,278

To see which agencies are getting abstinence funding in your state and how much they are receiving, go to http://www.siecus.org/policy/states/.

Almost one billion dollars has been spent on abstinence-only-until-marriage program—and the funding is *still increasing every year*. Remember, their whole goal is persuading young people to not have sex until they marry, not as a means to an end (say, to take care of themselves), but as an end in itself (*the only way* to take care of themselves). And since almost three-quarters of high school kids have sex before they finish high school, much of this one *billion* dollars is aimed at telling kids who have already had sex that they shouldn't start, or that if they've started, they should stop.

So we have a huge income stream being spent in unaccountable ways by ideologically driven people who are afraid of their kids' sexuality. There's so much money to be made from insisting on this perspective, maybe it's unrealistic to expect these people to see the basic flaws in their programs' structure. But given the idealism of these people, is it unrealistic to expect them to *care* that their programs don't work?

So they rationalize the programs rather than seriously evaluate them. Abstinence proponents have *nothing* to gain by having their programs evaluated. They're already traveling first class on the gravy train, which gets bigger every year. They can afford to be disingenuous about evaluation, claiming their opponents are "using" science for their own ends, because science can't help them.

These funds, of course, find their way to those with political connections. The Best Friends Foundation received $1.5 million between 2003 and 2004; it's run by Elayne Bennett, wife of William Bennett, and Alma Powell, wife of Colin Powell. The Medical Institute of Austin, Texas, receives more that $500,000 annually; its founder, Joe McIlhaney, has been friends with George W. Bush since he was governor. And disgraced House Majority Leader Tom DeLay's (R-TX) congressional district receives almost a half million dollars in funding annually.[14]

Your money is being used to persuade your kid to not start having sex or to stop having sex, and, either way, to feel bad and to mistrust contraception and disease protection. Your money. Your money.

SO WHAT'S WRONG WITH ABSTINENCE?

But most of all, *these programs don't work.* Here's proof:

- In Minnesota, sexual activity of junior high school participants in an abstinence program doubled.[15]
- Young people who took a virginity pledge are one-third *less likely* then nonpledgers to use contraception when they become sexually active.[16]
- Young people who took a virginity pledge have the same rates of STDs as nonpledgers.[17]
- Teens who pledge abstinence and haven't had intercourse are *more likely* to have oral and anal sex than nonpledgers who haven't had intercourse.[18]
- Two-thirds of Northern Kentucky University students who pledged celibacy until marriage broke that pledge while still in college. Of those who remained "abstinent," more than half acknowledged having oral sex while describing themselves as celibate.[19]

Did you know this? Probably not.

With all the media discussion of the abstinence mission and programs, with all the confident assertions that this is what's right for the country, why don't you know this? It should be front page news—"Billion-dollar program crucial to saving youth of America *doesn't work.*"

Despite these programs' failures, abstinence advocates still seem to think that ignorance and fear will motivate young people. If they'd only read the social science literature, they'd know that doesn't work. But they proudly declare their beliefs to be more valid than science. For example, last year, over 2,000,000 kids smoked their first cigarette. Three-quarters of a million of those kids will become regular smokers. One-quarter of high school kids smoke. Four-and-a-half million adolescents smoke. This despite hundreds of millions of dollars spent nationwide to discourage them, and radical age restrictions on tobacco advertising, marketing, and retail sales, and its near-disappearance from primetime TV and a dramatic reduction in films and video.

Does anyone think kids haven't been told enough about the dangers of smoking? And unlike sex, which you can get as a kid, you can't even buy the stuff legally. Somehow, kids want to do it anyway—even though they know relatives, friends' parents, and even popular figures die from it.

Does anyone think the desire to try a cigarette is stronger than the desire to try sex?

EVALUATION? NO THANKS

When confronted with questions of effectiveness, the motto of abstinence programs is, "Just say, 'I don't know.'"

One of the most damning facts about abstinence programs is their dramatic lack of interest in fact and science. The material actually delivered, as well as the mission of and marketing of the programs themselves, bear only a coincidental relationship with fact. Here are common untruths the abstinence movement repeats:

- Condoms don't work
- Premarital sex is emotionally poisonous
- Premarital sex is physically disastrous
- People who make abstinence pledges are the only ones who respect themselves

In 2004, Congressman Henry Waxman (D-CA) released a report, "The Content of Federally Funded Abstinence-Only Education Programs." It's a concise evaluation of the thirteen most popular abstinence-only sex education programs.[20] It documents that "over 80% of the abstinence-only curricula used by 2/3 of [federally funded programs] contain false, misleading, or distorted information about reproductive health." Especially common were:

- false information about the effectiveness of contraception;
- false information about the risk of abortion;
- blurring religion and science;
- treating stereotypes of girls and boys as scientific fact;
- scientific errors.

Here are actual quotes from these federally funded programs that actual children in actual American schools are now reading and hearing:

- "In heterosexual sex, condoms fail to prevent HIV approximately 31% of the time"
- Touching another person's genitals "can result in pregnancy."
- "The popular claim that condoms help prevent the spread of STDs is not supported by the data."

- "Women gauge their happiness and judge their success by their relationships. Men's happiness and success hinge on their accomplishments."[21]
- "Following abortion, according to some studies, women are more prone to suicide."
- Personal problems "can be eliminated by being abstinent until marriage."

The Religious Right's response (e.g., Morality in Media, Focus on the Family, Agape Press) was predictable: they trashed Waxman. They link him to same-sex marriage. They attack him for quoting Planned Parenthood data. They criticize his acceptance of campaign contributions from "groups that financially benefit from abortion" like the American Medical Association. They complain that he didn't mention all the funding for safer sex programs.[22]

Since they say they care about kids, you'd imagine they were concerned, wanted to fix the programs, increase their credibility, ability to serve kids, and so forth. But no. They attacked the report, the Congressman, his district, and his supporters. They attacked science.

No programs attempted to improve themselves. No one apologized for or attempted to remove inaccuracies. This is clear proof that these programs are far less interested in their results than in their ideological purity—and their hundreds of millions of dollars in funding.

In 2002, Congressmember Lois Capps (D-CA) offered an amendment to an abstinence funding bill that would have required abstinence programs receiving federal money to be scientifically accurate. Nothing fancy.

But no. They say they don't trust science—they simply "know" the programs work—and it was soundly defeated. In subsequent years, this was attempted again and again. In 2006 it was reintroduced with 120 cosponsors. You'd think this would be a slam-dunk—who doesn't want their kids to have accurate information, especially about protecting their health? But a majority of congressmembers resist this. Abstinence proponents say, "Whose science?" as if they could provide competing data showing that abortion does lead to infertility, premarital sex does lead to suicide, gays are mentally defective, or condoms do fail to protect against disease.

Senate Majority Leader Bill Frist is particularly hypocritical about this, as he proudly struts his support of health care outcomes research. In 2000, he said that outcomes research was a priority "of federal efforts to improve the quality of health care in the United States."[23] And in 2003, he said, "We must continue to move forward in the collection and the evaluation, dissemination, and analysis of information related to everyday health care."[24] The outcome data on sex education programs already exists, *and he promotes federal policies contraindicated by the data.*

Program evaluation is a sophisticated science used by trained experts across the industrial world, including the United States. It *is* possible to know how abstinence programs affect both thinking and behavior in its recipients—if someone wants the facts.

Proponents of comprehensive sexuality education have wanted to know for decades. Here's what peer-reviewed, validated, and replicated studies have conclusively shown; that is, here is what American civilization now knows:

- Does sex education make kids have sex?
  No
- Do condoms work?
  Yes
- Does the availability of condoms in school clinics increase kids' sexual activity?
  No
- Are gays mentally defective?
  No
- Does premarital sex itself lead to problems?
  No
- Does abortion lead to breast cancer?
  No
- Do abstinence programs stop kids from having sex before marriage?
  No

The biggest lie of abstinence is that it works every time. It *doesn't*. In the most comprehensive study ever done on adolescent health and sexuality, Columbia University's Dr. Peter Bearman's investigators interviewed more than 20,000 young people about virginity pledges. Twelve percent (12%) of the students who pledged virginity kept their promise. That's a 12 percent success rate with this supposedly perfect method. That means abstinence fails 88 percent of the time—*six times as often as condoms fail in typical use,* six times as often as the method that abstinence advocates say is unreliable.[25]

Kids using abstinence *this weekend* will have sex. They've promised they won't, but they will. How do we want to prepare them for this? We tell kids to wear seat belts, even though we don't want them to crash. We tell kids to call if they'll be late, even though we want them home on time.

What do we offer kids who don't refuse sex the way we want them to? Nothing—no backup plan, no mnemonic devices, no support, no information to protect themselves. Ask an abstinence proponent what a kid should do if he or she has sex, and they reply, "Don't have sex." Denny Pattyn, founder of Silver Ring Thing, says if "my own 16-year-old daughter tells me she's going to be sexually active, I would *not* tell her to use a condom."[26]

Abstinence "educators" disregard kids who have sex like so much trash. It's a disgusting form of hostility toward our young people. It would be like withholding vitamins from kids who refuse to eat vegetables (after promising they will), or withholding toothbrushes from kids who drink pop (after promising they won't).

CONSEQUENCES OF ABSTINENCE EDUCATION

We shouldn't be surprised, then, that America has inherited the consequences of the failure of all three of these strategies (lie about safer sex, claim that beliefs are facts, and provide forums for abstinence pledges). Kids don't abstain—whether they think sex is dangerous or not. Kids don't abstain—whether they make public pledges or not. Kids don't abstain—whether they think God will be mad at them or not. Over 90 percent of Americans have sex before marriage. The only question is whether they will have it in a physically and emotionally healthy environment. The goal of abstinence programs is to assure they won't.[27]

Although the emotionally abusive messages of abstinence programs don't shape adolescents' sexual *behavior* much, they do shape the *emotional context* of their sexual behavior. So these young people use contraception less, understand less about how sex actually works, feel worse about themselves, and talk less about their sexual feelings or experiences with their parents. So abstinence programs create the worst of both worlds: nonabstinence, lower rates of contraception and disease protection, and less intelligence about sex—not only logistically, but emotionally and spiritually.

All this from people who say they care about the children.

Without question, many young people would be better off if they postponed sex by a year or two or more. (Of course, many adults would, too.)

But no social policy is cost-free. And every public policy has unexpected consequences—some of them quite unpleasant.

So what do kids pay for abstinence programs?

- Unfamiliarity with, and mistrust of, contraception
- Increased contraceptive risk-taking
- Reinforcement of the belief that sex is bad and dangerous
- Reinforcement of traditional gender roles
- Unrealistic expectations of marital sex
- Unrealistic expectations of their own future—that they'll be chaste, when most won't be
- Ignorance of appropriate, personal sexual decision-making
- Shame, guilt, and isolation when chastity vows are broken
- Healthy experimentation made complicated and more dangerous
- Feeling rejected and judged by parents and/or God

Abstinence advocates say that a comprehensive (they call it "mixed") message teaches kids that we expect them to fail. That assumes, of course, that shunning sex is the only form of "success."

But what does it do to young people when we actually do set them up to fail? We are training a whole generation that "if" (actually *when)* they have sex before marriage, that they have failed, that God will be angry, that they lack discipline or self-respect or love for their future partner. They will also learn that they can't plan effectively. What kind of parents, citizens, lovers will they then be? With how many bad feelings will they associate sex—thereby undermining thoughtful sexual decision-making?

"Abstinence" is a huge gamble—if kids "fail," they can't protect themselves. So even if a few kids benefit, the rest—the majority—pay the price. Is this a reasonable social policy—gambling that a few will make it and abandoning the rest?

Finally, as award-wining educator Bill Taverner asks, how are programs preparing people to make the transition from using abstinence to using a different method of contraception and disease prevention? After all, almost 90 percent of abstinence pledgers have intercourse before marriage—and they protect themselves and each other at a lower rate than nonpledgers. Even if abstinence programs do help teens postpone sexual involvement, morality—yes, morality—dictates that they prepare these kids for the time when they will switch to a different way of life, with different challenges. So long as abstinence programs ignore this reality, their claims of "morality-based sex education" are hollow. What's left is the simple—and dangerous—antisex message.

KIDS AS A MINORITY TARGETED FOR DISCRIMINATION

When it comes to sexuality, Americans under 18 are a repressed minority. In most or all states,

- information is systematically withheld from them;
- government, school, and church programs deliberately lie to them;
- health services are withheld from them;
- health products are withheld from them;
- in many states it is against the law for them to have intercourse with *anyone;*
- it is against the law for them to take photos *of themselves* in provocative poses.

In other arenas, kids have rights, regardless of the needs and feelings of adults. There are laws, for example, requiring school attendance and certain vaccinations, and restricting child labor and corporal punishment, regardless of how parents or other adults feel about these issues.

But when it comes to sex, young people have no rights. Not *insufficient* sexual rights—*no rights.* Their rights have been taken away in response to adults' hysteria about their safety, anxiety about their morality, anger about their autonomy, confusion about their decision-making, and rejection of their human needs.

Sure, we regulate kids' access to tobacco, alcohol, and driving. But there's science backing these decisions, and kids are allowed access to unlimited, accurate information about these subjects. And we rarely tell them that young people who smoke or drink (or have car accidents) are bad, selfish, and immoral, no matter how much we want to discourage them.

Not so regarding sex.

When the United States has treated other minority groups similarly (Native Americans, the handicapped, women, etc.), scandal has eventually ensued, and discrimination has decreased. There is still no scandal about the way America targets children and young adults for discriminatory treatment.

International human rights law establishes that every person, including every child, has the right to the highest attainable standard of health; the right to seek, receive, and impart information of all kinds; the right to nondiscrimination and equal protection of the law; and the right to an education.[28] This includes the right to information and education concerning the prevention and control of prevailing health problems.[29]

The United States has signed international treaties guaranteeing these rights, including the International Covenant on Civil and Political Rights,[30] the International Covenant on Economic, Social, and Cultural Rights, and the Convention on the Rights of the Child. Participating countries affirm their legal obligation to refrain from "censoring, withholding or intentionally misrepresenting health-related information, including sexual education information."

The 1998 United Nations guidelines on HIV/AIDS and human rights recommends that states "ensure that children and adolescents have adequate access to confidential sexual and reproductive health services, including HIV/AIDS information, counseling, testing and prevention measures such as condoms."[31]

But according to the 2002 report of the internationally respected Human Rights Watch, "[American] Federally funded abstinence-only programs, in keeping with their federal mandate, deny children basic information that could protect them from HIV/AIDS infection ... these programs not only interfere with fundamental rights to information, to health and to equal protection under the law. They also place children at unnecessary risk of HIV infection and premature death."[32]

And now the United States has become an obstacle to HIV prevention on a global scale. Our government has decided that no forms of HIV prevention or pregnancy prevention besides abstinence shall be allowable in programs it funds anywhere in the world.[33] The government of the United Kingdom recently pledged over $5,000,000 to International Planned Parenthood Federation, specifically to fund programs made ineligible by American rules. Today's

U.S. government stands alongside Sudan (clitoridectomy), Saudi Arabia (limiting girls' education), Nigeria (stoning adulterous girls), Malawi (forced marriage of girls to old men to settle debts), and Pakistan (honor killings) in their violations of human rights standards of child treatment. How proud can we be of our way of life when we stand alongside these states and their barbaric customs?

What a humiliating contrast to Europe and Canada, whose teens have intercourse at roughly the same rate as Americans, but whose national policies on sex education and health have been dramatically more successful in curtailing teen pregnancy, abortion, and STDs.

The United States is a signatory of the UN and other international treaties that specifically state that children have a right to sexual health information and the entire range of treatment and prevention options. America violates this commitment as a matter of national policy.

The Geneva Convention says that children under fifteen "shall neither be recruited in the armed forces or groups, nor allowed to take part in hostilities." To satisfy the lust of their elders, American school children have been dragged into the War on Sex.[34]

Children as collateral damage in America's War on Sex? That would be bad enough. But the repulsive truth is that, in this war, children are a primary target.

Chapter Three

The Most Powerful "Minority" in the United States

I'm confused. Exactly who is this "they" that the Religious Right keeps saying has hijacked the country?

The Religious Right keeps bragging about how they are responsible for electing the President, Vice President, and Congress. They say they are effectively pressuring Washington to get conservative federal judges appointed. They claim they are electing mayors, state legislators, and governors across the country. So who exactly is passing the laws we all live under?

And who are the consumers of the cultural products the Religious Right constantly criticizes? Who do they think is watching *Desperate Housewives*, going to see *Maid in Manhattan*, buying *Cosmopolitan*, and downloading Janet Jackson's half-second nipple? At the mall, who do they think is giving their 13-year-olds money to buy belly shirts, iPods, and cell phones?

The three fastest-growing recreations in America are NASCAR races, TV wrestling, and poker. All involve beer and half-undressed pretty girls. Who are the fans for these?

And pornography: The Right keeps complaining that we're "flooded" with it. OK, there are 50 million Americans consuming porn—and they aren't all Al Gore and Michael Moore. So who are these 50 million people? When the Right complains that hotels are making a fortune selling in-room porn, who do they think stays in those hotel rooms in Topeka, Provo, and Memphis?

The Religious Right has masterfully portrayed itself as the voice of the sex-sober majority being oppressed by the sex-crazed minority. They demand sympathy and righteous indignation about the way "children," "families," "tradition," "morals," "values," and "decency" are under attack. They have gotten the government and media to support them as defenders of America's wholesomeness—against some mythical, incredibly powerful "them."

But the Right is like the kid who kills his parents and asks for mercy because he's an orphan. Somehow, they neglect to mention that it's the consumer choices and other preferences of *their own constituents* that are the so-called problem. It is average, working-class and middle-class Republican voters in

Charleston, Abilene, and Spokane that are watching porn, having affairs, buying vibrators, going to strip clubs, and keeping *Sex & the City* on the air. People may tell pollsters and even politicians that they want more "decent" programs and products. But that's not what these people are discussing, buying, and watching. Religious people, conservative people, "decent" people demand, and get, the *Gilmore Girls,* a Hitachi magic wand, Jenna Jameson, a lap dance.

The Right portrays America as under siege by a dangerous ideology, a villainous intelligence, which simply doesn't exist. The evil that the Right is battling so energetically isn't evil, and it isn't out there. It's the simple decision-making *of its own people.* And they make the same choices people around the world make whenever they have a chance.

Unfortunately, the idea of a tangible Satanic force that must be battled out in the world is familiar to tens of millions of fundamentalist and evangelical Christians. At various times, the group said to embody this Evil has been identified as pagans, Jews, Muslims, Catholics, and communists. These days they're homosexuals, liberals, and pornographers.

To the Right, these three symbolize choice. Valuing pleasure. The rejection of fear of Evil. A loss of group control over individual impulse.

The Religious Right plays to the literalist expectation of Evil exquisitely; for example, look at its portrayal of less than civilized, less than adult, conscience-less, seductive homosexuals. Somehow, this group of five or six million people, with no guns, two congressmen, and Ellen Degeneres is positioned as a threat to the most powerful country in the history of the world. That is a brilliant political accomplishment.

What exactly *is* this "homosexual agenda" from which the Christian Right is protecting you and me? The idea that gay marriage hurts straight marriage is staggering. "Honey, I'm sorry I had an affair, but you know how those gays are undermining our marriages . . ." The Bush administration has cut funding for student loans, funding for alternative fuels research, funding for grandma's medication, funding for poor people's birth control, and funding for job retraining. But they say the real danger is a bunch of men and women who want to marry each other instead of, uh, each other.

The Right is correct about one thing. The American family and American community are, today, spinning out of control. But it isn't because of the Axis of Moral Evil—homosexuals, liberals, and pornographers. Rather, it's the unintended consequence of a wildly successful advanced capitalist system, which gives spending money and privacy to teens, while overworking two parents who can't afford healthcare, geographically dispersing their families, and increasing their grandparents' lifespans while decreasing their dignity. It's a sociopolitical economic system that values computer networking over intimate connecting.

Our alienation and sense of powerlessness is the unfortunate result of getting what Americans said we wanted—more and more and more *stuff,* more low-density housing in car-dependent suburbs, more guarantees of physical security, and more certainty about the most uncertain anxieties of human existence—no matter how deadening our jobs, how unhealthy our environment, how corrupt our politics, how meaningless our entertainment, or how atomized our families and relationships. Americans have asked for lives that require less thinking, and we've been handed them. At a soul-searing price.

We ought to be sympathetic about the fear, grief, and resentment of people watching their lives and communities spinning out of control, and their kids spinning away from them. Men and women across America are brokenhearted. And the primary political group addressing this heartbreak is the Religious Right. Unfortunately, they do it in a fundamentally disempowering way. They say, "Let's give in to our fear, let's restrict our choices, let's attempt to control everything and everyone else." Sexuality—messy, idiosyncratic, unpredictable, transgressive—is high on the agenda of what needs controlling.

They don't encourage us to grow up and face our own role in creating lives we fear and resent. But as the only political group discussing heartbreak and isolation, they attract listeners, listeners who become disciples. And so although Christians damn the very activities the public values—soft-core entertainment, hard-core stimulation—the public somehow feels comforted. When the Right talks about an idealized, wholesome past that never existed, it's code for wanting to address how frightened and lonely people feel now. That makes them feel acknowledged. They then want to say "yes" to whatever solution is proposed, even the loss of dignity, freedom, and adulthood that is the core of the Religious Right's program.

So when the Religious Right hyperventilates, sputters, rages, and prophesies doom regarding premarital sex, extramarital sex, nonmarital sex, and pornography, abortion, *Grey's Anatomy,* STDs, and dildoes, they're talking about themselves, but blaming a "them." People who feel powerless are cheering this war on "them," even though it's ultimately a war on *themselves.* But people who feel powerless and ashamed of their own sexuality can't possibly stand up for themselves in this battle. They will continue to cheer Senator/Reverends Rick Santorum, Sam Brownback, and Ted Stevens, and Reverend/Senators James Dobson, Tony Perkins, and Brent Bozell as they demonize porn and Fox TV—even while voters buy porn and watch Fox. And manipulated by these cynical senator/reverends, the same voters will continue to spit on the American Civil Liberties Union while it protects their rights to buy porn and watch Fox.

There's a good chance that the Christian Right will continue scoring serious victories. They actually could criminalize abortion, restrict porn, abolish strip clubs, eliminate gay adoptions, purge and re-closet homosexuals, and make adultery and premarital sex excruciatingly frightening and costly.

But no government, no religion, can eliminate the desire for sex, for sexual experimentation, for the taboo, the naughty, the novel, the intense. Read a century of science fiction: no one can stop people from somehow creating erotic entertainment and pleasure *outside* the bounds of whatever is considered "decent."

We know that the most notable figures on the Right—including Rudy Giuliani, Jimmy Swaggart, Bill O'Reilly, Strom Thurmond, Robert Livingston, and Newt Gingrich—have participated in extramarital affairs, visits with prostitutes, and sexual harassment. Who would *they say* is the "them" who's hijacking the country?

Chapter Four

<u>Battleground:</u> *Reproductive Rights*

"**I** would like to outlaw contraception. It is disgusting—people using each other for pleasure," says Joseph Scheidler, national director of the Pro-Life Action League. Some people are obsessed with the rights of sperm to fertilize eggs, and with fertilized eggs to implant. Operation Rescue founder Randall Terry says, "I don't think Christians should use birth control." In fact, some in the antichoice movement have attacked others for not opposing contraception. As University of Dallas Professor Janet Smith says, "It is foolish for pro-lifers to think they can avoid the issue of contraception and sexual irresponsibility and be successful in the fight against abortion."[1]

Clearly, their logic is backward: Obviously, the way to eliminate abortion is to eliminate unwanted pregnancy. They should ardently *support* birth control, but they don't. Probable Presidential candidate Senator Rick Santorum (R-PA) says he cannot support availability of the Pill. During a recent Senate debate intended to minimize contraceptive coverage by insurance plans, Senator Dick Durbin (D-IL) said, "I was stunned when I came to Congress many years ago to find that the people most vehemently opposed to abortion were equally opposed to contraception. How can that make sense?"[2]

WHY REPRODUCTIVE RIGHTS?

Other than your partner, and possibly your mother, why would anyone—especially a stranger—care about whether or not you use a condom, keep emergency contraception (EC) on hand, or have an abortion?

It starts with a belief that the only legitimate purposes of sex are reproduction and marital intimacy. Contraception symbolizes sex for other purposes, that is, pleasure. Thus, an attack on contraception is an attack on sex-for-pleasure. And that's what the battle over reproductive rights is all about—limiting sex for pleasure.

So forget "pro-life." Forget "birth control pills cause cancer." Forget "condoms don't protect against a broken heart." Listen to what else the antisex conservatives are saying:

- "When people are less afraid of sex, they have it more."
- "Birth control causes promiscuity."
- "People need to understand that their actions have consequences."
- "God doesn't want anyone using birth control or getting an abortion."

These are not public health messages. They are the strategic thinking of people trying to control the amount and type of sex that *everyone* has.

Why *everyone*? After all, if you think abortion is horrible, don't get one. If you think an intrauterine device (IUD) dehumanizes you, don't use one.

While many Americans believe that whatever two adults do privately is their own private affair, many others disagree. For them, sex is either authorized or unauthorized. And sex is authorized only between legally married heterosexual couples, generally limited to penis-vagina intercourse. The only legitimate reasons for this sex are reproduction and, according to some clergy these days, strengthening the bond of holy matrimony.[3] This means that most Americans are having unauthorized sex. Put another way, most of the sex people have in America is unauthorized, including most religious conservatives.[4]

Those who war on contraception and abortion don't just want to discourage everyone from having unauthorized sex. They want to prevent it, or at least make it as difficult as possible. They may call themselves pro-life, but they're really antichoice. Anti *your* choice.

Why do these people want all unauthorized sex to stop?

They feel it pollutes their world. Obsessed by unauthorized sex, they feel it degrades everyone, even those not participating in it. They don't seem to have the psychological tools to ignore what others do behind closed doors.

Because they are attempting to adhere to a very strict sexual standard, temptation appears everywhere. Understandably, they fear their own (generally rather ordinary) sexual impulses, which they project onto others. Fearing their own sexual decision-making, they mistrust others'. They even talk about "slippery slopes"—that if you think you can "get away" with, say, premarital or extramarital sex, there's no limit to what else you'll do, imagining sex with minors, group sex, even bestiality as the logical conclusion of unmarried people using condoms.

Ultimately, they characterize sexuality as dirty, and therefore incompatible with spirituality, which they claim is what drives them—and legitimizes their attack on your rights.

American government at the national, state, and local levels has created public policy to discourage unauthorized sex and minimize contraceptive use. This itself is a breathtakingly radical development. The policy isn't quite perfectly sealed yet: you can still buy condoms in Safeway (although Safeway can't freely advertise them); most single Americans do have sex (although getting birth control pills and EC is becoming harder); and abortion is still legal for *some* people *some* of the time (if you aren't a teenager, are less than 18 weeks pregnant, can travel several times, and if you can find and afford a provider). But these current parameters aren't the point.

The point is that your government has decided to care about what you do sexually. Again. This time it isn't what you do with your eyes, mouth, or imagination, it's what you do with your genitalia. Our government cares about what you do with your genitalia way more than it cares what you do with your arms or legs. And they aren't even honest about the reasons.

FEMALE EMPOWERMENT

There's another reason some people want to limit or eliminate access to contraception and abortion: it enables women to transcend the limited role of mother, which studies from around the world show is the gateway to more financial and psychological independence.[5]

Reproductive knowledge and practice has always been part of female folk culture. Birth control techniques were practiced in virtually all societies, including herbal potions, ritual infanticide, abortion, magic, withdrawal, vaginal inserts, douches, and cervical caps.

The nineteenth-century bans against abortion and contraception were partly introduced to eliminate midwives, seen as competition by increasingly professionalizing doctors, and to undermine women's emerging reproductive control. And America's industrialization and westward expansion led government and religious groups to desire population growth. In 1905, President Theodore Roosevelt attacked birth control and the new trend towards smaller families as decadent, a sign of moral disease—and a dangerous response to the huge influx of immigrants who were "weakening" America's gene pool.

The new contraceptive technologies of the mid-late twentieth century were seen as particularly progressive because they could potentially sever the link between sexuality and reproduction. Shulamith Firestone emphasized this would free women from the "tyranny of reproduction," which dictated women's oppression.[6]

These technical advances were opposed by conservative and religious forces on so-called moral grounds. But their hypocrisy was exposed a few years later. Whereas abortion and contraception *challenged* the traditional equation of femininity and motherhood, new fertility technologies helped *fulfill* the traditional female role—and were therefore approved by most Christians. Artificial ways of *enabling* reproduction were OK, whereas artificial ways of *preventing* it were not.[7]

As one book put it, "The use of birth control requires a [social] morality that permits the separation of sexual intercourse from procreation, and is related to the extent to which women are valued for roles other than wife and mother."[8] But only a few years after the Pill and *Roe v. Wade*, it was no longer just contraception that disrupted the natural connection between mother and conception or fetus, it was the new kinds of artificially aided fertility, with human eggs and embryos moving in and out of a woman's body, or even from one woman's body to another. Sperm was being geographically manipulated as well.

In 1984, the British government debated regulating reproductive technologies, including restricting techniques such as in vitro fertilization, egg donation, embryo donation, and artificial insemination, to stable, cohabiting heterosexual couples. Such restrictions look quaint today, but they were an attempt to deal with the same question America struggles with today: who will have access to any new technology, and under what circumstances?[9]

Some attempt to frame this as a moral or spiritual or health question, but it isn't. It's a *political* question. Perhaps this is more easily seen if the question is posed as, "Who shall be allowed to access the Internet in North Korea?" Or, "Who shall be allowed to drive a car in Saudi Arabia?"

SEVERAL STRATEGIES

The war on reproductive rights is carried out in several ways at once. The strategies are:

1. Increasing the unwanted consequences of unauthorized sex.
2. Decreasing the motivation for using some or all kinds of contraception and abortion.
3. Limiting access to contraceptive and abortion equipment, technology, and information.

The churches, civic groups, and government agencies who promulgate these policies and restrict our choices uniformly claim that they care primarily about the disadvantages of various contraceptive/abortion technologies, and the personal consequences of their use. And these days, some believe that abortion is morally wrong.

But this is disingenuous. None of the disastrous results they say they're trying to protect us from are actually supported by science. For example, the idea that abortion leads to depression, infertility, and breast cancer, or that premarital sex leads to depression and suicide, are simply untrue. Scary, but *not true*.

Besides, don't Americans deserve the chance to evaluate the costs and benefits of their own choices—and aren't we used to doing so? For example, some people think flying is dangerous, and so they don't, while others think its benefits make flying an acceptable risk. The same is true with driving on New Year's Eve, smoking cigarettes, getting a facelift, and enlisting in the Marines.

Here's how your reproductive rights are being *successfully* challenged:

INCREASING THE UNWANTED
CONSEQUENCES OF UNAUTHORIZED SEX

Those who war on sex depend on a simplistic hypothesis proven wrong repeatedly throughout history, that if you increase the possible dangers of sexual expression, people will stop having sex. This shows such a dramatic lack of insight into their fellow creatures, one could be forgiven for imagining they had never met another human. Fear of AIDS has not prevented Africans from having sex, the risk of capital punishment has not prevented Iranian gays from having sex, and the possibility of unwanted pregnancy has not prevented millions of American teens from having sex.

And yet the fear (no statistics, just fear) of your "promiscuity" is routinely cited as justification for public policy: The belief that giving teenagers access to contraception will reduce their fear of pregnancy and STDs enough so that they'll begin to have sex, or choose to have more sex. The same is true about ending condom distribution in American prisons—as if fear of STDs actually stops some incarcerated men from connecting with or brutalizing others. Or that a reduced fear of STDs would entice some inmates to start having male-male sex they otherwise wouldn't.

This was the idea the government and Christian conservatives trotted out in attempting to restrict your access to EC (the "morning after pill" or Plan B). They said they feared that the drug would lower the risks of sex, thereby encouraging you to have more sex with more partners. In December 2003, Dr. David Hager, one of the four Food and Drug Administration (FDA) committee members who voted against Plan B approval for over-the-counter (OTC) sale, said, "What we heard today was frequently about individuals who did not want to take responsibility for their actions and wanted a medication to relieve those consequences."[10]

Discouraging such behavior is a function of the family (and church), *not* the government. Besides, studies show that access to the drug does *not* increase contraceptive risk-taking.[11] Unfortunately, this *fact* (and very positive safety data) has not influenced the antisex movement's desire to discourage access to and use of the drug (for details about the government's campaign against Plan B, see below).

The latest twist in this irrational saga is the development of a vaccine that can *prevent* HPV—the Right's favorite STD, because it can lead to cervical cancer ("see, sex kills!"). To be effective, the vaccine must be administered *before* a girl becomes sexually active. Remember, the Right is always pointing to HPV/cervical cancer as a tragedy people should avoid by abstaining from unauthorized sex.[12] Then it attacks this medical marvel by claiming, without any data whatsoever, that the vaccine will increase promiscuity by reducing the possible consequences of sex. ("That's OK, Kevin, I'm vaccinated so I can't get HPV, which can lead to cervical cancer. Come on inside me!") Thus, they're against *anyone* using it.[13]

Their alternate strategy for unmarried women to avoid getting HPV when they have sex? Unmarried women shouldn't have sex. "Abstinence is the best way to prevent HPV," says Bridget Maher, of the Family Research Council. "Giving the HPV vaccine to young women could be potentially harmful, because they may see it as a license to engage in premarital sex."[14]

This clearly illustrates that they are far less interested in supporting people's health than they are in controlling others' sexual behavior. They have the right to want this, of course, but their intellectual dishonesty about it is spectacular.

DECREASING THE MOTIVATION FOR USING CONTRACEPTION AND ABORTION

Although reliable contraception is a modern marvel, waging war on sex requires undermining people's motivation for using these products and procedures.

Contraceptive information is, of course, systematically withheld from sex education in most American schools—often by legal requirement. Any young person who develops the habit of using contraception to prevent unwanted pregnancy will have to do so in spite of what he or she learns in school. (For more information, see chapter 2.)

Antisex forces lie about the effectiveness of condoms. After years of urging condom use to prevent HIV, the Center for Disease Control's (CDC) Web site suddenly doubted their efficacy until criticism forced this down in 2005. That same year, physician Senator Bill Frist equivocated on national television about condoms' value in protecting users from HIV. A few months later, after he backed away from that, the FDA proposed requiring labels on condom packages that warn that they are probably less effective against certain STDs, including herpes and HPV, than others.[15] President Bush had been lobbying for such condom labeling for years.[16]

It isn't only the American government that is willing to lie about condoms to discourage their use. For years, James Dobson (Focus on the Family), Jan LaRue (Concerned Women for America), and many others have been talking about how condoms don't protect people very well. In 2003, the Vatican stirred international controversy with its false claim that the HIV virus can pass through condoms, and request that governments "act accordingly."[17]

The "effects" of contraception and abortion have been lied about so often that the lies have acquired the patina of accepted fact. The most common lies are:

- contraception and abortion encourage promiscuity in young people;
- abortion leads to physical problems such as infertility and breast cancer (in Mississippi, those requesting an abortion are required to undergo "counseling," which *must* include the warning that abortion may lead to breast cancer. Both the National Cancer Institute and *Lancet* medical journal refuted this in 2004.);
- abortion leads to mental problems such as depression or suicide;
- RU486 leads to infertility.[18]

No one has pro-
duced any scientific
evidence that these are
true. But antisex con-
servatives obviously
don't trust the faith
of their flock enough
to give them access to
medical and scientific
truth about contracep-
tion and abortion.

The Right attempts
to discourage people
from using abortion
by making the process
so difficult or repulsive
that many women just
give up. Increasingly,
individual states are
using techniques such
as mandatory waiting

THE POPE ON AIDS

The Catholic Church's continuing stance against
condoms as being somehow "immoral" extends to its
opposition to using them to prevent AIDS. In January 2005, Pope John Paul II reaffirmed church teaching urging abstinence and marital fidelity to stop the
spread of AIDS and forbidding condoms. As Nicholas
Kristof commented, "The worst sex scandal in the Catholic Church doesn't involve predatory priests. Rather,
it involves the Vatican's hostility to condoms, which is
creating more AIDS orphans every day. The Vatican's
ban on condoms has cost many hundreds of thousands
of lives from AIDS. Historians . . . will count its anticondom campaign as among its most tragic mistakes
in the first two millennia of its history."[a]

[a]Nicholas D. Kristoff, "The Pope and AIDS, *The New York
Times,* May 8, 2005, http://select.nytimes.com/search/restricted/
article?res=F10A14FD3E540C7B8CDDAC0894DD404482.

periods, forced exposure to photos or ultrasounds, and mandatory, propaganda-
filled lectures.

Thirty-two states *require* that women receive scripted "counseling" before
receiving an abortion, something not required prior to far more dangerous
procedures such as plastic surgery or heart bypass surgery. In 2004, South
Dakota passed a bill requiring that a woman be informed that abortion "will
terminate the life of a whole, separate, unique, living human being." Three
states require disclosure of a supposed link between abortion and breast cancer. Three others require information on possible psychological impacts of
abortion. In 2005, three states introduced bills that would require patients
to view ultrasounds of their fetus, or "unborn child," as South Dakota wants
to require.[19]

Twenty-four states currently *require* a waiting period (usually 24 hours) between counseling and abortion, with bills pending in 10 other states. This ne-
cessitates two separate trips to a clinic, an enormous burden for poor women
or those responsible for children—especially in states where women have to
travel hundreds of miles to get to an abortion provider.

Three states now require women be told that the fetus may feel pain during
abortion, and they must be offered anesthesia provided directly to the fetus. In
2005, 15 more states introduced requirements that informed consent materials must include the claim that the fetus can feel pain. Bills were introduced in
Colorado and West Virginia that would *require* fetal anesthesia *regardless* of a
patient's consent or additional risk.[20]

Eleven states sell "Choose Life" government-issued license plates.[21] In addition to sponsoring this religious propaganda, those states then give the government-collected fees to antiabortion pregnancy crisis centers. In fact, states introduced two dozen bills in 2005 to support these centers. Terrified pregnant women, often young, alone, poor, arrive there and are promised comprehensive information and choices. But they *never* learn their full range of options, and *never* learn the truth about the safety and efficacy of early abortion.

Kansas, for example, now provides grants to organizations that encourage women to carry their pregnancies to term, and prohibits grants to groups that provide abortion. Minnesota just appropriated $5,000,000 to encourage women to carry their pregnancies to term.[22]

DECREASING THE OPTIONS FOR CONTRACEPTION AND ABORTION

Given how clumsy and ineffective our government is in pursuing many of its goals, it has assembled an impressive array of methods to deliberately decrease our contraceptive options.

For starters, the federal and state governments are committed to reducing access to contraception, abortion, and sterilization for anyone under their legal or financial supervision. Women in prison who want legal abortions face tremendous obstacles which are not supposed to exist. Medicaid and Medi-Cal funding for contraception, abortion, and sterilization have been drastically cut. Those on welfare—for whom unwanted pregnancy really can be a matter of life and death—are in terrible trouble. And in 2004, Congress passed a bill denying federal funds to women in the military seeking abortions *even in the case of rape or incest.*[23]

In 2005, 52 state measures were enacted that restrict access to reproductive health care.[24]

Early in 2006, South Dakota made it a felony for doctors to perform any abortion, except to save the life of a pregnant woman. The law was designed to challenge *Roe v. Wade;* its sponsors want to force a reexamination of abortion law by the Supreme Court. According to Republican sponsor Rep. Roger Hunt, lawmakers defeated exceptions for rape, incest, or the health of the woman to maximize the law's impact on the national scene (rather than because it was best for the pregnant women of South Dakota).[25]

And in a dramatic restriction of contraceptive availability, Kansas has now made sex between teenagers more dangerous than ever. Attorney General Phill Kline now demands that doctors, nurses, counselors, and all other care providers report, as abuse, *any* sexual interaction between teens under 16, even when it's consenting and there's neither injury nor complaint. He claims this is to discourage and punish child abuse, but providers are already mandated to report *abuse.* He admits he periodically gets these reports from physicians and others, but, "I do not get them from the abortion clinics."[26] So that's his goal—to continue harassing abortion providers.[27]

In the process he has made it even less likely that teens will request contraception, STD and HIV testing, or simple information about sexual function and health. Quite a repulsive legacy for someone who claims to care about young people. This is a typical example of how the Religious Right's ideology of "protecting life" actually undermines it.

EXILING EMERGENCY CONTRACEPTION

Wouldn't it be great to have a product that could minimize one of the worst heritages of rape and incest; help prevent families from self-destructing; give foolish or unfortunate young people a second chance at a mature, responsible future; and in general, reduce the problematic consequences of sexual intercourse?

There is such a product: emergency contraception (EC). Essentially a high dose of conventional birth control pills, it has been available in Europe and the United States for decades. It prevents pregnancy for up to 72 hours after intercourse. That's the window—72 hours. The common side effects are uncomfortable, but nothing out of any woman's ordinary experience, and certainly absolutely nothing compared to an unwanted pregnancy.

First, the government was pressured against making it available here. Then it was approved, but only for prescription use. Obviously, though, a person needing it needs it immediately. So it must be available OTC and kept on hand. Although there's absolutely no rational reason it shouldn't be, a few key government officials and religious leaders have successfully prevented all of America from having this access.

Faced with an application to make EC available OTC, the FDA first cited bogus safety issues. Then it created a long series of unexplained delays. When the director of the FDA's Office of Women's Health resigned in frustration, and several senators demanded an explanation, the government and religious establishment finally admitted their objection: easier availability of EC would cause "promiscuity."

For example, Dr. David Hager, one of only four FDA committee members who voted against OTC availability, said, "What we heard today was frequently about individuals who did not want to take responsibility for their actions, and wanted a medication to relieve those consequences." And Tony Perkins of the Family Research Council said that making EC available OTC "would make the morning-after pill the new Saturday night party favor of choice."[a] Americans' response should have been simple and direct— "So what?"

Concerned Women for America has trashed the drug, saying it "can lead to promiscuity; it's for the promiscuity lobby." By which, presumably, they mean all those people lined up demanding that young people ruin their lives.[b]

(continued)

(continued)

Those ranting that EC leads to "promiscuity"—a life of depravity which is, of course, every American's God-given right—have clearly failed to read the boring social science literature that shows conclusively that EC *doesn't* increase "promiscuity."[c] The sad truth is that it wouldn't matter if they did, because this government and its religious allies don't trust science. They don't trust sex, and they don't trust you.

At a news conference on August 26, 2005, FDA Commissioner Lester Crawford announced that the agency had "completed its review of this application, as amended, and has concluded that the available scientific data are sufficient to support the safe use of Plan B as an over the counter product, *but only for women who are 17 years of age and older.*" Although there was no reason to insert this age restriction (younger women had been taking oral contraceptives for decades), the conclusion for women over 17 would seem to be simple and positive.

But Crawford then said the possibility of selling the drug both OTC (to consumers 17 and older) and by prescription (to consumers under 17) presented "novel regulatory issues"—which he didn't know how to solve. And so he established a period for public input, delaying the entire matter of OTC availability again.[d]

Later that week, Senator Orrin Hatch (R-UT) called it not "a pharmaceutical issue as much as it's a social issue."[e] Although most people nodded in agreement, this is a staggering admission for a modern democratic nation. What exactly *is* the social issue? It's the technological reduction of the risks of sexual activity, challenged by the desperate desire to maintain those risks.

Ten weeks later, Susan Wood, who had resigned as head of the FDA's Office of Women's Health in protest, said she was "very worried" that political pressure from the same conservative groups who had blocked OTC for EC would also delay availability of a new vaccine that protects against HPV, and therefore against cervical cancer. And for the same reason—that reducing one of the risks involved in sexual contact could lead to "promiscuity" among young women. As we saw above, she turned out to be absolutely right. "I also worry when and if we reach an HIV vaccine," she said, "that they will raise the same argument."[f]

---

[a]http://www.motherjones.com/news/update/2005/11/planb_timeline.html

[b]http://www.cwfa.org/articledisplay.asp?id=7967&department=CWA&categoryid=life

[c]Reproductive Health Technologies Project, at http://www.rhtp.org/news/media/documents/Factsheet-ThecaseforOTCPlanBAug05.doc

[d]http://www.fda.gov/bbs/topics/news/2005/NEW01223.html; http://www.alertnet.org/thenews/newsdesk/N16618935.htm

[e]New York Times, 9/2/05

[f]http://www.alertnet.org/thenews/newsdesk/N16618935.htm

ABORTION TRAINING AND AVAILABILITY

The number of abortion providers in the United States fell from 2,400 in 1992 to 1,800 in 2000,[28] while our population increased by nearly 50 million. Meanwhile,

- in 1996, 86 percent of all counties in the United States lacked an abortion provider; 32 percent of all American women aged 15–44 live in those counties;[29]
- one out of every four women must travel more than 50 miles to obtain an abortion;[30]
- three states have only *one* abortion provider.

At the same time, fewer and fewer medical residents are receiving training in reproductive health services. Only 20 percent of the nation's OB-GYN residency programs require first- and second-trimester abortion training. More than a third of chief residents in family practice receive no training to fit a cervical cap, fit a diaphragm, or insert an IUD. In Maryland, 97 percent of family practice residents and 36 percent of OB-GYN residents had no experience in elective termination of pregnancy in the first trimester. Of their family practice residents, half had never inserted an IUD, 43 percent had never inserted an implant, over a third had never prescribed emergency contraceptive pills, 30 percent had never fitted a diaphragm, 90 percent had never fitted a cervical cap, and 83 percent had no experience with tubal sterilization.

Keeping medical professionals ignorant or biased isn't the only way to limit reproductive choice. Even if a woman can get a prescription for EC, retailers are being successfully lobbied against stocking it. When a woman can't get her prescription filled at Wal-Mart or Target for example, she might have to drive hours for it—which for some people is just impossible.

CATHOLIC HOSPITALS

American hospitals affiliated with the Catholic Church are the nation's largest single group of nonprofit medical facilities. They operate some 600 hospitals, almost 400 nursing homes, and dozens of healthcare systems managing so-called public facilities.

These institutions provide some of America's finest health care. Their beliefs and regulations about sexuality, however, conflict with the needs of many patients. The National Conference of Bishops' "Ethical and Religious Directives for Catholic Health Care Services" unambiguously *forbids:*

- abortions;
- providing contraceptive information and devices;
- issuing or providing information on EC;
- voluntary sterilizations;
- disseminating AIDS and other STD information involving condoms.

And indeed, a 2002 study showed that over 50 percent of Catholic hospitals refused to offer EC to patients under *any* circumstances, including rape.[31]

This is particularly onerous as Catholic hospitals buy up secular facilities across America. Of the 127 mergers involving church-run and secular facilities between 1990–1998, nearly half resulted in the immediate termination of some or all reproductive services. For example, a Poughkeepsie, New York hospital ended abortion services after merging with a Catholic hospital, and a Gilroy, California hospital ended sterilization and contraceptive services after such a merger. As fewer institutions offer reproductive health care, the elimination of a single facility can add hours or even days to the task of getting legitimate services.[32]

Health care at Catholic colleges is similarly compromised. Of 133 Catholic colleges responding to a 2002 survey, only 16 made contraceptives available to students.[33]

TIMELINE: YEARS OF DELAYING OTC APPROVAL OF PLAN B

May 1960	FDA approves oral contraceptives by prescription. It becomes common for doctors to prescribe a combination of oral contraceptive pills for off-label use as EC.
July 1999	FDA approves Plan B as prescription contraceptive.
February 2001	Seventy medical and public health organizations including the American Medical Association petition the FDA to make Plan B available OTC.
May 2001	The Journal of Adolescent Health publishes a study showing that teens who receive advance provision of EC do not use condoms less.
February 2003	A study published in the Journal of Adolescent Health shows that teenage girls with increased access to EC were not more likely to have unprotected sex.
April 2003	Makers of Plan B apply for OTC status, with 15,000 pages of data and research from 39 clinical studies.
December 2003	Forty-three Republicans in Congress, including Majority Leader Tom DeLay, send letters to the FDA urging it to reject OTC status for Plan B.
December 2003	Two scientific panels of experts at the FDA vote 23–4 to recommend Plan B for OTC sales.
February 2004	FDA postpones its decision on Plan B's OTC status for 90 days.

(continued)

(continued)

May 2004	FDA bows to political pressure and denies the application to switch Plan B to OTC status, citing concerns about adolescent use ("promiscuity" and STDs).
January 2005	FDA delays its decision on Plan B again.
July 2005	Secretary of Health and Human Services, Michael Leavitt, promises Senators Hillary Clinton and Patty Murray that the FDA will rule on Plan B by September 1, 2005.
August 2005	FDA announces it will miss its deadline for the third time. Susan Wood, Director of the FDA Office of Women's Health, resigns in protest against FDA Commissioner Lester Crawford's unprecedented interference in agency decision-making.
September 2005	FDA announces it will invite public comments on whether it can approve the OTC application, and whether it could enforce any regulation stopping girls under 17 from buying it.
November 2005	Government Accountability Office (GAO) report confirms the FDA's decision process denying Plan B OTC status is "unusual," and cites evidence of uncharacteristic high-level participation and obstruction.[a]

[a]http://www.prochoiceamerica.org/womenarewaiting_web/index.html

FETAL RIGHTS LEGISLATION

In 2005, 115 fetal rights measures were introduced in almost 40 states. If passed, many would grant a fetus the same rights guaranteed to people in state constitutions. This is critical not only in criminalizing abortion should *Roe v. Wade* be overturned. It will also figure in battles over the *definition* of abortion. For example, some legislators, pharmacists, and religious crusaders are calling EC, which *prevents* pregnancy, an abortion drug. If a fetus has significant legal rights, a legislature could outlaw EC on the grounds that it *may* harm the fetus. Indeed, a Michigan lawmaker has introduced a bill to ban over-the-counter sales of EC in his state in case the FDA legalizes it.[34] In many states, killing a pregnant woman counts as killing two people. This language was conspicuous in California's 2004 Scott Peterson "double murder" trial.[35]

Legal recognition of fetuses' rights is *not* the same thing as criminalizing abortion—it's *worse.* Nor is it the same as declaring when life begins. It's more pervasive, with a cascade of awful effects. This is not an incremental change, it is an earth-shaking event counter to every founding document and principle in American history. The fact that it isn't seen this way is very dangerous. In essence, law has enshrined beliefs—not facts, beliefs—into legal entities. Law has taken moral and metaphysical beliefs and made them facts.

This *can't* be done without compromising the rights of women, whose bodies keep fetuses alive. Mothers are always free to not get abortions, always free to treat their fetuses as if they have legal standing—say, by leaving them money in a will. *But giving a fetus legal standing diminishes the rights of the mother in whose body it's growing.* This is a radical step which places an unfair burden on any pregnant woman (and her partner and any other children).

As the Feminist Women's Health Center says, "The life of a fetus cannot be separated from the life of the pregnant woman. [Doing so] is unique in medicine and law. No one can create a set of medical or legal principles giving a right to life to the fetus, because doing so inevitably limits the woman's rights."[36]

And this is no abstraction. Both pro-choice and antichoice thinkers have discussed the possibility of jailing pregnant women for behavior deemed detrimental to their fetuses. Lynn Paltrow, founder of National Advocates for Pregnant Women, had to file a federal civil rights challenge to a South Carolina hospital policy of searching pregnant women for evidence of drug use and giving the information to police. In 2001, the Supreme Court agreed that this policy violates Fourth Amendment protections against unreasonable searches and seizures.[37]

The antichoice movement clearly cares far more for fetuses than for babies, although babies are *at least* as human as fetuses, thus deserving equal protection. But controlling how people treat already-born babies doesn't help the religious community in their project of controlling sexuality. So we should not be surprised that Mississippi has the most stringent restrictions on abortion in the country, *and* the highest infant-mortality rate. So much for the moral, "pro-life" culture of which they are so proud.

EXAMPLE: INVENTING THE RIGHT TO REFUSE

In response to the legalization of abortion in 1973, federal and state policymakers started enacting "refusal clauses." These laws allowed doctors to refuse to perform or assist in abortions, and hospitals to refuse to allow abortions on their premises. It was a creative and effective way to circumvent the new law.[38]

Since then, refusal clauses have spread to an ever-expanding group of workers and activities—always involving sex. Last year, for example, a Wisconsin pharmacist refused to fill, and actually confiscated, a single woman's prescription for birth control pills. An Illinois ambulance worker refused to transport a patient suffering severe abdominal pain to a clinic for an emergency abortion. Now some hospital workers are refusing to clean surgical instruments or handle paperwork they believe tied to abortion.[39]

MANIPULATING SCIENCE VIA COMMITTEES

Slightly less visibly, but no less importantly, President Bush has been stacking various reproductive science advisory and research positions with ideologues opposed to reproductive services. Here are just a few:

- Tom Coburn, cochair, Presidential Advisory Council on HIV/AIDS—pledged to "challenge the national focus on condom use to prevent the spread of HIV."
- Joseph McIlhaney, CDC Director's Advisory Committee—anticondom activist who, according to his close friend James Dobson, "rather than expecting science to solve our problems, says a better solution involves a return to the spiritual and moral guidelines that have been with us for thousands of years."
- David Hager, Reproductive Health Drugs Advisory Committee of the FDA—opposes prescribing contraceptives to unmarried women, seeks to revoke FDA approval of the RU-486 abortion pill.
- Dr. Joseph Stanford, Reproductive Health Drugs Advisory Committee of the FDA—refuses to prescribe contraceptives of any kind, because "medicine is permeated with attitudes toward sexuality and fertility that are incompatible with Christian values."

Comments Donald Kennedy, past president of Stanford University and editor of Science, "I don't think any administration has penetrated so deeply into the advisory committee structures as this one." Added David Michaels, professor of public health at George Washington University, "They're stacking committees to get the advice they know they want to hear, which is a charade." Even some Congress members are concerned. In 2003, a congressional committee on government reform noted that leading scientific journals have begun to question whether scientific integrity at federal agencies has been sacrificed to further an ideological agenda, finding "numerous instances where the administration has manipulated the scientific process and distorted or suppressed scientific findings."[a]

[a]U.S. House of Representatives, Committee on Government Reform, Minority Staff Office (Washington, DC: Government Printing Office, 2003). (Cited in) The Planned Parenthood Federation of America, "The Assault on Birth Control and Family Planning: Executive Summary" (New York: The Planned Parenthood Federation of America, 2003), 16.

At the moment, medical facilities in 46 states can refuse to provide abortions. This creates huge obstacles for women who can't afford (or aren't healthy enough) to travel the hundreds of miles now sometimes necessary, not to mention the problem of followup care. Many states now protect any institution that refuses to *mention* EC to women who have been raped—and the federal government wants to protect this inadequate medical care nationally.

Another pending federal measure would forbid state or local governments from requiring any individual or institution to perform, provide, refer for, or pay for an abortion under any circumstances. This would virtually end states' ability to ensure abortion access for low-income women, even in cases of life endangerment, rape and incest, as required under Medicaid.

Congress and many states are now attempting to extend refusal rights to virtually anyone involved in health information or services, for any reason. For example, a 2005 Mississippi law allows "any employee of any hospital, clinic, nursing home, pharmacy or medical school to refuse to participate in counseling, diagnosis, research or administering of any type of drug, device, surgery, care or treatment by asserting an objection on moral, ethical or religious grounds."[40] This same law allows payers of health care to refuse to cover any service to which they object on moral grounds, which could include sterilization, HIV treatment, STD diagnosis or treatment, contraception, or even prenatal checkups for women who "shouldn't" be pregnant.

"Moral grounds." Today, that's code for *sex*. "Morality" hasn't led pharmacists to demand the right to refuse to fill prescriptions for drugs tested on animals, or drugs whose manufacture pollutes the environment, or drugs that are too expensive for anyone but the wealthy or well-insured, or drugs with awful side effects, or drugs that make children violent or adults submissive zombies. No, "moral grounds" means, "Makes sex safer or more enjoyable."

Shockingly, most states now allow pharmacists to refuse to fill any legal prescription, and new laws protect pharmacists who then refuse to refer patients to other pharmacies that will help them. The American Pharmacists Association wants to protect "pharmacists' rights to not dispense drugs they are opposed to." The Christian Legal Society's Center for Law and Religious Freedom says it's un-American to ask pharmacists to sacrifice their rights for their jobs. The Family Research Council wants the Workplace Religious Freedom Act passed to protect pharmacists' rights to uphold their "morals" at work.

Pharmacists do not have this "right." Your Aunt Mabel does—*in private.* Indeed, pharmacists have the same rights as your Aunt Mabel to withhold, cajole, persuade, and bully in order to shape your behavior—in private.

Pharmacists and pharmacies are licensed by the state to provide health care. As such, they must adhere to standard U.S. medical practices and serve the entire community, regardless of race, ethnicity, age, height, eye color, and shoe size. Or medication requested, or condition it's designed to treat. That's the responsibility pharmacists take on in exchange for the privileges of their license. Anyone is free to believe that some people should not have access to certain medications—but acting on this belief disqualifies a person from being a pharmacist.

Discrimination is discrimination, whether a pharmacist bases it on *your* religion or *his.* Refusing to sell medication to help a single woman have responsible sex is just as bad as refusing to sell a black family a house in a white neighborhood.

The government's job is to set standards based on science so consumers, who can't possibly evaluate professional competence, are safe. Consumers can use any criteria they like, including moral values, to decide which medications and procedures to use or avoid. *That's* the American promise.

The Bible, while silent on abortion, repeatedly demands humility and compassion. Pharmacists who won't dispense EC to a woman who has only a few hours left to prevent an unwanted pregnancy need to have their Viagra prescription denied, their blood pressure medication delayed, and their eyeglass prescription confiscated. Since their religion hasn't taught them compassion, perhaps these experiences would.

ENFORCING MORALITY ON OTHERS

Shall there be any limit on people's right to enforce their morality on others? If pharmacists demand this right, what about other people demanding their rights? These might include:

- a cab driver refusing to take you to a Planned Parenthood clinic;
- a 7–Eleven clerk who won't sell you alcohol because you shouldn't drink;
- a Bloomingdale's clerk who won't let you spend any money on goods made in China;
- a toy store clerk who won't let you buy toy guns or sexy Barbies;
- a physician who won't let you have a blood transfusion that's against God's will;
- a lawyer who won't write a will leaving your money to your lazy son;
- a high school counselor who won't help a girl get into MIT because girls shouldn't be scientists.

Since some pharmacists demand the right to withhold any medication that facilitates sex-related behavior of which they disapprove, we can also expect to hear the following rationales for being refused legally prescribed medication:

- "No, that estrogen for your sex-reassignment interferes with God's creation of men and women."
- "No, you're gay, and you'll use that Viagra to have abominable gay sex."
- "No, treating your vaginal infection will allow you to resume sex—which, since you're single, you shouldn't be having."
- "No, that medication will relieve the pain of a vasectomy you shouldn't have had."
- "No, antidepressants will make you a more feisty woman, disrupting family harmony."
- "No, Prozac will make it hard for you to ejaculate, indirectly limiting your family size."
- "No, testosterone will increase your postmenopausal sex drive, and there's no need for that."

Chapter Five

The Sexual Disaster Industry

There is so much money to be made scaring the hell out of Americans about sexuality that no one on this gravy train can afford to slow it down. Any outsider who questions this juggernaut is immediately labeled insensitive, anti-family, immoral, or a pedophile.

The Sexual Disaster Industry (SDI) involves federal and local government, conservative religion, so-called morality organizations, right-wing think tanks, victim-parade daytime talk shows like *Montell* and *Maury,* and news programs looking for a bump ("Isn't it awful the way people go to strip clubs? Film at 11!"). Honorable mention goes to the psychotherapy profession (current motto: "You're *sure* you were never molested?") and to the nighttime adrenalin-rush crime shows like *CSI.*

Acting independently (while reacting to common cultural imperatives and personal anxieties), these institutions daily overstate the amount of sexual violence, sexual danger, sexual immorality, and sexual *freakiness* around us. They've created the illusion of an enormous sexual "other" living in our midst—tens of millions of sexual predators, bisexual sadomasochist anarchists, satanic molesting sex educators, wanton husband-stealing strippers, and malevolent shyster pornographers.

The Industry is continually inventing and warning us about new sex-related disasters in the making. And although government, religion, and civic groups are working overtime creating more and more solutions, everyone agrees that our safety and peace of mind is further away than ever. It would seem that our sex-related problems are just too big, that American sexuality (actually, human sexuality) is just too degenerate. That's why programs need more money, citizens need to be more vigilant, people need to give up more rights, and government has to pass ever-stricter laws.

There's a better explanation.

The contemporary American narrative of sex-as-danger is a rich one. In this well-known tale, our country is filled with pedophiles and date rapists; pornography drives people to destroy their marriages and to commit violence and perversion; sexual entertainment damages communities; sex education seduces children into having sex; premarital sex leads to STDs, pregnancy, depression, and suicide; contraception leads to promiscuity, ruining lives; and abortion leads to breast cancer, sterility, and crippling guilt.

Almost all sexual choices are morally wrong, physically dangerous (for self or others), and economically and politically disastrous. Managing one's own sexuality, or the sexuality of one's neighbors and community, therefore, involves reducing anxiety and minimizing danger, not maximizing intimacy, self-exploration, pleasure, or spirituality. It's a full-time job.

The SDI translates this abstract cultural narrative into tangible problems that frighten real people. Some of the alleged threats they've recently cooked up that will require our anxious attention include people watching porn videos in the backseats of SUVs; couples who go to sex clubs to meet other couples; a vaccine that could prevent cervical cancer, which will, of course, encourage teens to have more sex; the Gay Agenda, which intends to abolish heterosexual pair-bonding and childrearing; kids hearing swear words on network and cable TV; and Amazon.com selling sex toys as if they were just another consumer item. Every single one of these has been criminalized or is the target of a powerful "morality" pressure group.

Government hearings periodically bless the latest problem from which we must defend our families. Some of Washington's recent crusades involve "promiscuity," cybersex, and alleged over-reliance on contraception (in the country with the highest rate of unintended pregnancy in the industrialized world). The idea that the U.S. Senate would hold hearings with titles like, "The Science Behind Pornography Addiction" and "Open Forum on Decency" sounds like a Jay Leno gag. If only.

The government selects the witnesses to these hearings who will provide the exact outcome it wants. Junk science, like Judith Reisman's antiporn delusion about "eroto-toxins," is common. The basic qualification of many who get to testify is that they're *really* upset. Or a reformed pervert. So ex-porn junkies like Phil Burress create Citizens for Community Values, and demand action about porn addiction. Concerned Women for America lectures senators about contraception causing promiscuity. Donna Rice Hughes washes out as Gary Hart's eye candy and is reborn as an expert on abstinence and Internet porn. It's like credentialing someone as a doctor because she's really worried about illness, or choosing an accountant because he's flunked several audits.

Oh, for some actual expertise: sexologists, sociologists, psychologists. But expertise would contradict the media-religion-civic group-politician Disaster Axis (religion and the media terrify people, civic groups offer solutions, politicians fund them). Science, statistics, historical perspective—they might tell us that our kids, our property values, and our bodies are safer than we think. Americans don't want this good news. Given our guilt and shame about sex, problems and anxiety make more sense. So problem-oriented faux expertise ("Look at me, I know how dangerous sex is") carries the day.

Every industry promotes basic assumptions about the world in which its customers live, and how its products improve lives. Despite a lack of evidence—despite *contradictory* evidence—the SDI has effectively persuaded Americans that the following (unproven) beliefs are principles of modern life (which, of course, justify the very existence of the Industry):

1. Kids are damaged by exposure to sexual words, pictures, and concepts.
2. America is full of sexual predators—and the situation is getting worse.
3. Ultimately, people can't explore sexuality safely.
4. People interested in sexual stimulation, exploration, or unusual stuff, are "them," not "us."
5. Eliminating venues for sexual experiences will eliminate sexual behavior.
6. Feeling scared about sexuality is responsible citizenship and common sense.

Together, these six assumptions create a landscape of danger and power-lessness, in which suspicion of one's own and others' sexuality is sensible. Surrounded by this much danger and potentially explosive eroticism, fear (and resentment) isn't just plausible, it seems responsible.

This is the context for the SDI's marketing of its products: programs, laws, investigations, new psychological diseases. Allegedly designed to make our lives safer, in reality they make people more frightened. And when people are more frightened, they don't ask questions about whether programs are making them safer—they just want *more* of them. The constant reminders of the Amber Alert system makes parents feel more afraid, not less (while rescuing a tiny handful of kids); date-rape awareness classes make dating scarier, not easier (while date-rape reports increase).

And so regardless of the alleged problem being addressed (porn addiction, stranger abduction, date-rape drugs, blight surrounding strip clubs), the Industry's solutions (its product) always involve the same things: desexualize the environment, reduce the opportunity for sexual expression, increase the costs of sexual activity, increase community anxiety, divide people into the sexually "safe" (us) and "dangerous" (them).

The true product of the SDI isn't safety, but fear. If it were safety, the Industry would encourage:

- condom use among men and women;
- comprehensive school sexuality education;
- regular, ongoing parent-child discussions about sex;
- preventing or relieving childhood guilt about masturbation;
- widespread understanding that most childhood sexual exploitation is done by familiars, not strangers;
- making the new HPV vaccine routine for all preteen girls;

- funding actual research into the cause and treatment of childhood sexual exploitation;
- including sexual orientation in national antidiscrimination law;
- training marriage counselors and psychologists to understand, rather than demonize, pornography use;
- licensing swing clubs instead of driving them underground.

That's just for starters.

The SDI's newest product is fear of same-sex marriage. It's crazy, but of course they predict disaster: straights won't marry anymore, people will demand the right to marry animals or their own children, no one will have kids anymore, children will no longer aspire to couple, too many children will be raised (poorly) by gay parents.

It's all nonsense.

If they were honest, they'd say, "We're against same-gender marriage because it's against our religion. We don't think anyone should have the right to do that." But that doesn't inflame people. The SDI doesn't want people annoyed, it wants them frightened and angry. It can then channel those feelings into political power and financial gain. Annoyed people don't donate time or money. Angry, frightened people do.

The Religious Right's hypocrisy is astounding. They claim to care about the children, women, men, and families supposedly at risk from the sex-related disasters they describe in fetishistic detail. They tell us to support this or that law, give up these or those rights. But they disappear when it comes to addressing the actual risks Americans really do face—*risks that the Religious Right is creating and exacerbating every day.*

These include the child who's feeling more guilt about sex, the teen who's more vulnerable to unwanted pregnancy, the prostitute who's more subject to police shakedowns, the swinger who loses custody of her son, the newlywed who can't buy a vibrator, the lesbian unfairly dismissed from her job, and the couple who can't get emergency contraception. They aren't abstractions—theirs are real lives, compromised or ruined by the self-righteous, ultimately worthless flailing about of the SDI.

The SDI's goal isn't to address the real problems of real people. It's to 1) inspire us to fear sex, and 2) provide society with excuses to restrict sexual expression.

No, they won't fix the problems they say they're so upset about. The only thing they fear more than sex is going out of business.

Chapter Six

Battleground: *Broadcast "Indecency"*

Some people are so upset about what *they* see on TV and hear on the radio that they'll do anything to prevent *you* from seeing or hearing it. That's not the American way, and it's not in the spirit of democracy. But rather than shut the set, rather than change the channel, rather than use tools like the V-chip or filters, these people are using the most primitive, blunt instrument they can—destroying *everyone's* right to see and hear what they want.

Is it just the stuff that comes into your house for free, whether you asked for it or not? No. They even want to destroy everyone's right to *pay* to see and hear what they want. And, of course, the stuff they're upset about has to do with sexuality—sexual health, words, themes, jokes, and relationships.

As I write this, Congress is talking about regulating the content that can be transmitted over premium cable channels like HBO and Showtime—which you can get only if you pay for them. "Morality" groups and Congress want to criminalize sexuality-related programming of all kinds. It's a new version of Prohibition, in which a small group of people decides how everyone is going to live.

Let's briefly list the kinds of "sex-related programming" under fire:

- Sexual themes in sitcoms, dramas, movies, talk shows, news shows, and cartoons (adult or children's)
- Erotic activity—on or off camera, including kissing if it's two men or two women
- Descriptions of erotic activity, whether poetic, funny, clinical, or dramatic
- Exposure of breasts, buttocks, and genitals, whether in sexual context or not (e.g., autopsy in crime show, famine victims in the news, mammogram in health feature)
- "Vulgar" or "curse" or "bad" words, or references to bathroom activities
- Commercials for sex-related products such as Viagra, condoms, and tampons

If that appears to cover practically every program and every kind of situation, you're right. They want to censor every show and every commercial you watch.

Erotophobes and government officials say they think it's all vile. They want it controlled, or, at the very least, eliminated from 6:00 A.M. to midnight, the time period that virtually all Americans are watching or listening. That leaves midnight to 6:00 A.M. as "adult time" (how much do you use TV or radio after midnight?), although they say they want this regulated as well—just not quite as much.

These government officials and nongovernment morality groups want something that's unknown in any other Western country—to eliminate virtually any depiction of or reference to sexuality on TV and radio, whether programs are free or paid. They present this goal as reasonable, but it represents a radical change in how America is governed. And it represents the triumph of fear over freedom.

Because the war over broadcast "indecency" is a national power struggle. It's a struggle over how sexuality will be perceived: as a danger to be feared and regulated, or as an inevitable part of life that challenges us to grow and demands to be understood and celebrated. Even more than that, the war over broadcast "indecency" is about the nature of pluralism: is *it* something to be feared and regulated, or is *it* a unique and precious part of our American heritage that must be continually protected from both external and internal threats?

This, more than the right to see Janet Jackson's nipple, is the crucial political issue every freedom-loving American should care about. The War on Sex is the battlefield on which the issue of pluralism will be fought. The War on Sex is a Theater of Power.

The very way the public debate is framed—"the problem of indecency"—is problematic. It's similar to expressions like "the Jewish problem" or "the gay problem," which assume that the conflict is caused by the presence of Jews, gays, or alleged indecency. Such constructs dramatically limit the solutions that can be generated. I say we don't have an indecency problem. How different it would be if the contemporary discussion was about "the contrast in values problem" or "the some people's discomfort with sex-related programming problem," or "the intolerance problem." Even if we did not solve such problems, this formulation would be progress—over people frantically trying to solve the wrong "problem."

WHAT EXACTLY IS THE ALLEGED HARM?

In what way are the so-called F word (is there a more juvenile expression?), tampon commercials, and talk shows about threesomes harmful to Americans? Here's what The Parents Television Council (PTC) claims, without any documentation whatsoever:

> Thousands upon thousands of clinical studies [really?!] show a direct, causal relationship between the messages children see in the media and their behavior and development . . .
>
> Time and time again, we see our children being disrespectful. We hear them using language that would never have been used in our grow-

ing up years, ever. We see a sexual awareness that at the very least is disturbing. What will these youngsters be like when they are adults? Won't they exhibit the same antisocial behavior that is a part of their world today? I'm afraid that is so.[1]

The typical anti-indecency arguments ultimately come down to:

1. exposure to sexual themes and words is dangerous for kids;
2. exposure to sexual themes and words damages adult relationships;
3. the broadcast of sexual themes and words forces adults to have conversations with kids that adults don't want to have;
4. sexual themes and words in the media "coarsens" our culture;
5. "moral" people deserve to have their "morality" validated, and deserve to have others' "immoral" interests eliminated from the public sphere;
6. some people are mentally unbalanced, and hearing "bad" words or seeing "bad" body parts might motivate them to commit sex crimes.

Let's answer these one by one.

1. Exposure to sexual themes and words is dangerous for kids.

Prove it.

Actually, the kind of sexuality typically portrayed and referenced *isn't* the best for kids to see or hear—it's stupid and stereotypical and sometimes really unrealistic. But even at its stupidest, the simple fact that it's sexual doesn't make it dangerous for them.

2. Exposure to sexual themes and words damages adult relationships.

Prove it.

Are most adults and their relationships so fragile, so vulnerable to sexual themes and words? Are adults never bored or selfish, violent, unfaithful, or imaginative without TV or radio?

As a marriage counselor for 25 years, I'm pretty familiar with the limitations of many relationships around communication and intimacy. I see this with my couples every week, and it's pretty independent of what they're listening to or watching. Seeing a breast on Howard Stern that isn't digitally covered or hearing raunchy language on a radio show makes no difference in a couple's ability to negotiate differences or trust each other. Watching a condom commercial or actors tongue-kissing may make a couple uncomfortable, but it doesn't damage them. And if their discomfort about such harmless stuff is strong enough to make them retreat from each other, the couple's problems go way deeper than what's on TV or radio.

3. The broadcast of sexual themes and words forces adults to have conversations with kids that adults don't want to have.

Yes, that's right. And that's *good*; it's called "parenting." TV and radio offer an unending series of teachable moments, of opportunities for adults to talk with kids about sexuality, relationships, decision-making, gender, and values. This is the antidote to whatever is bothering parents about any possible harm from sex on the media. The solution to dumb talk is smart talk, not no talk.

Talking with your kids about references to sexuality on TV and radio isn't a problem, it's a solution. If some adults are uncomfortable with this opportunity, that's no reason to eliminate it for other parents, and no reason to punish non-parents.

4. Sexual themes and words in the media "coarsens" our culture.

Our culture has indeed changed in the 58 years since television was invented. During this time America has also participated in four wars and lived through the invention of the Pill, a huge increase in the number of women in the full-time workforce, a dramatic increase in the age of first marriage, a huge exodus of middle-class people from the core of every big American city, the decriminalization of contraception, abortion, and sex between unmarried people, a huge increase in the daily privacy of school-age children and teenagers, and the geographic dispersion of most families. Not to mention the invention of the Internet and cell phone. America has changed even more radically in the 90 years since the start of commercial radio.

If American culture has become coarsened, every one of these demographic changes is responsible along with sexuality themes in the media. This general trend is worrisome to many people. Feeling helpless to turn back the clock, some of them try to reduce their anxiety by attempting to censor the media. It's a selfish and desperately retrograde strategy that hurts others, but they don't seem to care.

"Sexual themes in the media has coarsened our culture" is a statement that sounds reasonable, is impossible to prove or disprove, and is a substitute for actual thinking or facts. It's just as easy to suggest that sexuality in the media has *enriched* our culture—for example, by discussing breast cancer treatments, advertising condoms, exposing sexual exploitation, supporting the sexual function of older people, and encouraging couples to talk with each other about their sexual concerns.

5. "Moral" people deserve to have their "morality" validated, and deserve to have others' "immoral" interests eliminated from the public sphere.

For starters, *whose* morality? People who are certain that there's only one morality have a simple answer—theirs. People who understand that there's more than one way of understanding life don't have that same certitude, and so their voices on this, unfortunately, are typically not as loud.

The value judgment that sexual inhibition equals morality is by no means a fact, and is by no means universal. More importantly, the U.S. Supreme Court (in *Lawrence v. Texas, 2004*) challenged the very idea that enhancing "morality" was a valid government function. Using government power to restrict the content of broadcast media for this reason, therefore, should be clearly seen as both inappropriate and illegal in a secular democracy.

6. Some people are mentally unbalanced, and hearing "bad" words or seeing "bad" body parts might motivate them to commit sex crimes.

Prove it.

This is the desperate plea of last resort. "If everyone were normal, the sex stuff on TV and radio might be OK, but some people are disturbed, and we must limit everyone's rights so we don't encourage these disturbed people to do dangerous things."

Public policy generated by the fear of a handful of crazies is *never* sensible, and isn't the norm in American life. We don't limit food distribution because of bulimics, we don't limit car distribution because of terrible drivers, and we don't limit lotteries or casinos because of compulsive gamblers.

I challenge the sincerity of would-be censors' fear of "the crazies." If they were seriously concerned, they would have eliminated all guns following the 1999 school shootings in Columbine—but they didn't. They would have eliminated college fraternities because of the periodic injuries or deaths during hazing—but they haven't. The "What about the crazies?" argument is just another strategy for lowering the acceptable standard of adult media experience (along with "What about the children?"). It's intellectually indefensible, and we shouldn't give it any weight.

As talk show host Dick Cavett said about TV causing violence and other social problems, "There's so much comedy on television. Does that cause comedy in the streets?"[2]

There's one more point about the alleged harm of sexual imagery on radio and television. Western Europe has been running the experiment America refuses to, for decades. Western European radio and television feature words, themes, and pictures (including nudity) that are prohibited to American audiences and broadcasters. According to the predictions of America's moral crusaders, Europe should therefore be a cesspool of sexual perversion. But it's just the opposite. Table 6.1 shows some convincing facts.[3]

It's what parents are always telling their eight-year-olds: "I know you're afraid, but that doesn't mean there's something real to be afraid of."

THEY SEE SEX EVERYWHERE—AND THEY HATE IT

Let's return to the list of sex-related broadcasting that the crusaders are trying to eliminate. You'll recall it's a long, long list.

That's a big problem for them—they see sex *everywhere*. Where you might laugh (or not) at a simple joke on Comedy Central about penis size, crusaders

Table 6.1
Teen Birth and Abortion Rates, by Country

Nation	Teen Birth Rates (per 1,000 women ages 15–19)	Teen Abortion Rates (per 1,000 women ages 15–19)
United States	48.7	27.5
Netherlands	4.5	4.2
Germany	12.5	3.6
France	10.0	10.2

feel assaulted. Where you might ignore a tampon or douche commercial, they feel assaulted. Where you might be turned off (or intrigued) by an *Oprah* episode about teen hookers, they feel assaulted. That's a lot of assault. If you're not obsessed with sex, you might not even put these three experiences together in your mind. You might casually observe "dumb joke + health product + social problem (exaggerated or not)." They perceive "sex + sex + sex." And for them, it never stops; people obsessed with sex they resent never have a nice day.

When people are obsessed by sex—not about doing it, but by the subject— they see it *everywhere.* Like a four-year-old in a candy store or an eight-year-old at a scary movie, they are simply not emotionally equipped to ignore what they see. We should feel sympathy for these people, but they make it difficult, because they deal with their upset in such an aggressive way. You know how some people have a frustrating day at work, come home, and kick their dog? People who are obsessed by sex regularly feel assaulted by yet another on-air example of it (remember, they don't know how to ignore it), and in response they kick *you.*

And then they claim it's for your own good. Nice touch. Do they say that to their dog while kicking it, too?

What if such people saw sex everywhere, but *didn't* fear it? It is, after all, possible to see the erotic *potential* around us—sexual issues in healthcare, the needs of teens to be better prepared for relationships, the beauty of people talking honestly about difficult sexual feelings, the complexity of adultery, the poetry of everyday eros—and rather than feel repulsed and desperate to escape from it, to feel intrigued, compassionate, bemused, and involved in the human parade, the Divine Comedy.

We could argue that moral crusaders *can't* evaluate the "community standard" around sexuality, because they don't see *any* sex-related issue *in context* (and seeing things in context is part of the legal requirement for determining the community standard). Consider their outrage about the soldiers' language in *Saving Private Ryan,* or the shriveled, bare breasts of Holocaust prisoners in *Schindler's List*—crusaders literally can't see these as non-erotic, because once a theme or word or picture in any way relates to sexuality, it belongs to the single, simplistic category they have—"sexy."

Moral crusaders have also invested magical, demonic powers in certain combinations of syllables. They have spent millions of dollars pursuing NASCAR driver Dale Earnhardt's "s-word expletive," Bono's "F word expletive," and Comedy Central roasts that "bring unspeakable vulgarity" into U.S. households.[4] The legislature and courts of our proud democracy have actually spent thousands of working hours debating whether Bono used "fucking" as an adjective or a sexual reference[5]—a legal point that would determine whether adults were allowed to hear it on TV.

Seeing sex everywhere, and hating it, explains censors' desperate grab for power, and their desperate demand for action *now*. But asking these people about a "community standard" regarding sexuality is like asking an anorexic to evaluate a movie for its possible connection to food or eating—which they'd see in every frame.

When the government or crusaders refer to a "community standard," should it be the standard of people who see sex everywhere, or of healthier people who have a less obsessive perspective? We must acknowledge that for people who see sex everywhere, cleansing the environment so that they see none is virtually impossible. They will never be satisfied, as we'll see below in the section on children's programming.

"WHY MUST YOU INCLUDE SEX IN EVERYTHING?"

This is a common complaint of those who want less eroticism in the public sphere. But that's the wrong question, a phony question. And once moral crusaders get everyone looking at the wrong question, it doesn't matter what answers people come up with.

The right question is, "Why must you *delete* eroticism from everything?"

Sexuality is an enormous part of human life. That's why, whether on cave walls, pottery, papyrus, or the Internet, it's been a central theme of art since the beginning of recorded history.[6]

The choices faced by the broadcast media (and of all performing, literary, and fine arts) are to portray sexual themes well, portray them poorly, or omit them. Erotophobes want America to move from portraying sexuality poorly to omitting it. We actually need to move in the opposite direction—from portraying it poorly to portraying it well.

Unfortunately, the sexual material on TV and radio is either stupid (e.g., sitcoms, shock jocks) or extreme (e.g., *CSI, Nip/Tuck*). Broadcast media typically portray sexual themes, situations, and feelings as less interesting, less rich, and less sophisticated than they can be, not to mention less accurately and more stereotyped. That actually *is* a problem, but antisex crusaders don't see it.

We need more everyday, real stuff in between these poles—an idea which, oddly, many observers consider too radical. The intensity of *CSI*-type sexual references may be in bad taste, but it's inevitable. It's how both Hollywood and audiences act out their frustration with the lack of realistic sexuality in broadcasts. It's why the second a show announces that it's pushing the edge on language or nudity—*NYPD Blue*, *The Sopranos*, *The Daily Show*—people rush to tune in. Imagine—characters talking or behaving like real people—incredible!

Methodically stripping sexuality from the public arena not only distorts all portrayals of life, the process itself is socially devastating. We saw this in Europe's witch hunts, Victorian England, and again in Afghanistan under the Taliban.

We must stop being defensive about this and say unequivocally, "Yes, eroticism *belongs* in broadcast media presentations—because it's part of the lives the media portrays, and the lives of its audience. Coming to terms with sexuality is part of growing up. This involves a process that may not always be comfortable, but it is essential for emotional, spiritual, family, and community health. The opposite? Think Salem, Massachusetts. Think about turn-of-the century American children who were literally handcuffed to their bedposts each night to prevent them from destroying their health through masturbation.[7] Think about the sexually tormented J. Edgar Hoover, and Joseph McCarthy tormenting the rest of us.

Stories about real life, commercials about real situations, jokes about real misunderstandings—the media doesn't *insert* sex into these, sex *lives* in these. Americans need and deserve to see it and hear it, in recognizable, sophisticated, normal-seeming ways.

Morality groups and many elected Congress members want the airwaves sanitized to be "family friendly" or "safe for children." This assumes that families never observe or discuss sexual themes, and it begs the question of what *is* safe for children; morality crusaders apparently mean it to be reducing all programming and advertising to themes and words that won't challenge kids' alleged innocence.

This would give children way more rights than adults—which, by the way, is exactly what these same groups are trying to do regarding the Internet (see chapter 8). But as Mark Twain said, "Censorship is telling a man he can't have a steak just because a baby can't chew it."

It is dangerous for a democracy to restrict adults to what's (supposedly) safe for kids. It keeps citizens from facing and exploring different ways of addressing adult challenges. It encourages passivity and narrow thinking. But to those in power, desexualized adults are less threatening than full adults. And for morality groups, convincing a million people that F words in the living room are more dangerous than toxic waste across town, or overcrowded classrooms down the street, creates a constituency that is frightened and therefore motivated to donate money and time to morality groups.

INDECENCY VS. OBSCENITY VS. "I HATE IT"

The legal and political issue of "indecency" is confusing for two reasons. First, the very idea of a democratic government giving itself the right to determine what adults can see and hear is bizarre. Second, because this bizarre idea contradicts the guarantees of our Bill of Rights, Congress and the courts have had to erect odd ways of defining what is and isn't permissible.

Speech and broadcasts related to sexuality fall into three legal categories: (1) obscenity, (2) indecency, and (3) non-obscene, non-indecent stuff that some people hate. The three are defined below. If the legal language sounds like subjective nonsense, that's because it is. But our government takes these criteria seriously. Prosecutors and morality groups depend on these definitions to help them limit what you can hear or see.

1. "Obscene" material must meet a three-prong test:

   - An average person, applying contemporary community standards, must find that the material, as a whole, appeals to the prurient interest (i.e., characterized by an inordinate and unhealthy sexual interest or desire);
   - The material must depict or describe, in a patently offensive way, sexual conduct specifically defined by applicable law; and
   - The material, taken as a whole, must lack serious literary, artistic, political, or scientific value.

Obscene speech is *not* protected by the First Amendment and cannot be broadcast at any time.

2. "Indecent" material, in context, depicts or describes, in terms patently offensive as measured by contemporary community broadcast standards, sexual or excretory organs or activities.

It is illegal to broadcast anything indecent between 6:00 a.m. and midnight.

3. It is *not* illegal to broadcast non-obscene, non-indecent things that some people hate.

You can see that when a civic group or elected officials want to restrict your access to certain words or pictures, getting the government or the courts to decide that it's indecent or obscene is a phenomenally powerful tool. Once something is ruled indecent or obscene, the government then has the right (actually, the obligation) to restrict or ban it.

The Federal Communications Commission (FCC) could decide, for example, that the word "breast" is indecent, in which case, adults wouldn't be allowed to hear it on the air between 6:00 a.m. and midnight, seven days per week. It could even decide that the word "breast" is obscene, in which case it wouldn't be allowed on any show at any time. Farfetched? Well, groups like Citizens for Community Values are pushing legislation that redefines certain words and images. And already, we take it for granted that Jay Leno can't say the words clitoris or fellatio, much less show examples of either.[8]

As these definitions show, a bureaucrat, judge, or Congress have wide latitude in determining which words and pictures you do not have the freedom to hear, see, or broadcast. "The problem is, the indecency 'standard' is not a standard," argues Cato adjunct scholar Robert Corn-Revere. "It's basically a test for what people find distasteful, which is entirely in the eyes and ears of the beholder."[9] Too much of the War on Sex is described as allowing or restricting broadcasters from doing this or that. While this is accurate, *your* rights to hear and see are equally under attack. This crucial point seems to get lost over and over.

THE FCC: PROTECTING YOU FROM . . . YOURSELF?

The FCC's original mandate was to (1) encourage diversity of programming, (2) make sure there was programming specifically designed for children, and (3) assign unique frequencies to radio and television broadcasters from the usable spectrum that was limited by the technology of the day.

The FCC has pretty much given up on its first two mandates. And now that satellites, coaxial cable, and broadband have expanded our viewing choices almost infinitely, the "public airwaves" are an entirely different kind of resource, which virtually eliminates the third rationale for the FCC as currently constituted.

When the FCC started insisting it could and should police broadcast *content*, it justified its interference because "TV and radio come into the privacy of people's homes."[10] It was a ridiculous argument, but the courts agreed. The rise of satellite radio, cable TV and pay-per-view TV has demolished that audience-as-passive-victim argument.

But under a series of activist commissioners, the FCC has recently assumed the highly dynamic role of government watchdog of what Americans can see and hear. There are only two precedents for this, both disastrous: the 1873 Comstock Act severely punished anyone mailing anything "lewd" (including contraceptive information) and lasted for 100 years. The Motion Picture Production Code stifled American film production from 1930–1968, promising that "No picture shall be produced that will lower the moral standards of those who see it. . . . Correct standards of life . . . shall be presented. Law, natural or human, shall not be ridiculed."[11]

The FCC has blown its original mandate—they've overseen the unprecedented concentration of media ownership into just a few corporate hands, leading to the near-destruction of local commercial radio, as well as the news

THE FCC HALL OF SHAME

Here are a few recent incidents involving alleged broadcast indecency that clearly illustrate the seriousness of those pursuing the War on Sex. Speculate, for a moment, on what the next such incident could be. More importantly, speculate on what the impact of that incident would be on America's writers, producers, directors, and programmers...and citizens.

Censored: New Orleans Mayor Nagin

On September 1, 2005, New Orleans Mayor Ray Nagin was interviewed on WWL-AM radio about the devastation of his city. His anger at the slow federal response and his grief at the resulting destruction were clear.

And they were censored.

Radio and TV stations around the country carried parts of his interview, with his language bleeped:

"I keep hearing that this [help] is coming and that is coming. And my answer to that is BS.

"These goddamned ships that are coming, I don't see them. . . .

"They [President Bush and others] flew down here one time two days after the doggone event was over with TV cameras, AP reporters, all kind of goddamn—pardon my French, everybody in America, but I am pissed..."

The destruction of New Orleans last year was a turning point in our nation's economic, cultural, and political history. The Mayor's experience of Washington's betrayal, honestly expressed with a few "goddamns" and "BSs," were a newsworthy part of that history—and considered inappropriate by the nation's media.

The interview ends with the Mayor and his interviewers in silent tears.

Censored: Garrison Keillor

Yes, that Garrison Keillor, the tapioca-voiced sage of the Midwest, who ends his Prairie Home Companion shows with the wish to "be well, do good work, and keep in touch."

A Kentucky public radio station refused to air an episode in August 2005 because of two poems containing the word "breast." As in heart, as in soul, as in conscience.

"I don't question the artistic merit, but I have to question the language," WUKY general manager Tom Godell said. "The FCC has been so inconsistent, we don't know where we stand. We could no longer risk a fine."[a]

Was Godell paranoid? Crazy? Illiterate? Station managers like him felt forced to imagine the most prurient kind of mind—and program around it. We're living in very dangerous times.

Chased off Radio: Howard Stern

In early 2004, the FCC fined giant Clear Channel Communications $495,000 for sexual material on Howard Stern's daily radio show. The

(continued)

(continued)

allegedly offensive material was aired, of course, on a show that everyone—listeners and non-listeners—knows is sexually oriented. Soon after, the nation's largest radio chain dropped the show. "Mr. Stern's show has created a great liability for us and other broadcasters who air it," said John Hogan, president of Clear Channel.[b]

Two months later, Clear Channel agreed to pay a record $1.75 million to settle a series of indecency complaints, including sexual discussions on Stern's show. By year's end, the FCC had proposed more than $15 million in fines against Clear Channel, the nation's largest owner of radio stations.

In October 2004, Howard Stern signed a five-year deal to appear on Sirius Satellite Radio. As a pay-for-listening outlet, it is not currently subject to the same indecency standards as free broadcast radio. If Senators Brownback and Stevens, Congressman Blunt, FCC chairperson Martin, and others have their way, however, that will soon change.

The cost of listening to Howard Stern on satellite radio is now some $200 per year. Until the FCC came after him, it was free. They call this protecting the public.

Preemptively Cancelled: *Saving Private Ryan*

By November 2004, the FCC had filled the broadcast environment with fear. It was increasing its scrutiny of content, assessing higher and higher fines, practically soliciting complaints to justify these fines, and still would not specify exactly what they would pursue and punish. Forced to guess at what would be punished as "indecent" and fearful of the resulting fines, broadcasters became terribly cautious. Dozens of TV stations cancelled the Veterans Day showing of the World War II drama, *Saving Private Ryan*—which had been scheduled, ironically, to honor the soldiers who died to preserve the American way of life.

Threatened: All Broadcasters

In 2005, members of Congress introduced the Broadcast Decency Enforcement Act. The BDEA is the anti-Janet Jackson-nipple bill that makes broadcasters liable for fines of up to $500,000 for any obscene, indecent, or profane material they disseminate.

The size of these proposed fines suggests a nipple-phobia that is simply impossible to comprehend. Can our Congress actually believe the Republic is in such grave danger?

---

[a]Ken Tucker, "Station Pulls Keillor for 'Offensive Content'," Billboard Radio Monitor, August 12, 2005, http://billboardradiomonitor.com/radiomonitor/news/business/net_syn/article_display.jsp?vnu_content_id=1001014255.

[b]John Hogan, in Clear Channel press release, April 8, 2004, http://www.clearchannel.com/radio/pressrelease.aspx?pressreleaseID=489.

departments of most local TV stations. In 2003 they attempted to pass new regulations allowing an even smaller number of companies to own an even larger percentage of communities' radio, TV, and newspaper outlets. This was such a greedy giveaway that even the Republican-controlled Congress resisted, and the proposal was challenged and ultimately rolled back in 2004.[12]

As public interest attorney Marjorie Heins notes, the public desperately needs the FCC to take its original responsibility seriously—regulating media *structure,* not *content.* It seems "there are a million channels, but there's hardly a true diversity of ideas out there in the mass media."[13]

So what is the FCC doing instead? Protecting America's children from the F word. Reacting to public "concern" with all the finesse of a 400-pound Romanian weightlifter.

In 2005, Kevin Martin, a lawyer for the 2000 Bush/Cheney campaign and later a White House aide to President Bush, was appointed FCC chair. He says that if obviously "inappropriate" material isn't kept off the air, the very definition of indecency may have to be changed. And he's keeping up with the times, looking at new media as well; he's committed to ending the relatively unregulated state of cable and satellite TV.

Audience rights? Broadcaster rights?

"Certainly broadcasters and cable operators have significant First Amendment rights, but these rights are not without boundaries," Martin said. "They are limited by law. They also should be limited by good taste."[14] *Whose* taste, of course, is the critical question. Our Constitution is cleverly designed to make that question irrelevant by excluding subjectivities like "good taste" or "blasphemy" or "indecency" as criteria for government action.

The FCC has it exactly backwards: it favors deregulation of *industry,* but regulation of *content* and *consumers.* They cite the wisdom of the marketplace when justifying corporate giveaways—and ignore it when censoring content that the same market would allow.

Remember that the FCC is required to refer to "community standards" when making judgments of any kind. If taken seriously, this would help prevent the FCC from becoming a bureaucratic kingdom running amok, or from being used as an agent of government tyranny. By ignoring this reasonable and far-sighted limit, however, the FCC has used its punitive powers to reward the censorship groups that support members of the Congressional Commerce Committee that oversees the FCC, as well as the President himself. By baldly favoring the interests of one group of Americans over another, the FCC has horrifically damaged American democracy and artistic freedom.

THE UNHOLY ALLIANCE OF THE FCC AND PRO-CENSORSHIP GROUPS

People who want to restrict everyone's choices are often active in organizations like Family Research Council and Concerned Women for America.

Others are in positions of government power, like Senators Ted Stevens (R-AK) and Sam Brownback (R-KS), and Kevin Martin at the FCC. Crusaders and government are going after your viewing choices as a team.

That makes sense from their point of view. Crusaders see that their beloved economic marketplace refutes their values—shows and commercials involving sexuality don't go away for lack of viewership, they thrive. And crusaders have learned, to their dismay, that their beliefs don't win in the marketplace of ideas either—they haven't convinced nearly enough people that their families are in danger from broadcast material, that they should change their media habits, and that they must enforce these beliefs on others.

And so, crusaders want the government to enforce restrictions that neither the commercial marketplace nor the intellectual marketplace can. It's like school yard politics—if you can't bully someone yourself, get your bigger brother or older cousin to do it.

Many in government, unfortunately, agree. They see their role as providing the big stick the anti-indecency lobby needs when its ideas aren't persuasive enough to their fellow citizens. These government officials are happy to lend their power to morality crusaders. The White House backs this "big government" agenda because it can point to the FCC's work and show its core constituency that it's responding to them. Morality crusaders like PTC president, L. Brent Bozell, then take credit for "cleaning up" the airwaves. It's a win-win for the War on Sex.

But it's wrong, simply wrong. The FCC has aggressively asserted itself where it doesn't belong, and it now represents a small group of Americans—leaving the rest of us unrepresented. The FCC has stated its agenda of being more powerful ("active," they call it), regardless of the damage it inflicts or how far it strays from its mandate.[15]

And so, FCC fines for indecency have gone from a total of $48,000 in 2000 to $99,000 in 2002 to $7.9 million in 2004—without any substantive change in broadcast content to motivate this. The only visible motivation for the increased fines is the Bush administration's desire for votes and campaign contributions. And in June, 2006, Congress passed, and the president signed, the Broadcast Decency Enforcement Act, which *astronomically* increases the penalties against broadcasters for "transmissions of obscene, indecent, and profane material."[16] Because there is no objective definition of indecency, "the increased fines will create a chilling effect on otherwise protected speech," says attorney Larry Walters. "The censorship will be real, but it will be inconsistent, leaving broadcasters in the dark. This is not good for the First Amendment."[17]

While "decency" and "morality" groups have littered the American landscape on and off for three centuries, there are few times in America's history they have had more influence over ordinary citizens' lives than they do today.[18] Since 1980, we've seen the emergence of Focus on the Family, Concerned Women for America, Moral Majority, and other groups. Since 2003, two particularly frightening new players have emerged, Morality in Media (MiM) and Parents Television Council (PTC). The FCC has adopted these groups with terrifying speed and absolutely no counter-balance whatsoever. According to *Time* magazine, "Almost single-handedly, the PTC has become a national clearinghouse for, and arbiter of, decency."[19]

In the past two years, the FCC has been in bed with the morality crusaders more times than either would allow the word "sex" on TV—with no comparable room at the inn for people who tolerate or want sexy material. This cozy arrangement, which has produced the largest broadcaster fines in American history, was recently exposed by journalist Jeff Jarvis as government-facilitated tyranny of the minority. Here's the story:

In late 2004, the FCC leveled an incredible $1.2 million dollar fine against the Fox TV network for an episode of *Married by America* that suggested—not depicted, just *suggested*—sex. The justification for this enormous fine, said the FCC, was the huge number of complaints it supposedly received.

How many complaints? According to the FCC, 159. Is that staggering enough, that 159 complaints can trigger the largest broadcaster fine in American history, against a show watched by millions?

Wait, it gets better.

When the FCC's actual data was released in response to Jarvis's Freedom of Information Act request, it showed that the complaints came from only 23 individuals. Twenty-three.

It gets even better.

Reports Jarvis,

> All but two were virtually identical. In other words, one person took the time to write a letter and 20 other people photocopied or emailed it to the FCC. They all came from an automated complaint factory. . . . Only two letters were not the form letter. So in the end, that means that a grand total of three citizens bothered to take the time to sit down and actually write a letter of complaint to the FCC. Millions of people watched the show. Three wrote letters of complaint.[20]

This shocking story is all over the Web—and yet there's been virtually no broadcast media coverage. Could the media possibly be feeling intimidated about reporting this, about exposing the shocking bias at the agency that could subsequently fine them and even revoke their licenses? Is this what our free American media have come to?

In the summer of 2005, the FCC announced the formation of yet another battalion in its war on "indecency." It hired Penny Nance to work in its Office of Strategic Planning and Policy Analysis to "advise on indecency issues."[21] Nance founded the Kids First Coalition, a group that fights abortion, cloning, and indecency in the name of "pro-child, pro-family public policy."[22] Long a vocal antipornography crusader, she has frequently testified before Congress. During the 2004 presidential campaign, she appeared on Fox News as a "suburban stay-at-home mom" to say that women believe President Bush will "protect our children."[23]

In public talks, Nance describes herself as a "victim of pornography"[24] because she says a man who once tried to rape her watched porn. In January 2005, Nance signed, along with other activists, an open letter to President Bush, complaining of a "huge indecency problem" on basic cable and a growing indecency threat on satellite radio.

The "indecency problem" Nance was hired (with your tax dollars) to resolve is the currently legal recreation of tens of millions of law-abiding Americans. She will *not* attempt to solicit or provide a balanced view or scientific evaluation of broadcast content and its consequences. She will invite input from sincere censors who *believe*, sincere self-described victims who *hurt*, sincere parents who are *concerned*. She doesn't want input from any of the millions of people who now consume the legal products she will help criminalize. This is not a modern democracy at work.

Attorney Paul Cambria has argued many Supreme Court cases, and is past president of the First Amendment Trial Lawyers Association. "What a lot of people don't understand on this indecency thing for broadcast standards is that it has a community standard element in it, just like the obscenity law does. But who is speaking for the community? In all the congressional hearings and everything else they're having, what component demonstrates the pulse of the [mainstream] adult community as to what . . . they think the standard should be? Shouldn't the community have a voice in that? Where's the survey of the community?"[25]

There are certain rights even democracies don't put up for popular referendum, such as laws about racial discrimination or murder. Laws limiting what we can see or hear should be among those. Americans live by a body of non-negotiable guarantees; the PTC wants to change the rules, and government seems eager to go along. As Rush Limbaugh, our era's archetypal conservative, said in *opposing* government efforts to censor Howard Stern:

> If we are going to sit by and let the federal government get involved in this, if the government is going to 'censor' what they think is right and wrong . . . What happens if a whole bunch of John Kerrys, or Terry McAuliffes start running this country, and decide conservative views are leading to violence?
>
> I am in the free speech business. It's one thing for a company to determine if they are going to be party to it. It's another thing for the government to do it.[26]

Says Jim Dyke, executive director of the advocacy group TV Watch, "What has become clear is this really isn't about protecting kids. This is about changing television. A politically active, savvy group of Americans has figured out a way to make TV in their own image."[27]

IGNORING/CIRCUMVENTING THE MARKETPLACE

What happens when the morality campaign goes head to head with *Desperate Housewives*? In red states, in religious areas, in every single state that passed an antigay marriage law, it's all the same: *Desperate Housewives* is a runaway hit. Ditto *Will & Grace,* ditto *Monday Night Football* and its half-naked cheerleaders, ditto Viagra commercials.

Sure, Christian TV and radio sell—but that's not where people go for entertainment. They're ghettoized, as they haven't succeeded in the mainstream; there isn't enough of an audience to drive "the sex stuff" off the air. So crusaders want to truncate the market mechanism and enforce their taste on the entire public.

They use a circular argument—the marketplace should make decisions except where it makes poor decisions. The media's decisions about sexuality are poor because they're bad for people. How do we know? They contradict "moral" values.

Both our current government and anti-indecency groups claim the heritage of conservative ideology. But "[FCC commissioners] Powell, Martin, and the corporate-friendly GOP have green-lighted big media companies to capture near-total market control over cable and broadcast television," says Ben Scott, policy director at Free Press. "Now, the same bunch is upset over the low-cost, high-ratings schlock that media conglomerates pump into the marketplace. Martin must soon decide if he's a free market Republican or a local-values Republican. When it comes to regulating the media, you can't have it both ways."[28]

As TV started its third decade, 20 years before the Internet, TV critic Clive Barnes put it this way: "Television is the first truly democratic culture—the first culture available to everybody and entirely governed by what the people want. The most terrifying thing is what people do want."[29] Needless to say, "what people do want" still involves sexual themes, as it has since the days of Shakespeare and the ancient Greeks. As proof, look at the PTC Web site's listing of "worst TV shows of the week." Month after month, it's a who's who of the most popular shows in America.

How do would-be censors explain this continuing popularity? Do they honestly think people would choose different programs if they had more choice? If so, public radio and TV wouldn't have such a small audience, a fact that free-market Republicans gleefully point out regularly.

Whenever something on TV is punished—for example, Janet Jackson's nipple, the Madonna/Britney kiss—Americans vote immediately. And they always vote the same—they want to see it. First they vote by downloading or recording the video clip. For example, the clips of each of these moments are among the most downloaded in Internet *history.* And "Janet Jackson is still the most TiVo'd moment we've ever measured," according to a company spokesman, eclipsing—what else?—the Madonna/Britney kiss.[30] People then vote again by watching the news about the moment and its aftermath. TV stations across America replay the stuff over and over because they know people want to see it. So the moral crusaders' claim that broadcast indecency is being thrust on us is simply inaccurate, just like the claim that porn is thrust on us.

You may recall the fuss over the racy Terrell Owens/Nicollette Sheridan ad promoting *Monday Night Football* in November 2004. The *New York Times* columnist Frank Rich noted[31] that the spot was replayed around the Internet and dozens of TV shows for several days, among them *The View*, where Ms. Sheridan's bare back had been merrily paraded at the child-friendly hour of 11:00 A.M. As Aaron Brown of CNN wryly observed, "People were so outraged they had to see it 10 times."[32]

The recurring Internet downloading and ubiquitous TV rebroadcasting of taboo moments is *real* democracy in action, not some spam farm that fakes mass indignation. When the FCC fines a broadcaster for violating "community standards" and the public actively pursues the very broadcast moment being fined, why isn't this considered straightforward evidence of the "community standard?" Why isn't it given the same weight as mass-produced e-mails?

CHILDREN'S PROGRAMMING

One of the most crucial goals of media crusaders is shielding kids from all sex-related content, advertising, language, jokes, and situations.[33] We should recognize that this is a radical enterprise. It's such a comprehensive goal that attempting it (much less succeeding) would *have* to create broad collateral damage—which crusaders brush off as a distant, secondary consideration compared with their crucial goal.

What are they trying to accomplish? To raise children who are ignorant about sexuality except in the vaguest sense; that it's an adults-only thing reserved for spiritually oriented, procreating married couples, and that it can kill you or ruin your life. This would make our kids the least sophisticated, least prepared for sexual adulthood in the Western world.

Given the fundamental importance of sexuality in human life, eliminating it from children's programming and advertising requires constant vigilance. Remember, it's a crusader's job to notice sexual themes and references, so they can be eliminated. And crusaders see sex everywhere because they're obsessed with it.

Especially homosexuality. Although their fear of homosexuality is absolutely serious, it's so exaggerated and baseless it's hard to take seriously. Has a gay person ever told you he or she is out to "recruit" straights? Has a gay man or woman ever told you that they believe a hot same-gender experience can turn a straight person gay? One more reality: the overwhelming majority of adult-child sex offenders are heterosexual.[34] So what are the practical reasons to panic about homosexuality?

If we don't want kids to think homosexuality is normal, OK, but what's the harm if they do? If our kids become more tolerant of others, that will help them in life. If we really think our children are going to say, "Homosexuality as a lifelong choice? Sounds interesting, think I'll try it," we completely misunderstand them (as well as homosexuality). Most kids experiment with their same-sex pals at some point,[35] a normal developmental stage that antigay crusaders desperately deny.[36] Very, very, very few children become gay adults. America's professional community is virtually unanimous that it isn't a same-sex kiss or jack-off session with a buddy at age 10 that makes Mary or Johnny gay. If it were, 90 percent of American adults would be gay.

If we're really paranoid about our school-age sons having sex with an adult man, we should remember to keep them away from *heterosexual* men. They're the ones involved with almost all of the sexual exploitation between men and boys. These guys are often married, have rarely had a man-man sexual experience, and, in fact, often say they hate gays.

Looking for sex in every corner, searching for homos in the same paranoid, bug-eyed way that their cultural predecessors looked for "Commies" a half-century ago, the crusaders have gone after kids' TV programming, both commercial and noncommercial.

They've gone after Barney and Big Bird for sexual offenses. The only explanation is that these adults are obsessed with sex. They see it where their kids don't—actually can't, developmentally—and want to protect their kids from something that doesn't exist. That says a lot about their obsession and their fear.

Here's just a partial honor roll of those who have been attacked or killed in the War on Sex (and no, we are *not* making this up):

SpongeBob SquarePants and Barney the Dinosaur

In 2005, a video was distributed to 61,000 schools across the nation to celebrate National We Are Family Day. Sponsored by FedEx, the video was broadcast several weeks later on Nickelodeon, PBS, and the Disney Channel.

The American Family Association (AFA) criticized it as "homosexual indoctrination," saying "homosexual activists are using popular children's TV characters such as SpongeBob SquarePants and Barney the Dinosaur to surreptitiously indoctrinate young children into their lifestyle." AFA researcher, Ed Vitagliano, sees the project as an "open door" to a secondary discussion of homosexuality, noting that children and adults are encouraged to sign a "tolerance pledge," which includes sexual orientation, on the sponsors' Web site.[37]

Buster

On her second day on the job in early 2005, new Education Secretary, Margaret Spellings, contacted PBS. Citing "strong and very serious concerns" about an upcoming episode of *Ready to Learn* (RTL) in which Buster the cartoon rabbit visits a family headed by two lesbians, Spellings insisted that PBS refund RTL money used to make the program if the network distributes it.

The challenge came at an interesting time, as PBS was preparing to compete for renewed Ready to Learn funding from the Education Department—money they had previously been awarded yearly. PBS officials decided to cancel the episode.

Postcards from Buster is a series designed for four- to eight-year-olds (particularly those who speak English as a second language) that celebrates the nation's cultural diversity as it teaches language awareness. In the canceled episode, "Sugartime!" Buster visits rural Hinesburg, Vermont, where he meets a family with three kids and two moms during maple sugar season. Same-gender civil unions are legal in Vermont.[38]

Teletubbies

In 1999, Jerry Falwell suggested that Tinky Winky, one of the Teletubby characters, is gay. The February edition of Falwell's publication, the *National Liberty Journal,* notes that Tinky Winky has the voice of a boy yet carries a purse. "He is purple—the gay-pride color; and his antenna is shaped like a triangle—the gay-pride symbol," the story says.[39] Falwell, the founder of the now-defunct Moral Majority, contends the "subtle depictions" are intentional, and said, "As a Christian, I feel that role-modeling the gay lifestyle is damaging to the moral lives of children."[40]

* * *

Media crusaders and the FCC don't trust American parents at all. They don't believe most parents can make good judgments for their own kids. They say they're speaking on behalf of all caring parents, but of course they aren't. Presumably, if all parents felt the way the FCC and crusaders are portraying them, the market would have eliminated these shows, these commercials, and the entire Comedy Central network. It's an old story: censors feel equipped to make the "right" decisions when they're certain that others are not. As Clare Booth Luce said, "Censorship, like charity, should begin at home. Unlike charity, it should end there."

They think sexual words and themes are more dangerous for children than sugar, fat, toy ads, and stereotyping (gender, racial, age, etc.). In fact, as Nicholas Jackson says in *The Conservative Voice,* "The sexualization of our young people is perhaps the greatest threat we face in our nation today."[41]

These crusaders continually say they want to parent free from government interference. They want home schooling, exemptions from inoculating their children, local control of public school curricula, and the right to opt out of sex ed class. But at the same time, they want the government to intervene regarding the content of broadcast media so *no* parents have independence or control about the media choices *made in their own home.*

TOOLS THEY WON'T USE—WHY?

Parents already have many tools they can use to completely control what their kids see on TV. But this doesn't satisfy would-be censors. Obviously, the goal of morality groups and pro-censorship government isn't really to protect kids, it's to control what *adults* can see or hear.

Parental tools for controlling their kids' viewing now include:

Off Button

Every TV has one. A perfect solution for all parents who don't want their kids to see inappropriate material.

Channel Changer

Every TV has one. It not only takes kids away from what parents don't want them to see, it guides them toward what parents want them to see.

Ratings System

In the mid 1990s, the broadcasting industry created a voluntary ratings system evaluating violence and sexuality. A monitoring board ensures accurate and consistent ratings. There are seven categories (three more than big-screen movies use) to help parents determine which programs are suitable for their children.

Rating labels appear in the corner of the screen during the first 15 seconds of each program, and are digitally encoded into the program itself.

V-Chip

Every TV larger than 13 inches manufactured after 2000 contains this technology, allowing parents to block programs they don't want their children to watch. Using the remote control, parents can program the V-chip to block shows based on their ratings or other criteria—so the blocking works *even if parents aren't home.*

Cable Filter

All cable TV subscribers can request a "lockbox" from their cable operator, which can be set to prevent the viewing of any channel a parent dislikes. All U.S. cable operators are required to make lockboxes available.

Satellite TV Parental Controls

All satellite providers such as DIRECTV allow parents to easily restrict their kids' unsupervised viewing by blocking shows with certain ratings, locking out entire channels, setting limited viewing times, or blocking specific shows or movies.

"No-curse" Products

A variety of products can be purchased and installed which delete offensive language from programs. Generally, when a word that's in their dictionary (e.g., "ass," "jesus," "boobs") is detected, the sound is momentarily muted. A substitute word is then either spoken or flashed on the screen. This allows viewers to watch a broader range of programs without fear of hearing something unwanted.

* * *

By giving parents powerful and sophisticated ways to finely tune the exact TV viewing kids can do in their homes, these tools render blunt, society-wide or community-wide restrictions obsolete. The cable and satellite industries have recently launched a campaign to educate parents about these technologies, but this helpful program has been opposed by a powerful alliance of family advocacy groups and activists with close ties to major evangelical ministries and the Bush administration. "It will be war," says Rick Schatz, the president of the National Coalition for the Protection of Children and Families, a Christian ministry, of the coming battle over cable and satellite regulation. "There will be tremendous grassroots pressure brought to bear."[42]

They still don't get that television viewing is a *choice*, not a *right*.

SUMMARY

Pro-censorship groups like Morality in Media bemoan the "trash" on TV and radio. Observing the gradual changes in the language and situations being broadcast, they demand to know, "How far will it go? Where will it end?"

The answer is simple: the evolution of radio and TV broadcast of sexual themes and language will "end" when audiences, through their viewing choices, want it to. Despite the political manipulations of pro-censorship government and civic leaders, American viewers are still not prepared to end this evolution.

There's also the trivial issue of the U.S. Constitution that's in the way. God Bless America.

Chapter Seven

Yes, They Really Said That

The federal courts, and the Supreme Court in particular, have "systematically attacked Christianity."

Tony Perkins, president, Family Research Council[1]

Course materials and instruction relating to sexuality or sexually transmitted diseases should include "emphasis, provided in a factual manner and from a public health perspective, that homosexuality is not a lifestyle acceptable to the general public and that homosexual conduct is a criminal offense."

Texas Health and Safety Code 163.002(8)[2]

America must pursue a civil society "that will democratically embrace its essential moral duties, including . . . caring for children born and unborn."

Proclamation of President George W. Bush,
declaring January 18 "Sanctity of Life Day"[3]

"I personally object to vaccinating children against a disease that is 100% preventable with proper sexual behavior."

Leslie Unruh, director, National Abstinence Clearinghouse[4]

"If Marriott wants to make another sizable contribution or to build another building in their name, we want people at Brigham Young University to think, 'Maybe we don't want to have a building built with porn dollars.'"

Randy Sharp, American Family Association, which demands
that Marriott hotels, which has given the Mormon University
$12 million, stop offering in-room adult films[5]

"If a woman wants to give birth to a healthy baby, Planned Parenthood kicks her out the door with a referral slip. After all, adoption is not where the money is."

Douglas Scott, president, Life Decisions International[6]

"I don't believe the principal problem facing America is the battle in Iraq, as important as that is, or federal spending that's out of control. Let's face it, the current leadership of this nation, led by Congress, has to make a basic decision sooner or later: Will we as a people acknowledge that God exists?"

Former U.S. Representative Bill Dannemeyer
(R-CA), for the Family Research Council[7]

"Even legislation that is largely symbolic...has significant pedagogical value. Laws teach people what they should and should not do....The states should not be required to accept, as a matter of constitutional doctrine, that homosexual activity is harmless and does not expose both the individual and the public to deleterious spiritual and physical consequences."

William Pryor, Attorney General of Texas, in Lawrence v. Texas[8]

After taking Garrison Keillor off the air for reciting two classic poems with the word "breast," "I don't question the artistic merit, but I have to question the language. It's not that he's behaving like Howard Stern, but the FCC has been so inconsistent, we don't know where we stand. We could no longer risk a fine."

Tom Godell, General Manager, WUKY (national public radio)[9]

"Labor to keep alive in your breast that little spark of celestial fire called conscience."

George Washington[10]

"The Parents Television Council does not censor. The First Amendment was instituted to guarantee precisely the type of activities pursued by the PTC: free speech and disseminating information."

Parents Television Council, which pressures the
government to remove "objectionable" TV shows from the air[11]

"Hardcore pornography, or material depicting actual sex acts, promotes the idea that human beings can be sexually used and abused without consequences. If we tolerate pornographic material that encourages people to indulge their darkest sexual fantasies, we cannot act surprised when millions do so in real life as well."

Daniel Weiss, senior analyst for media and sexuality, Focus on the Family[12]

"I announce the formation of the Moral Majority Coalition. A primary goal of TMMC is the registration of 10 million new evangelical voters for the 2006 and 2008 general elections."

Jerry Falwell[13]

"We need to yell it to the top of the rooftops that these condoms we're sending down to you don't protect you.... [You] have a false sense of security. So I think we're sending the wrong message when we use taxpayer dollars to give condoms out to these kids and we don't tell them, 'By the way, you'll probably be dead at age 24 by cervical cancer. But we're giving you condoms, so go do your thing.' To me, abstinence is the only way."

Representative Jo Ann Davis (R-VA), at Congressional Hearing on Cervical Cancer and HPV [14]

"Middle America better take note. Last night Hollywood exposed its own corrupt agenda. [It] is no doubt out on a mission to homosexualise America."

Stephen Bennett of "Straight Talk Radio," about the 2006 Golden Globe Awards, which conservative Christian groups accuse of promoting films with gay themes [15]

"We are trying to create a town [Ave Maria, Florida] with traditional family values and a wholesome environment. That's why we are saying we will not allow adult bookstores, massage parlors or topless bars."

Paul Marinelli, CEO of Barron Collier (The town is being developed through a 50–50 partnership with Domino's Pizza founder Thomas Monaghan, who is investing $250 million. Barron Collier and Monaghan will control all commercial real estate) [16]

References to "the exclusion of gay couples and other minority groups" by other religious bodies, and "the fact the Executive Branch has recently proposed a Constitutional Amendment to define marriage as a union between a man and a woman" make "this spot unacceptable for broadcast."

CBS TV network, rejecting United Church of Christ paid ads affirming their nondiscrimination policy [17]

"[Journalists and politicians like you] are in what we call the reality-based community, people who believe that solutions emerge from the judicious study of discernible reality. That's not the way the world really works anymore."

Senior advisor to President Bush, in conversation with journalist Ron Suskind [18]

"Top priority should be placed on an effort to recover our most fundamental founding belief that our national objectives, policies and laws should reflect obedience to the will of Almighty God."

Former Senator Jeremiah Denton (R-AL) [19]

"Consider that the average age now of exposure to pornography is 5 years of age."

Nicholas Jackson, The Conservative Voice [20]

Signing the Unborn Victims of Violence Act, "We widen the circle of compassion and inclusion in our society, and we reaffirm that the United States of America is building a culture of life."

President George W. Bush (The legislation gives a fetus rights distinct from a pregnant woman) [21]

"When two people of the same sex ... adopt children ... I think what you have in many respects is state-sanctioned child abuse."

Radio host Janet Parshall, on CNN's Larry King Live[22]

"No wonder many in America seem to believe that the Court has become one more inclined to protect pornography than to protect religious expression. Most people in America don't believe that God is a dirty word. But the sad fact is that some Americans are left to wonder whether the Supreme Court might have greater regard for it if it was."

Senator John Cornyn (R-TX), at the Senate Hearings on Judge Samuel Alito's Nomination to the Supreme Court[23]

Porn users "give lame justifications for their behavior like: 'It's harmless,' or 'Everybody's doing it.' By doing this, they ignore the effect their problem is having on the people around them. This behavior is not OK, it's not even almost OK. This habit is a perverse and ridiculous intrusion into [a] relationship."

Dr. Phil McGraw[24]

"Broadcasters and cable operators have significant First Amendment rights, but these rights are not without boundaries. They are limited by law. They also should be limited by good taste."

Kevin Martin, chair, Federal Communications Commission[25]

"I'm always a little bit irritated when I hear the criticism of abstinence, because abstinence is absolutely 100 percent effective in eradicating a sexually trans-mitted disease."

First Lady Laura Bush, apparently unaware that absti-nence fails in 88% of teens who pledge it[26]

Pornography is "capable of poisoning any mind at any age and of perverting our entire younger generation." The rising tide of obscenity is "part of the Communist Conspiracy."

Charles Keating, founder, Citizens for Decency through Law, and mem-ber of the Meese Commission on Pornography, later jailed on four counts of fraud in connection with the Lincoln Savings and Loan scandal[27]

"Giving the HPV vaccine to young women could be potentially harmful because they may see it as a license to engage in premarital sex."

Bridget Maher, Family Research Council[28]

"The first step toward reducing demand for sex slaves is to prosecute those dis-tributing material that violates obscenity laws and serves as a veritable training manual for abuse."

Daniel Weiss, senior analyst for media and sexuality, Focus on the Family[29]

"It isn't the American people who are clamoring for more pornography on the Internet and in their communities, and for more sex (including pornography), vulgarity and violence on TV."

Letter to President George W. Bush signed by the leadership of Morality in Media, Citizens for Community Values, Union of Orthodox Rabbis of the United States and Canada, Family Policy Network, American Decency Association, Concerned Women for America, Focus on the Family, Family Research Council, American Family Association, and Parents Television Council [30]

"Procuring stem cells from an embryo destroys the tiny human being."

Tom Strode, Baptist Press News [31]

"The new Helms School of Government at Liberty University . . . [will] train young people to enter public service with a Christian worldview and a bold passion to confront a liberal-oriented culture. Students will spend weekends and summers working hand-in-hand with pastors and staff members of evangelical churches all over America, registering voters in the churches and neighborhoods along with educating parishioners."

Jerry Falwell [32]

"If the public can be convinced that condoms offer certain—or nearly certain—protection from pregnancies and STDs, then the [proponents] can argue that the only thing holding people back from free sexual expression is outdated, irrelevant religious restrictions."

Focus on the Family, on why they must discourage trust in condoms [33]

Those who rent or sell adult materials should be jailed, because, "In the Garden of Eden, the virtue of man was stripped away, and the only way that that virtue can be returned is by Jesus Christ being Lord over our sexual desires."

Don Kohls, chairperson, Omaha for Decency [34]

"The sexualization of our young people is perhaps the greatest threat we face in our nation today. It will only be a matter of time before we are absolutely snowed under with filth and perversion in our libraries and communities."

Nicholas Jackson, The Conservative Voice [35]

President Bush's decision to allow the tiniest possible amount of stem cell medical research is "A covenant with the Devil; he has this nation chasing the illusion of eternal life by depending on science rather than on the Lord Jesus Christ."

Neil Horsley, creator of The Nuremberg Files Web site, which advocated "eliminating" physicians performing abortion [36]

"Other police investigation [TV] programs…do not include child actors describing sexual acts and graphic abuse. To involve innocent child actors in the dramatic process not only creates an extra-disturbing episode; it also can negatively affect the young actors and actresses."

Parents Television Council[37]

"For 25 years, I would have said that the pro-life issue is the most pressing threat to America morally, but pornography has overtaken it. More people's lives are being destroyed on a daily basis by addiction to pornography than through abortion."

Rev. Richard Land, prominent leader in the Southern Baptist Convention[38]

If "my own 16-year-old daughter tells me she's going to be sexually active, I would *not* tell her to use a condom."

Denny Pattyn, founder of Silver Ring Thing, popular abstinence pledge program[39]

"This is just a short note to express my heartfelt thanks to you and the entire staff of Focus on the Family for your help and support during the past few challenging months. I would also greatly appreciate it if you would convey my appreciation to the good people from all parts of the country who wrote to tell me that they were praying for me and for my family during this period. As long as I serve on the Supreme Court I will keep in mind the trust that has been placed in me. I hope that we will have the opportunity to meet personally at some point in the future. In the meantime my entire family and I hope that you and the Focus on the Family staff know how much we appreciate all that you have done."

Supreme Court Justice Samuel Alito, to James Dobson after
Alito had been confirmed to the Supreme Court[40]

Chapter Eight

<u>Battleground:</u> *Adult Entertainment—*
Feverish Dreams, Real Estate Nightmares

L ast year, New York's Mayor Michael Bloomberg famously said, "I don't want a porn shop in my neighborhood, and you shouldn't have one in yours."

On the one hand, there's something fundamentally silly about grown-ups running around, tripping all over each other to prevent lap dances and the sale of blowup dolls. You would think the dancers, dolls, and customers alike were wielding grenades, threatening to destroy cities in which people don't patronize strip clubs.

On the other hand, there's something profoundly scary about the ferocity of these continual attacks, the absolute self-confidence with which sexually conservative people damn the beliefs and recreation of their fellow citizens. They unashamedly embrace civic coercion—genteel political and financial violence—in a commitment to manipulate government in whatever way necessary to accomplish what they want. Their passionate crusade has an almost erotic sheen to it. If violence can spiritually purify, these people are spiritually pure.

The target is "adult entertainment": strip clubs, massage parlors, art galleries, home sex toy parties, erotic theater, topless bars, adult bookstores. And whatever else is designed to provide sexually oriented entertainment.

With communism gone, with racial integration accepted in public and abandoned in private, with terrorism an enemy no one can fight in his own backyard, lust-and-perversion is the identified menace of our day, an infinitely expandable threat as handy as Satan—and just as omnipresent, if you're of a mind to see it.

Adult entertainment is a little different than pornography. With pornography, people look at "bad" pictures or read "bad" words, which are *representations* of "evil impulses." The personal *enactment* of those impulses—*actual* swinging, bisexuality, bondage, exhibitionism—is "pure evil," creating an enormous category of sexual minorities that suffers legal persecution and discrimination every day (see chapter 14).

Adult entertainment falls in between; not simple *representation*, not entirely *enactment*. Entertainment. America has a long love-hate tradition about these transactions. We can't, apparently, live without them; we won't, apparently, admit we can't live without them.

Civic censors make a point of calling this eroticism "public," even though it's all behind closed doors and is off-limits to the underage or those who can't pay. Since it isn't "private" in the traditional sense, they condemn it as non-intimate, stripping it of any respect, dignity, or legal protection. They've been saying for decades that an erotic experience can't be meaningful if it isn't "intimate."

Society desperately needs a third category, a name for sexual behavior that lies between public (orgies in the street) and private (two people behind closed bedroom doors). We could easily call it "commercial," but that's the precise kiss of death in Puritan America. Other linguistic options are "nonpublic," "erotic entertainment," and "recreational." None is perfect.

As a large group of Americans increasingly accepts and participates in taboo sexuality, the repressive part of society cracks down with increasing fervor. The Internet and the modern lap dance didn't invent this schizophrenic civic morality, it existed during Victorian times, in Thomas Jefferson's home, during the Salem witch trials, as part of the Inquisition, in Chaucer's London, in Paul's own life, and backwards through time beyond that.

But Americans—who typically think "history" is whatever happened before the Dodgers left Brooklyn—see this conflict as uniquely contemporary. And empowered by a sense of American exceptionalism, sexual conservatives are devoted to finally, completely winning this conflict by any means necessary short of nuclear weapons. Nothing is to stain God's shining city on a hill, not even the semen of people whose rights are supposedly inalienable, endowed by their Creator.

The ways in which communities across America are successfully limiting their neighbors' expressive and recreational opportunities are endlessly creative, as expensive as necessary, and at the very top of the civic agenda. The coalitions driving this are typically religious (meaning, in America, Christian) at the core, but they attract other constituencies as well. These include worried parents, greedy business people, conflict-hungry media, savvy law enforcement departments, and cynical politicians who know a good bandwagon when they see one. In the good old days, the scurrilous political tactic of choice was accusing one's opponent of being soft on communism. That smear pales beside the power of today's smear of being soft on hard-core sex.

This is a War on Sex, you know. They can deplore the negative impacts on neighborhoods, the exploitation of those poor strippers, 10-year-olds being lured into massage parlors (which happens only in *Reefer Madness*-type propaganda), and all the marriages destroyed by husbands preferring lap dances to home cooking. In contrast, everyone jokes about golf widows;

no one blinks at the number of blown-out knees young athletes suffer, small towns are begging to be destroyed by Wal-Mart, and marriage, well, marriage is in trouble across America.

So it's not the busted neighborhoods, ruined virginal strippers, kids playing Nintendo with hookers, or bored, philandering husbands that are the real issue. It's sex as entertainment. It's people arranging for sex to serve them, rather than people being enslaved by sexual repression. It's the acknowledgement that erotic novelty is not only desirable, it's possible. And it's the assertion that men and women who choose to use sex in this way can make responsible choices in the rest of their lives.

For those who fear sex, tolerating adult entertainment means collapsing their crucial distinction between good people who repress their sexuality and bad people who don't (and who suffer as a result). If someone can get a lap dance and be a loving father and husband at the same time, the fundamental principle that sexual interest is dangerous is ruined. And there are too many people invested in that principle to let it be spoiled. They will stop at nothing to uphold it. They will use state-sponsored violence, discriminatory zoning, public shame, deceit and misrepresentation, fear, even threats of the Lord's wrath—whatever it takes.

Municipalities say this persecution is because of the so-called secondary effects (increased crime, decreased property values, general "blight," increased "immorality"), but it's far more visceral than that—it's having to admit that "that stuff" exists. And some people are willing to destroy the rights of others to make that awful feeling go away.

What's interesting is that while most people don't feel they have the legal (or moral) right to exclude, say, an unwelcome Scientology center or Muslim butcher from their neighborhood or town, many do feel they have the right (indeed, the obligation) to exclude adult businesses. There's a cultural agreement that privileges people's discomfort if it's about sexuality. If you're uncomfortable about blacks, you're a racist; uncomfortable about Jews, you're an anti-Semite; uncomfortable about sex, you're a civic leader. Indeed, politicians vie to show who is the most disgusted with nonconforming sexuality, and who works hardest to protect their constituents from having to face their discomfort about it.

This being America, of course, there are limits to how much you can eliminate sexual expression and adult businesses. But this being America, courts all the way to the Supreme Court have agreed on various ways of doing so. Relying on alleged secondary effects and concern for public morals are good ones. So is wanting to limit child porn, exploiting women, and stopping "trafficking," the new favorite. Laws designed to stop "sex trafficking" in West Virginia or Oklahoma will have the same effect as the elephant gun I keep in my office: True, I haven't had an elephant problem, but I want to keep it that way. And since the purchase, I haven't seen a single elephant, so the gun must be working.

"We're not a town that tolerates sin," says mayor after assemblyman after minister. Does an American town really have the option of *not* "tolerating sin"? Supposedly, the reason taxpayers give organized religion so many privileges (regarding taxation, zoning, governance, use of the mails, etc.) is that it provides the social good of seducing people into behaving morally. If a town isn't satisfied with how effectively its churches are doing this, it has no legitimate legislative recourse. In a democracy, people *don't* have the right to live in a morally pure place. They can attempt to live in a pure home, but that's it. Besides, let he whose home is without sin . . .

ZONING

Zoning laws are a physical embodiment of our residential dreams and self-image. But America has decreed limits to the use of this tool. For example, cities can't use it to subtly encourage or support racial discrimination or air pollution. Using zoning to prevent specific businesses from locating anywhere in a town simply because "we don't like your kind" is *illegal*. Since the Supreme Court (in *Lawrence v. Texas*) has said government can't legislate with the primary goal of enforcing a moral code, using zoning to do so should be banned as well.

Of course, there are graceful ways to use zoning as a crushing hammer. New York City, for example, has proposed to allow adult entertainment—as long as it's at least 1,000 feet from a residence. In the shoulder-to-shoulder high-density world of Manhattan, that leaves thousands of locations for strip clubs—all beneath the Hudson River. Similarly, ordinances in small towns that ban adult entertainment within 500 or 1,000 feet of a school, church, park, residence, or government facility eliminate every site in town.

If *New York* is considering this, you know that cities across the country are. It must seem almost too good to be true for zealots: "You mean, all we have to do is pass a law saying those nasty businesses can't be here—and they can't be here?!" Other than the customers, business owners, and citizens who value the right to be left alone, who could object?

It's amazing that many Americans complain about government being too big, then feel frustrated when they can't use it in unlimited ways.

HOW A BUST WORKS

Cities and counties across America spent way over $50 million last year harassing adult clubs and bookstores. That's a lot of librarians' salaries, a lot of updated firefighting equipment, a lot of preschool classes for poor kids—*not*.[1] It is estimated that various jurisdictions in Florida alone spent as much as $5 million pursuing strip clubs and other adult entertainment venues in 2005.[2] The *City of Erie v. Pap's A.M.* case cost Pennsylvania taxpayers at least one million dollars.[3]

Here's how it usually works:

A community has one or more adult businesses—topless bars, adult bookstores, whatever. Each has paid the necessary business tax (often astronomical, compared to similar non-adult businesses), and is generally content to limit their signage and advertising. People who want to find these places find them. Many residents or businesses a few blocks away don't even know they exist.

Somebody decides their very existence is awful. It may be a politician running for office, a police department wanting a boost, a religious leader looking for a new cause, an exposé by a local newspaper or TV station in search of a story. It is virtually *never* a bunch of people *actually noticing,* "Gee, there's more crime, less virginity, and unhappier wives in the neighborhood of the Kit Kat Klub ever since it opened. Maybe the club is the reason—let's get rid of it!" It's never that way, because that's simply not the reality.

So someone decides to make a fuss, gets some other people riled up, and they pressure the police, mayor, district attorney, or grand jury. Or the police decide to be entrepreneurs, looking for a popular bust that will increase their political and financial support. Either way, two or three police officers then go undercover. These underpaid, overworked cops sit in a strip club, and carefully, professionally, observe the activity there. They take covert photos. If they're in an adult bookstore, they buy some nudie magazines or overpriced dildos. To get the best quality evidence, they go back night after night, and stay hour after hour. You would too, if you could do that instead of responding to domestic violence calls or muggings.

When the police voyeurs are sated, they typically close the place down. If it's a shop, they seize the inventory. If it's a club, they arrest anyone they please— dancers, ticket takers, janitors. They note any broken lightbulbs or bathrooms missing soap for the scrupulous health inspections which inevitably follow. If only our restaurants were inspected that thoroughly.

Evidence in hand, the prosecution begins. The narrative is always the same: wholesome town versus greedy, disgusting businessman. Sometimes a jury is impaneled to decide whether the dancing or material for sale is "obscene." In other cases, one or more judges rule on whether the business has violated an ordinance that restricts nudity, obscenity, prostitution, or other victimless crime. The municipality will spend no less than $250,000 for this first round of harassing the business. If the business wins, the municipality will frequently appeal, throwing good money after bad. Many of these cases go on for years, as cities and counties attempt to eliminate adult businesses, and courts keep reminding them that this is America.[4]

But this isn't a Jimmy Stewart movie with a simple, happy ending. Many clubs and stores win their cases, but are destroyed by the costs of doing so. Pastors who haven't learned to turn the other cheek when it's a buttock say they don't care, as long as the businesses leave town.

Sometimes it works in the opposite direction. Municipalities will attempt to zone adult businesses out of existence, and the businesses take the city or county to court. Local, state, and federal courts are all over the legal map on the rights of adult businesses to exist and the rights of communities to ban them.

When courts do affirm the right of adult businesses to exist, locales typically respond by changing the rules: nude dancers have to wear pasties, or have to stay a prescribed distance from the audience (in a restraining order neither the dancers nor the audience want), or aren't allowed to touch or be touched, or must be clothed when not on stage. One city requires nude dancers to buy permits, which they have to display *while dancing*. They say they're concerned for the dancers' health and safety.[5]

UNICORNS AND SECONDARY EFFECTS: IS ADULT ENTERTAINMENT DANGEROUS?

Concern about the "secondary effects" of adult entertainment is the last refuge of scoundrels.

Americans are guaranteed the broad right to express themselves regardless of the content they wish to convey. Theoretically, the government may not single out particular forms of expression (like, "The President is insane!" [which is illegal to say in Turkey]) for restriction. Legally defined "obscenity" is one of the few exceptions to this protection. But the citizenry's increasing acceptance of sexual materials in the 1980s made obscenity convictions harder to obtain.

In 1986, the Supreme Court finessed the Constitutional protections of free speech (*Renton v. Playtime Theatres*)[6] by creating a new, *non-content* criterion that municipalities could consider when limiting the operations of adult businesses. This was the "secondary effects" (coined by a dissenting Justice Stevens) which adult businesses supposedly have on the surrounding community. And, unlike in every other regulated industry, municipalities didn't have to prove these effects existed (nor would businesses have the chance to refute these assumptions).

The secondary effects that give local government a "compelling interest" in stopping adult entertainment have typically been crime, reduced property values, "blight," STDs, and a vague "lowered morality."

For years, cities and counties have had the luxury of banning adult entertainment because of these supposed effects. Americans have had no reliable right to enjoy sexually oriented entertainment; across the country, that right abruptly ended whenever local officials decided it was bad for the community. Some of our most respected jurists were uneasy about this. In 1988, Supreme Court Justice William Brennan warned that the secondary effects doctrine "could set the Court on a road that will lead to the evisceration of First Amendment freedoms."[7]

And that's exactly what happened. For two decades, the secondary effects doctrine has been used to restrict commercial and political speech, with cities citing concerns about noise, security, privacy, *appearances* of impropriety, competition, and of course, "harm to children."

Officials in Erie, Pennsylvania, for example, tried for over 10 years to prevent nudity in the Kandyland strip club. The city knew it couldn't simply ban nude dancing, which the Supreme Court has given some free speech protection, so Erie claimed it was addressing the club's alleged secondary effects on its neighborhood—even though it couldn't prove any.

In 2000, a split court used the secondary effects rationale to uphold the criminalization of nudity. Justice Antonin Scalia argued that society's "traditional judgment" that nude dancing is "immoral" was sufficient justification.[8] Justice John Paul Stevens dissented, saying, "To believe that the mandatory addition of pasties and G-strings will have any kind of noticeable impact on secondary effects requires nothing short of the titanic surrender to the implausible."[9]

When experts or businesses challenged municipalities to prove the existence of secondary effects, they couldn't. Fulton County, Georgia tried. When their studies didn't find the results they expected, the county ignored them and relied instead on old (and ultimately discredited) studies from other states. In 2001, a federal court looked disdainfully on this (*Flanigan's Enterprises, Inc. v. Fulton County, GA*).[10] The county was using deceit to uphold "moral standards." That's what desperation, and the narcissism of fundamentalism, will do.

In a blatant attack on Americans' civil rights, the government validated the secondary effects concept in 2002. In *City of Los Angeles v. Alameda Books,* the Supreme Court ruled, "It is rational for the city to infer that reducing the concentration of adult businesses in a neighborhood . . . will reduce crime."[11] The bookstore's attorney, John Weston, challenged the city to produce evidence of secondary effects. It had none.

Backed by the Supreme Court, municipalities have written their sexual prejudices into law. Ohio's 2005 law restricting adult entertainment, for example, "finds" it necessary in order to protect "health, safety, morals, and welfare;" asserts "convincing documented evidence" that clubs "have a deleterious effect," "lend themselves to ancillary unlawful and unhealthy activities," and that some employees "engage in a higher incidence of certain types of illicit sexual behavior."[12] "Morals," "illicit"—if that's where a law starts, you know where it will end. Similarly, a law banning swing clubs in Phoenix, Arizona, "finds" that these clubs are dangerous to the public welfare.

Municipalities and religious leaders also attempt to justify sexual censorship by appealing to "common sense," the same source of wisdom that mandated racial segregation, criminalized oral sex, and declared that rape wasn't possible between husband and wife.

For people who are unfamiliar with a broad range of sexuality, or the experience of adult entertainment, common sense can be very different from the facts. For example, among nightclubs that serve alcohol, those *with* nude entertainment have *lower* rates of crime than clubs that *don't* offer nude entertainment.[13] Contrary to common sense? Only if you assume that men go to strip clubs, see naked women, and get provoked into an uncontrollable frenzy.

In reality, strip clubs have clear rules about behaving respectfully, and most customers are delighted to have visual access to attractive nude women. Since everyone has the same limited access to them, there's nothing to fight about, and the patrons themselves subtly patrol the environment. Men are watching the women and aren't talking very much. At bars *without* nudity, men focus more on each other, or on the sports on TV, and they drink more, all of which can lead to violence more easily.[14]

In America, laws regulating virtually all industries have to be based on fact. You can't prevent markets from selling ham simply because you *believe* it leads to heart attacks or immorality, you have to prove it first. You can't require drivers to wear seat belts unless you can prove they reduce injury and save lives. But when the subject is sexual entertainment, citizens allow governments to assume it's bad for customers, bad for entertainers, and bad for neighborhoods. That's a fundamental weapon in their War on Sex, and it simply must stop.

America requires police to use science in detective work, and inspectors to use science in making food safe. It's time to require communities to use science to determine if a business actually ruins neighborhoods or harms families. This data is *already* being collected by police departments in every American city; it straightforwardly shows that adult entertainment doesn't usually have these negative effects—which is why cities have never used it, and don't want to.

As far as adult entertainment lowering property values, one club's attorney recently said, "Send all your neighbors to the tax assessor's office every time the tax assessment in the area goes up, and let them say, 'We are right next to an adult business, so our property values must be going down.' And the tax assessor is going to say, 'No, we track this, and the property values are going up.' That would be good evidence for court. There's a bookstore in Seattle next to a strip club, the tax assessment last year doubled. If that doesn't refute the idea that adult businesses reduce property values, nothing does."[15] Similarly, when the Phoenix, Arizona, club The Chute sold its building, it had *tripled* in value. Hardly evidence of plummeting property values.

Preventing property values from declining used to be an excuse to keep blacks from moving into white neighborhoods, which our courts have ruled was simply legitimized discrimination. Keeping strip clubs away for the same reason should be similarly banned.

But Ohio legislator Jim Jordan said studies that look at police reports aren't relevant. He believes people frequenting adult establishments are involved in criminal activity and use drugs and have illicit sex. "Common sense tells you these things are going on," he said. Jordan conceded that he would outlaw all strip joints if he could: "I think they're degrading to women."[16]

Canada has recently changed its approach to supposed secondary effects. In 2005, its Supreme Court ruled that swing clubs are legal, overturning the traditional test for indecency—whether an activity violates a "social consensus" of community standards. "Criminal indecency or obscenity must rest on *actual harm* or a significant risk of harm to individuals or society," wrote Chief Justice Beverley McLachlin in the majority decision. "Consensual conduct behind code-locked doors can hardly be supposed to jeopardize a society as vigorous and tolerant as Canadian society."[17] Some countries attempt to export democracy abroad. Other countries actually practice it.

It's not worth attempting to refute the claim that a certain sexually oriented activity—in this case, adult entertainment—decreases the "morality" of participants or the community. It is worth repeating that the effect of purchasing a product or service on the morality of consenting adult customers is *irrelevant*. Eating cheeseburgers or buying a motorcycle are both "immoral" choices because they're bad for your health (and, of course, send the wrong message to kids). But if you don't want those choices taken away from you, leave adult entertainment alone.

CUSTOMERS ARE FROM MARS, CIVIC LEADERS ARE FROM VENUS

There are no consumer groups lobbying to protect the rights of adult entertainment patrons. But who is paying for all this stuff that antisex activists are so eager to wipe out?

These are phantom customers—they don't exist in the polity.

Somehow this invisible group supports billions of dollars worth of commercial activity. This presents a logical conflict: if the crap is "everywhere," who are these millions of customers? If the entertainment is so perverse and marginal, who are all these perverts keeping them in business?

We need to acknowledge all these silent customers, and wonder why they're quiet. If they're ashamed to admit what they do, it's because of social pressure. Their shame doesn't keep them from doing it, only from acknowledging it. That's bad for people and towns. *There's* a secondary effect that should concern everyone.

These customers are getting shuffled from town to town. Some eventually give up and take their interests to the Internet and DVDs, although that's not necessarily what they want. They apparently want a *live* experience, and some clearly value the *group* experience as well. It's why many sports fans prefer bars or live events instead of watching at home. Consumers of erotic products deserve that opportunity, too.

Cities generally act as if these consumers are Martians who drop in for a few hours, throw used condoms and beer bottles around, then leave. Naturally, these cities try to make themselves as inhospitable to such aliens as possible. Indeed, less than three weeks after Sandy Springs became Georgia's newest city last year, its city council drafted new restrictions on the hours and location of adult establishments. Affecting at least half a dozen existing locations, Mayor Eva Galambos said that as far as she's concerned, adult businesses don't have a place in the young city. "They don't fit what the business community is trying to do," she said. Who does the mayor, city council, and the "business community" (hardly unanimous, according to newspaper reports) think patronize these adult businesses? The very people who lived there *before* incorporation, of course.[18]

Naturally, the demand for adult entertainment is somewhat elastic: if you make it inconvenient or dangerous enough, people will patronize it less. But what's the curve? How many units of increased inconvenience will create one unit of decreased attendance? How much of a city's money, civic energy, and dignity is that one unit worth?

And what will the people who are thereby dissuaded from consuming adult entertainment do instead? The desire for a lap dance is not exactly fungible with playing bridge or going ice skating. The reasons people want a lap dance won't go away just because the psychic or financial price goes up. Will they spend more time in church or listening to their spouses' feelings? Only someone totally out of touch with sexuality would think so.

It's obviously too scary for some of us to admit it's our neighbors who patronize adult businesses. If consumers of this stuff are bad, and my neighbors do it, then they are bad—and I can't trust my kids at their house, let them coach soccer, or borrow my lawnmower. Better to pretend *we* aren't like that. Just like *we* don't have same-sex fantasies or enjoy dominating or submitting during sex.

There's a fundamental narcissism of politicians and religious leaders regarding adult entertainment. Bluenoses assume that since *they* would feel ashamed, dirty, and withdrawn from their family if they went to a strip club, patrons who *do* go feel the same way. Antisexuals assume that everyone winds up at adult bookstores via repression and degradation (which is how an antisex person *would* get there), not via celebration or choice or even mild loneliness.

There simply aren't enough perverts to support thriving local adult businesses. So customers are either coming from surrounding towns—which is what *every* town implausibly says, too—or the customers are not perverts after all. For a would-be censor, which is more frightening, the idea that a bunch of perverts are watching a strip show, or the idea that the people watching a strip show are *not* perverts? If the former is true, they can mobilize about it. If the latter is, however, they have to change their entire view of civic life and reevaluate their goals and tactics. They might actually even have to think about whether customers had some political clout of their own. Thus, the Right is firmly committed to the customer-as-pervert model. There's just no motivation to see it any other way.

BUZZING AFTER VIBRATORS

More than 1,000,000 vibrators were bought in the United States last year. And the year before that. And, presumably, will be next year.[19]

Before there were DVDs, before there was the Playboy Channel, before there was videotape, there were adult bookstores. They sold "dirty magazines" and "adult novelties," and sometimes had booths in which you could watch so-called blue movies. They were often in seedy neighborhoods, frequented by people who slunk in, hoping to avoid notice. Most store owners had virtually no rights other than what they could buy from local cops.

Now adult stores are better lit, and often better located. They sell DVDs, videotapes, and magazines. They often have video booths, and they sell vibrators, dildos, and other toys. Customers include classy people and even couples, in addition to the grim, avoid-any-eye-contact guys. Nobody goes there looking for attention. Store owners are still treated like dirt.

Sex toys used to be expensive, crappy gadgets sold mostly in crappy places, but in 1977, San Francisco sex educator Joani Blank opened a new kind of well-lit, unapologetic store. Good Vibrations offered accurate sexuality information and quality sex toys—selected by female employees, sold to female customers. Stores operated by women opened in several more cities in the 1980s and 90s, and now they're in almost every metropolis in the country.

Nevertheless, those who fear the idea of women and men actually shaping their own sexual experience are trying to shut these stores down in every one of the 50 states. It's ironic, because sex toys are one of the best ways to improve sexual satisfaction, especially in long-term relationships that lack creativity, playfulness, or communication. Seeing them as some kind of threat is really page 1 in the sexual misunderstanding textbook.

The state of Alabama has been in and out of court, trying to criminalize the sale of vibrators *for a decade.* When a U.S. district judge ruled against the state ban on sex-toy sales—twice—the state appealed—twice. Finally, a federal court actually ruled that the government has a compelling interest in keeping "orgasm stimulating paraphernalia" out of our hands.[20] Were they concerned that women would stop having sex with their husbands if they could buzz off with a vibrator?

The court also ruled that Americans do *not* have a "fundamental right" to use "sexual devices," and so the men and women in the Alabama legislature have the right to police the sale of these devices. In a bizarre forecast (that shows just how frightened of sexuality the judges are), the court worried that if they established a right to sexual privacy, they might be required to uphold that right in cases "including, for example, those involving adult incest, prostitution, obscenity, and the like."[21]

So although every Alabaman has a fundamental right to own a gun, they don't have the same right to own a dildo.

Six other states (Georgia, Mississippi, Indiana, Texas, Louisiana, and Virginia) also outlaw the sale of sex toys. Even selling these items at home among friends can invite jail time, as Joanne Webb discovered. The church-going mother and former school teacher was arrested in a Dallas suburb in 2003, and faced a year in jail. She was charged with obscenity for selling a vibrator to undercover *narcotics* officers posing as a dysfunctional married couple. Where? At a neighbor's home, who was hosting a Passion Party. Has the narcotics squad finished cleaning up all the dangerous illegal drugs in town?

That's how common vibrator use is now—it's made it onto the Right's radar, making those who sell or enjoy them more vulnerable than ever before.

There's a recurring theme here. Adult entertainment involves women owning their bodies and sexuality, choosing to use them for self-expression and income. Sex toys are a way for women to own their bodies, taking charge of their sexual satisfaction. These are new concepts. Remember, rape used to be a crime against the victim's husband or father. And it used to be legally impossible to rape one's own wife—unlimited sexual access to her was assumed. One reason sexual entertainment is outlawed is that it legitimizes women's ownership of their own bodies and sexuality. Some people fear this will upset the whole social order. They're half right. It will upset any social order based on repression of, and male control of, female sexuality.

Would I want my daughter stripping at the local Kit Kat Klub? Do I encourage other women to? These questions are irrelevant. I wouldn't want my daughter to be an oil company executive, professional gambler, or to ride a motorcycle, but I don't want *anyone* to prevent her from doing so. Not even me.

ETHICS?

Since the ostensible goal of eliminating adult entertainment is improving the moral health of the community, it's appropriate to point out the unethical ways zealots pursue this goal.

They manipulate the public. They refer to danger that doesn't exist, making connections that aren't real. Religious and civic leaders acquire more power when citizens are frightened. They rely on anecdote or so-called common sense, pretending there's no science to guide public policy on adult entertainment. Ohio Assemblyman Jim Jordan said studies that look at police reports aren't relevant; he believes people frequenting adult establishments are involved in criminal activity, use drugs, and have illicit sex.

When New York City tried to virtually eliminate adult entertainment in 2003, it relied on the secondary effects argument. When police department figures showed there was virtually no crime attributable to adult businesses, the city then shifted its position, claiming that such businesses nevertheless lead to seedy neighborhoods.

These civic leaders pretend to speak for the whole community when they damn adult entertainment. They claim concern for exploited dancers, endangered kids, or the threatened marriages of customers, but rarely encourage or enact legislation to help any of these. Affordable day care? College tuition assistance? No, they'd rather put the money into busting strip clubs.

In fact, police departments and prosecutors often know that their cases won't stand up. They pursue them anyway, knowing that the costs of defending themselves will devastate many adult businesses. This is dishonest, and the federal courts have frowned on this,[22] but federal court is a long way from a Mormon county in Idaho or a small town in Indiana where morally indignant neighbors can destroy someone holding the wrong opinion.

The final ingredient in this discouragingly antidemocratic scene is raw political opportunism. For example, Donna Hughes Rice went from forgotten bimbo punch line to a star in the antiporn world; Ralph Reed found his financial calling first in antichoice politics, then used his contacts to become a political lobbyist.[23]

Phil Burress is another example of political ambition masquerading as moral concern. Calling himself a reformed porn addict, he founded Citizens for Community Values (CCV) in Cincinnati in 1983 to fight the existence of strip clubs and other adult businesses. He claimed they were all mob-affiliated and hotbeds of drug use, prostitution, and disease. He gradually attracted money and attention with his call to restore "Judeo-Christian values" to the area, and added more products to his organization's charter.

Like virtually all people who demonize sex, Burress went after gays, helping put the state's antigay movement on the map. In fact, he claimed Karl Rove urged him to get an antigay marriage referendum on the 2004 ballot, which Rove said would help mobilize the state's evangelicals to vote. He was right. While *Issue 1* ("no special rights for homosexuals") was passing statewide, 76 percent of Ohio's evangelicals turned out for Bush, whose two-point win in the state reelected him.

But soon enough, the high-minded Burress got caught looking like just another slick political operator. A local group, including Cincinnati's former mayor, has filed suit, investigating the clandestine fundraising operations of the antigay campaigns. And after Burress threatened any Republican assemblyman who didn't support a bill criminalizing nude dancing, 31 clergy from across the state asked the Internal Revenue Service to investigate if Burress's blatant political maneuvering should disqualify his tax-exempt status.[24]

ISN'T THIS WHOLE THING TRIVIAL?

Is the right to watch a bored 24-year-old gyrate topless really that important? Is a club's right to stay in business where powerful people don't want it really worth the litigation, the personal attacks, the possible jail time?

Yes.

Adult entertainment sits atop a steep and slippery slope.

Powerful people and institutions are *saying out loud* that regulating adult entertainment is *not* their end goal; they have further plans. Businessman Richard Enrico, whose group Citizens Against Pornography takes credit for eliminating the sale of *Playboy* magazine in all 1,800 7–Eleven stores in 1986, explained this to me clearly: "First we get *Playboy* out of stores, and soon it will be out of people's homes. Then we'll go on to other kinds of filth."[25]

The legal tools they are developing and using against adult entertainment are also being applied against other forms of sexual expression, such as the Internet and "indecency" on television and cell phones. As these groups win victories in adult entertainment cases, they acquire power, prestige, and funding for other battles over sexual rights.

It's crucial to see the connection between the battle over strip clubs and more "serious" issues like abortion, sex education, and the Internet. It's the same people, same philosophy, same money, same coalitions—backed by the same political/religious machine. The Family Research Council, Focus on the Family, and Concerned Women for America do not limit themselves to single issues; their goal is a broad transformation of American society.

Is this a conspiracy?

No.

It's worse—it's a war. They are straightforward about their goals and strategy. They *said* they would go after the Internet ten years ago—and the federal government has tried to censor what you can see there four different times. They *said* 20 years ago they would go after porn—and the federal government has empowered a multi-million dollar obscenity task force that, among other things, recently shut down the largest erotic video arcade network (over 60 stores, over 1,000 booths) in Texas. They *said* they would clean up radio and TV, and they chased Howard Stern off of free, *public* radio. They *said* they'd cleanse every state and city of tittie bars, and they are in the process of doing so. There is no conspiracy—just a war.

In 2000, Justice Stevens, dissenting in *City of Erie v. Pap's A.M.*, wrote, "Far more important than the question of whether nude dancing is entitled to the protection of the First Amendment, are the dramatic changes in legal doctrine that the Court endorses today. Until now the secondary effects of commercial enterprises featuring indecent entertainment have justified only the regulation of their location. For the first time the Court has now held that such effects may justify the total suppression of protected speech." Further, "The Court's use of the secondary effects rationale to permit a total ban has grave implications for basic free-speech principles."[26]

And there's a meta-slippery slope.

It's not just sexuality the antisex forces want to control. *According to them,* it's every aspect of American life. It's all part of a plan, as Dr. Judith Hanna says, to destroy the wall between church and state. For example, the mission statement for Citizens for Community Values is "to promote Judeo-Christian moral values, and to reduce destructive behaviors contrary to those values."[27] In addition to a $2,000,000 campaign to close every nude club in Ohio, CCV has proudly created political campaigns to oppose gay marriage, reproductive rights, and effective sex education.

When groups like CCV win battles around adult entertainment, they get stronger for further battles. According to *U.S. News & World Report,* CCV "has become one of the largest local grassroots organizations of its type in the nation."[28] Every victory validates the horrifying idea that morality can be the basis of American law.

In one sense, it doesn't matter in *what* context zealots are trying to loosen our rights—we must protect ourselves. If the battleground is sexuality, and some desultory tittie bar on the wrong side of the tracks where more people frown than smile, so be it. Those who find this battleground distasteful, or don't believe it's worth fighting over, aren't looking at the bigger picture. You don't have to have a child in school to oppose the teaching of Intelligent Design. You don't have to watch Howard Stern to oppose chasing him off the air. You stand up for the rights of sad people to watch other sad people gyrate—so *you* can watch, read, download, write, and listen to whatever *you* want. *That's* the American way.

UNDERMINING AMERICA

The willingness of these activists to behave unethically is bad enough. What is truly disturbing is their willingness to attack fundamental American rights to achieve their personal ends, typically the reduction of their personal anxiety, affirmation of their identity as pious, and accumulation of political power or money. Individual rights that no one would dream of attacking in any other (nonsexual) context are treated as an inconvenience, a simple challenge to the creativity of law enforcement, elected officials, and civic watchdogs. Communities object to many things, but it is only the patrons and purveyors of adult entertainment whose rights are so systematically limited and violated.

As insane as racial segregation was, at least blacks had their own drinking fountains. But communities are not trying to establish restricted places where people can watch a stripper or buy a whip—they are trying to eliminate such options altogether.

And while some observers smirk, wondering who would stand up for something as trivial as a lap dance, no one seems to be commenting on the amount of energy some people are putting into *eliminating* lap dances. In fact, anyone who put as much time into *preserving* the option of getting a lap dance as people are putting into eliminating it would be derided as an obsessive pervert.

Half a world away, America is spending mountains of money and buckets of blood to ease its fear about a group of faceless people trying to destroy the American way of life. But from Maine to California, Americans are doing it to

America right here. The Taliban would take away the right of a woman to wear short sleeves; Daytona Beach has taken away the right to wear thong bikinis. The Taliban would prevent men and women from watching each other dance; Alabama prevents men from having a beer and watching women dance if they show their nipples.[29]

And the governments of Daytona Beach and Alabama have enacted their bans for the exact same reason that the Taliban enacted theirs: they know what's right and wrong, and have seized the power to make people live accordingly. It's for *everyone's* good, you know.

Chapter Nine

How They Do It: Ammunition in the War on Sex

Those who war on sex have an extraordinary arsenal of weapons at their disposal. It includes:

- willingness to promote fear, anger, hatred, and anxiety
- ability to dismiss fact and focus on feelings
- huge circular flow of cash between government and religious groups
- lack of media scrutiny combined with extra media access
- establishment of so-called morality groups as legitimate spokespersons
- marginalization of moderate religious voices
- linguistic and category domination
- explicit policy collusion between government and religion—with the President himself straddling both worlds

How could *any* social movement with these advantages fail to accomplish its agenda? Let's look at some of the specific strategies of antisex forces. Enhancing our literacy about media, statistics, and oratory may not stop the War on Sex, but it will enable us to see it more clearly, and therefore make it visible to others.

WHAT'S THE PROBLEM?

The very framing of phenomena is the first step toward controlling the conversation about it. Americans hear about "the problem of indecency" and "the problem of pornography" constantly. This means that anyone who isn't concerned about indecency is *for* indecency, doesn't care about children, and so forth. It's far less common to hear about "the problem of censorship" or "the problem of others' discomfort with sexuality," which would make it easier for anticensorship people to appear in a positive light. Similarly, we hear a lot more about "the problem of gay marriage" than about "the problem of intolerance and discrimination."

Protecting our rights now requires standing up and saying, "We don't have an indecency problem, we have a censorship, intolerance, and hijacking of government problem." As George Lakoff says, "Framing defines the problem. Framing limits what you can talk about. They have achieved the ability to frame public discourse their way."[1]

CREATIVE USE OF LEGAL TERMS

The people who write our laws can make anything illegal. All you have to do is create a category of thing that's illegal, and then put behavior into it. By criminalizing "public sex acts," "mailing indecent substances," obscenity "in public view," material "harmful to minors," "contributing to immorality," and "undermining community morals," various communities have made an enormous range of activities illegal. These now include private swing clubs, lap dances, nude car washes, and, as 21-year-old Clemson University student Christine Vetter found out, mailing her worn, unwashed panties.[2]

CATEGORY MANIPULATION

Control a society's vocabulary and you control the society.

Normal conversation depends on many words that lack objective meaning but have emotional resonance—that is, subjective meaning. We agree to use expressions like "intimacy," "frustrated," "overcrowded," "rude," and "on top of things," even though we each mean something different by these words. We're all against "sex abuse," but exactly what constitutes it? We all want people to feel "respected," but what do you and I each mean by that?

There are many words associated with sexual problems, and those who war on sex keep expanding what those words mean. "Sex abuse" and "child molestation" used to mean the physical violation of children by adults. Now we hear that adults who go to strip clubs are molesting their kids "spiritually." And we have eight-year-olds busted for "sexually abusing" a classmate by casually peeking under her dress.

"Sex offenders" used to only be violently intrusive. Now the category includes harmless exhibitionists and those who solicit prostitutes. "Date rape" is a terrible thing, but at some colleges, if you change your mind the morning after sex and can prove you'd had a few drinks, you can claim you're a victim. Everyone's language has gotten saltier since the 1970s and 80s, but Morality in Media urges people to petition the Federal Communications Commission about "indecent" words like "butt" and "boob." And then there's the word "child." The War on Sex loves to talk about the horrible stuff "children" are seeing and doing—without mentioning how many of those children are 16, not 6.

Then there are the phony categories used to scare us. It's easy. Take two separate things, one common and one unusual. Put them together and watch how many things fit in. Like, um, "Millions of wives scold or even hit their husbands on the honeymoon," or, "Tens of millions of people leave restaurants feeling too full or even sick." How about these actual categories:

- "Sexual pressure or coercion" (one is subjective and part of dating; the other involves force)
- "Pornography and kiddie porn" (one is legal; the other isn't)
- "Prostitution and trafficking" (one is voluntary and common; the other is coerced and rare)
- "Victims of early sex(!) and molestation" (one is consensual, often with an age peer; the other is illegal, often forced, usually with someone much older)
- "Sadomasochism and abuse" (one is consensual; the other isn't)
- "Molestation and unwanted sexual attention" (one is illegal and destructive; the other is a part of life to be negotiated)
- "Missing and exploited children" (one is rare; the other terribly common)
- "Indecent and obscene" (two radically different categories; in most circumstances, the first can be legal while the second isn't)

A popular usage of this is attacking virtually *anything* by associating it with something bad. So the F word shouldn't be allowed on late night cable TV because "porn is bad for kids." *No one* is requesting porn on "American Idol." Another popular tactic is setting up and attacking a pointless straw man: "Sex education shouldn't encourage bestiality." Yes, even I can agree with that totally inane statement.

Or these popular Grimm's scary tales:

- "Giving condoms to children" (who are 16 or 17)
- "Legalizing marriage of groups, siblings, or a man and his horse" (is there *anyone* demanding this?)
- "Homosexualizing America" (like gays don't have enough sexual opportunities with each other? Like straights are so vulnerable to gay sex?)
- "Books on child sex instruction" (yes, books teaching kids *about* their sexuality—not *how* to have sex)

And here's my favorite, repeated endlessly (from Nicholas Jackson in *The Conservative Voice*): "The average age now of exposure to pornography is 5 years of age." I challenge Mr. Jackson to say exactly how he defines "pornography" and "exposure." I haven't seen too many five-year-olds down at Hollywood Hustler lately. If he's talking about kids seeing half a second of Janet Jackson's nipple, or some of Meryl Streep's cleavage at this year's Oscars, or ads for *Brokeback Mountain,* I can live with this. And I don't call that porn.[3]

THE LANGUAGE OF WAR

And while we're on the subject of language . . .

Pro-life	Sex addict	Childhood innocence
Porn addict	Cybersex addict	Sex and violence
Abstinence is 100%	Hard core, smut, filth	Activist judge
Baby killer	Pro-abortion	Traditional values
Promiscuity	Unborn child	Perversion
Culture of life	Pornographer	Normal
Abortionist	Victim of porn	Secondary effects
Partial-birth abortion	Morality group	Obscenity
Pro-family	Decency	Indecent
Homosexual agenda	Christian nation	Harmful to minors

DRAWING CONCLUSIONS FROM ANECDOTE

A week doesn't go by that we don't hear about some maniac, present or past, who

- has been arrested for rape, with porn in his pocket;
- has been arrested for child molestation, with kiddie porn in his pocket;
- has been sued for divorce after spending the rent money at a strip club;
- pushed his high school girlfriend to have sex the night after his first sex ed class; or
- well, you get the idea.

Correlation is not causality. Just because two things happen near each other doesn't mean that one caused the other. Buying nachos at Taco Bell at 8:00 doesn't make the moon rise at 8:15. *Of course* many rapists consume porn. Fifty million other Americans do, too. Every one of those 50 million drank milk as a kid, like every rapist did. You don't hear people saying, "Milk made him do it."

For a perfect example of this, see Jan LaRue's (Concerned Women for America) piece on victims of pornography, which cites "a lieutenant colonel who admitted killing his wife during an argument about his use of the Internet to view pornography."[4]

One staggering story doesn't constitute an analysis. As heartbreaking as the story might be, it doesn't even constitute information. As Alan Leshner, CEO of the American Association for the Advancement of Science reminds us, "The plural of anecdote is *not* data."[5]

DRAWING THE WRONG CONCLUSIONS
FROM SURVEY INFORMATION

The abstinence folks report teens tell surveys they want abstinence. Then 90 percent of them have sex before marriage. The decency folks report that viewers want wholesome programming. Then viewers make *Will & Grace, Desperate Housewives,* and *Grey's Anatomy* huge hits. Antiporn groups report that people want obscenity laws enforced. Then 50 million Americans look at porn, and hotel room porn skyrockets when antiporn groups come to town.

Perhaps these surveys are indicating something different than antisex groups think. They're actually proof that (1) people tell surveys what they think the desirable answer is, and (2) people say one thing and do another. Social psychologists have known the first for over 50 years, and everybody has known the second for about 50,000 years.

Of course, when survey statistics are based on heterogeneous categories, the results can mean anything a sponsor claims it does. For example, "Parents favor abstinence until a couple is married *or close to marriage,*" [emphasis mine] according to a Heritage Foundation survey.[6] They have the nerve to say that this proves public support for abstinence programs.

Other statistics are abused as well. Lifenews.com recently decried how both the absolute number and the percentage of American abortions being done by Planned Parenthood keeps rising. What Lifenews.com conveniently omitted is that the number of places Americans can get abortions has declined every year since 1982, and is at its lowest in three decades. Of *course* Planned Parenthood is doing more abortions. It is quickly becoming the only organization with the money and political courage to cope with the harassment and violence that abortion providers must endure.[7]

WE'RE ALL VICTIMS HERE

Conservative government and the Religious Right love to portray regular Americans as victims of porn and nasty TV assaulting their homes, and strip clubs invading peaceful neighborhoods. Exactly who do they think pays for these products? Or do they think *South Park,* Jenna Jameson, and the local tittie bar are brought to us by altruistic nonprofits? It is staggering that the Right can decry how much bad culture surrounds us, while simultaneously pretending there is no consumer demand for the things they damn.

Similarly, they somehow claim to be fighting an uphill battle against a flood of dangerous eroticism, while claiming that theirs is the voice of the majority that must be heard and given power.

OMITTING DISCUSSION OR PROOF OF KEY ASSUMPTIONS

The rhetoric in the War on Sex is ripe with assumptions that it never tests or proves—because it can't. It's easy to *say* that kids should be shielded from all sexual imagery because it destroys their alleged innocence and warps their moral vision, but where's the evidence? Without evidence, these assumptions shouldn't be the foundation of endless hand-wringing editorials, one-sided hearings, and apocalyptic states of emergency—and they *certainly* shouldn't be driving public policy.

Here are some other key assumptions of the War on Sex:

- The existence of porn hurts women.
- "Morality" involves limiting sexual expression and experimentation.
- It's best for kids to be kept innocent about sexuality for as long as possible.
- The value of keeping kids abstinent far outweighs any harm done by how you accomplish it.
- Adult businesses are "just in it for the money," which is worse than other businesses having the same motive.
- Those who want to limit sexual expression and sexual rights speak for the community.
- Undesirable social change is the fault of the various adult industries.
- Porn use leads to violent behavior (although America's rape rate steadily declines while the availability of porn steadily increases).
- Women are not actually interested in lusty sex—such as viewing porn, using sex toys, playing bondage games, or insisting on sex.

Local and federal government hearings feature these assumptions—invariably without giving anyone from the other side a chance to challenge them. Legislators and would-be censors alike describe their opinions in quasi-scientific ways ("we all know . . . " "it's clear that . . . " "the obvious connection between . . . ").

One enormous scam getting virtually no scrutiny is the well-intentioned but poorly conceived Megan's Law. Tens of millions of dollars are spent around the country maintaining complex databases and complicated notification schemes that scare the hell out of people. But there isn't a single study validating that this approach actually makes anyone safer.

QUOTING SELF-DESCRIBED "VICTIMS" AS IF THEY HAVE EXPERTISE

Phil Burress started Citizens for Community Values because, he says, he was a porn addict for 25 years. He isn't alone; many "decency" leaders have led lives of debauchery (an honorable tradition that goes back to St. Augustine). But having been dysfunctional doesn't provide expertise. That would be like selecting an attorney because he kept getting sued, selecting a marriage counselor because she is divorced, choosing an architect because his house came down in a storm, or looking for a doctor whose broken leg refuses to heal.

The real reason these "decency" crusaders are interviewed over and over is that their stories are titillating, and provide the perfect morality tale to reassure antisex forces (and it allows the media to showcase its "community concern"). "Look at how sex ruined me" promises a peek under someone's dress, as well as the "proof" that sex destroys us. Throw in some divine revelation, and you have a moralistic hat trick. If you have a decent bookkeeper, there's faith-based funding in it, too.

The late Senator Daniel Patrick Moynihan used to say that "everyone has a right to their own opinion but nobody has a right to their own facts."[8] Unfortunately, the War on Sex is being conducted by people who are extremely skillful at portraying their opinions as fact, and successfully ridiculing facts that challenge their opinions.

Chapter Ten

Battleground: *The Internet*

Along with the mobile phone, the Internet has become absolutely ubiquitous in American life. In just a few short years, we've acquired a new vocabulary to describe our daily activities: to log on, to google, to IM, to post, to blog. We've learned about new entities, such as cyberspace, e-mail, DSL, wireless, and ISPs. Our new adjectives include interactive, user-friendly, plug-and-play, and virtual. The Internet's alchemy has even changed our most familiar surroundings, turning our postal mail into snail mail, and our local mall into brick-and-mortar stores.

The spectacular penetration of the Internet gives us an opportunity to see social history unfold in our own lifetime: What happens when a brand-new technology is introduced into Western popular culture?

Watching the Internet, the result is frustratingly familiar, and pathetically predictable. For millions of Americans, the Internet is just the latest blunt instrument with which to terrify ourselves and others about sex. And so the most profound communications tool in the history of the human race has been transformed into a battleground in the War on Sex.

Having an existing War on Sex did hasten this destiny (although, as we'll see below, history suggests it would have happened anyway). Because the War on Sex had a sophisticated infrastructure already in place, powerful individuals and groups were able to fit the Internet right into their campaign.[1]

To do so, experienced groups were able to use the same vocabulary, psychological paradigm, and political machine they had used in prior battles (such as those over broadcast TV and VCRs), waged before the Internet was central to American life. The breathtakingly futuristic innovation of the "information superhighway" didn't matter to them; there was nothing modern about the fear they whipped up around it. We might as well have been witnessing the mystery of fire terrifying our pre-caveman ancestors.

TECHNOLOGY IS ALWAYS ADAPTED FOR
SEXUAL PURPOSES

The way the Internet actually became pervasive in America followed a well-known pattern, one which tells us a great deal about human nature and sexuality. This 10,000-year-old pattern tells us, in fact, that new technologies do *not* shove erotic imagery, words, and themes at a naïve public that hasn't invited it, wants to resist it, but simply can't. No, what has almost invariably happened for 100 centuries is that new technologies are used for sexual purposes *very early in their development.* And that's true regardless of a society's economy, religion, political system, or level of literacy.[2] *These sexual uses ultimately make the technology available to the general public for more general uses.*

One reason for this pattern is that sex is central to so many human endeavors. Another is that humans have an unlimited thirst for sexual expression, health, and comfort.

Consider:[3]

- When public baths were introduced in ancient Africa, China, Greece, and Rome, new communication tools, such as pictographs and writing, were immediately adopted for sexual purposes—the names and addresses of sex workers etched into the tile.
- Italian and English emerged as popular, national languages due to the publication of bawdy stories—Boccaccio's *Decameron* (approx. 1351) and Chaucer's *Canterbury Tales* (approx. 1387). Passed from hand to hand and read to a largely illiterate population, they made people want to learn how to read—the languages that had until then been local vernaculars.
- When the printing press appeared in 1452, it was used mostly to print the Bible and scholarly works. But Arentino's *Postures* and Rabelais' *Gargantua and Pantagruel*—filled with engravings of sexual positions, stories of exposed genitalia, and the most coarse scatology—were enormous and immediate hits, showing the press could make money. Although both were banned, Rabelais boasted that "more copies of [Gargantua] have been sold by the printers in two months than there will be of the Bible in nine years." This would apply to every new medium ever after: sex sells.[4]
- When still photography was invented, it was a complicated, staid affair requiring tremendous discipline from its subjects. But during the Civil War, soldiers demanded their sweethearts mail them erotic photos—a practice so common that by 1865 Congress outlawed it. The new medium of photography, however, had become an accepted part of life.[5]
- VCRs were terribly expensive when first invented. The first videos produced, in 1977, were straightforward pornography; the first non-porn videos followed a year later. People really desired the expen-

sive new technology, not to replace taking the family to the neighborhood cinema, but for the chance to watch porn in private. Sony bet wrong—predicting videotape would be used mostly to record TV shows, it created one-hour Betamax tapes. When the market for videotape proved not to be time-shifting but prerecorded films—porn films—the less-sophisticated but longer VHS format quickly won out and became the industry standard. With porn films available for home viewing, demand for the machines exploded, the price plummeted, and today 91 percent of American homes have at least one VCR.[6]

Whether a technological innovation involves transportation, communication, or new materials, the pattern looks like this:

- In the early stages of acceptance, a few people predict there will be sexual "abuses" (i.e., uses) of the new technology, which will lead to awful consequences (e.g., cars were predicted to give lovers mobility and privacy, leading to debauchery and white slavery).
- Indeed, people *do* use the new technology for sexual purposes, which can involve entertainment, expression, health, pleasure, and convenience (electricity was quickly used to light downtown cabarets, where people could meet or court unsupervised for the first time; mass printing was quickly used for salacious books and pamphlets).
- The sexual uses lead to the development of practical applications of the technology, enabling more widespread adoption of it (once perfected, systems to pay for Internet porn were adapted to make Internet shopping possible).
- When the technology is adapted for widespread nonsexual uses acknowledged as valuable, certain groups or individuals attempt to limit or eliminate the sexual uses (including "900" phone lines, the French minitel, and paperback books).[7]

It doesn't matter which people, which technology, or the format of the sexuality involved, the pattern is almost always the same. People upset about sexual adaptations of technology may blame it on the lasciviousness of a particular group (atheists, immigrants, homosexuals, liberals, perverts); or on the modernity or soullessness of a particular innovation (crocodile dung, the printing press, latex rubber); or on the temptations of a particular sexuality (kiddie porn, swinging, sodomy). All are missing the point: humans are hungry for sexual imagery. They fantasize about sexual opportunity. And they'll do so any way they can.

Just as humans yearn for an easier, richer, safer world regarding economics, food, childrearing, and health, they have the same yearnings regarding sexuality.

As people adopt technologies for enhancing nutrition, improving their health, and keeping warm and dry, so too they adopt them for making sex safer, easier, more exciting, more varied, less expensive, and more self-expressive. The Internet is only the latest chapter in this timeless story. And while most humans want privacy around their sexual expression, these same humans have been dying to know what their neighbors do sexually since privacy became the norm.

People will *always* respond this way to technology. You and I will live to see dire predictions, efforts at control, and moral hysteria about other technologies that haven't been invented yet. Because those yet-to-be-invented technologies will be adapted for sexual purposes. Count on it.

HOW IT WORKED WITH THE INTERNET

- The Internet, originally developed by the Department of Defense and later by the National Science Foundation, was limited to a small number of specialists—until it was used for sex.
- Once uses for sex were practical, money poured into the Internet. This propelled entrepreneurs to make the Internet less expensive and easier to access.
- This acquainted more people with the Internet, which spurred demand for access to it.
- When enough laypeople heard about the Internet, some started talking about the "bad" uses of it. They began to describe it with a fear-based vocabulary adapted from other antisex campaigns: inappropriate content, dangerous for children, online predators, exploitation of women, and so forth.
- These people demanded that the government do something to limit Americans' access to the Internet, and the Internet's access to Americans.
- To justify this, they developed a full-blown moral panic. They made it clear that the Internet posed a clear and present danger so intense that it justified compromising certain basic rights.

Why is this history important? Because we should look beyond the specifics of the attacks on the Internet. We should see today's battle over the Internet as one of a long series of such battles.

In this chapter we'll examine recent history and you can watch the War on Sex in action.

WHAT'S SPECIAL ABOUT THE INTERNET?

In its purest form, the communications technology known as the Internet has five key features:

- Anyone can add anything they want to the material available to everyone.
- Anyone can access anything that's available.
- Anyone can communicate privately with anyone else participating in the network.
- Both producers and consumers can participate anonymously.
- The network is infinitely expandable.

As one federal court put it, the Internet is a "vast democratic forum, open to any member of the public to speak on subjects as diverse as human thought."[8]

The combination of these features gives the Internet extraordinary potential. In less than two decades, three developments fulfilled this potential:

- An enormous volume of human culture is currently stored on this network: an estimated 11.5 billion pages in 2005.[9]
- This material can be searched very effectively, according to practically any criteria; the most popular search systems are intuitively usable by almost anyone.
- An enormous number of individuals currently participate in this worldwide network, with 167,000,000 in the United States alone.

The features described above make the Internet a revolutionary tool for human communication that is actually changing the way people think and interrelate—*subject to this caveat:* The criteria for what these 167 million Americans choose to write onto it, to read on it, to search for in it, and with whom to communicate are, *in the Internet's purest form,* not regulated by government, a corporation, or other authority.

And that's how it was until the mid-90s. But as with all technologies, when use of the Internet expanded beyond the initial technology-oriented, younger group of early adapters, the demand for legislation to control it grew. And that has triggered a fierce, take-no-prisoners battle in the War on Sex.

From the individual users' point of view, the Internet is a special world. To a degree unknown in the non-virtual ("real") world, the virtual world:

- empowers users—including minors—without punishment for feeling entitled;
- presents unlimited, typically anonymous opportunities for sexual talk, research, imagination, and fantasy;
- is an amoral universe, without the restrictions of an external moral code;
- tolerates an unlimited range of beliefs, desires, and imagination.

For those who wish to control others' sexuality, thinking, or family structure, the Internet is a nightmare come true.

Not coincidentally, the Internet—in its purest form—also represents the fulfillment of America's loftiest ideals:

- Democracy: equal rights for all participants
- Meritocracy: no one cares about your "actual" skin color or "true" physical beauty
- Liberal rights: people can do what they want if they're not hurting others
- Pluralism: the recognition that different people want different things, and the assumption that all will tolerate all

These are two different ways of describing the same phenomenon. Many people hate or fear the Internet precisely because its fulfills these lofty American ideals.

HISTORY OF THE INTERNET

The Internet started out as part of a multination physics research project, CERN. Computers had been around since the end of World War II. By the 1950s, deep in the Cold War, the U.S. government wondered how to keep its chain of command intact in the event of a nuclear war. The desired solution was to have a decentralized system that didn't physically exist anywhere. That system became the Internet. It won't, of course, survive a nuclear war, but today's typical Internet user rarely thinks about its military uses.

At first, participating in the Internet required technical skill and equipment that few people had or could acquire. The early participants were an esoteric group, members of a mostly invisible society that developed its own language, etiquette, and priorities.

During the 1980s, a long series of technical achievements was making the Internet more practical for more people. Things we take for granted today had to be, and were, invented: HTML, URLs. The World Wide Web project was announced in 1991. Three years later, Netscape released the first Netscape browser.

And the thing that drove the whole development was . . . sex. Pornography to look at. To read. To buy. Chat rooms in which to discuss sex or have "virtual" sexual experiences. Fetish sites which proved you weren't the only one who enjoyed your unusual fantasy. E-mail with which people could flirt, discuss sex, and masturbate together. People took pictures of themselves nude or having sex and posted them for others to enjoy. It was commonplace to note, for example, that online pornography is the first consistently successful e-commerce product.

With the Internet becoming more easily usable, people started going to it for a wide range of nonsexual activities: shopping (made possible because of porn-for-pay systems), research (via high-resolution, compressed images needed for porn), education (via CD-ROMs, developed to deliver porn), and e-mail, with the extraordinary opportunity to communicate with others around the world (a network financed by people using it for sexual purposes).

And so the whole country started finding out about this cool way to interact with others. And some people started freaking out about this sexual way to interact with others.

Which brings us to the predictable thing that happened next: people brought the War on Sex to the Internet. The frontline moved online.

THE MORAL PANIC OVER THE INTERNET

It wasn't long before the public was being told there was "too much" sex on the Internet, and that it posed a danger to many people, particularly children. There was already a powerful civic-political alliance battling against sexual rights relating to videotape, TV, radio, telephone sex, library books, and adult entertainment. Thus, there was an infrastructure of fear/danger already in place to explain that:

1. Sexual material on the Internet is dangerous.
2. An ever-growing group of people were "abusing" the new technology, increasing kids' vulnerability.
3. These people were themselves dangerous.

The supposedly out-of-control reader of Mickey Spillane was simply transformed into the out-of-control reader of Internet porn. The supposedly ever-present playground predator was easily transformed into the ever-present chat-room predator.

Since the special technology of the Internet makes an enormous range of words and images widely available, people who worried about uncontrolled access and experience were easily frightened. Sexual imagery formed an easy target on which to focus the anxiety of this group; for anyone who believes that access to the "wrong" material frees people's dangerous "latent tendencies," the Internet is the most treacherous thing ever invented.

Many institutions—churches, "morality" groups, think tanks, parent groups—devoted themselves to controlling online sexuality, while many more came into being with this specific mission. It was the focus of enormously successful fundraising efforts; indeed, it helped make some groups, like Concerned Women for America and Focus on the Family, the big players they are today. Like Jenna Jameson (and Senator Sam Brownback), they can proudly say, "We owe our success to Internet porn."

Since these groups' constituents were (and often still are) technologically unsophisticated, they were easily misled about the magnitude of the dangers the Internet posed. Those already participating in other moral panics (regarding, for example, homosexuality, child abduction, satanic abuse, feminism, or contraception) found it easy to believe almost any assertion about destructive sex on the web.

If they heard sensational claims about it, they rarely checked them out, and certainly weren't having experiences that contradicted these lies. If their pastor told them that kids can access millions of Web sites showing women having sex with horses, they didn't surf the web to discover it isn't true. If they heard that there are perverts molesting young girls in every chat room in cyberspace, they didn't go to chat rooms with their nieces and share benign experiences there.

The moral panic was fed by stories citing the explosive availability of, and interest in, sexual material on the Internet. It became commonplace to cite how sex was the most-searched for word on the Internet, a fact that has continued to this day.

Obviously, tens of millions of people, from every walk of American life, were eager to look at, think about, or discuss sex via the Internet. But antisex forces didn't consider the meaning of this very typical interest. Instead, the moral panic quickly grew to the point where some people demanded that the government take steps to control what others could see, read, and hear on the Internet. Congress responded with a series of measures in 1995 and 1996, addressing "Protection of Children from Computer Pornography," material "harmful to minors," and the use of morphing technology to create simulated child porn.

And still some people feared, and still they wanted more control. In 1998, Senator John McCain (R-AZ) introduced legislation "to ensure that pervasive, obscene, and violent material is screened out [of schools and libraries] and that our children are protected."[10] That year the government passed the outlandishly comprehensive Child Online Protection Act (COPA), which criminalized the sending of anything "indecent" (is that a broad enough, vague enough category?) over the Internet.

So the government joined in the Big Lie about (1) the Internet being a dangerous environment that (2) needed to be controlled.

The moral panic around the Internet needed villains, of course. Not surprisingly, the category of "dangerous people" is getting bigger and bigger. It now includes couples who post nude photos of themselves, adult women who dress in fantasy teenager costumes, political analysts and impolite bloggers, and people who publish sites providing information about sexual health, homosexuality, and nonmonogamy.

Antisex forces continually expressed outrage that so-called pornographers were allowed to do what they wanted on the Internet—as if the rights of people to consume what pornographers were producing was of no importance. So pornographers were a handy villain. And the people who protected Americans' rights to consume their online products—such as the American Civil Liberties Union, National Coalition Against Censorship, and People for the American Way—were branded as protecting pornographers' rights to poison America.

That strategy has continued to this very day—ignore the rights of consumers of sexually oriented materials when discussing possible harm and possible solutions.

A SPECIAL KIND OF PANIC—STATE BY STATE

As the panic spread, the Internet was increasingly looked upon as an enormous pipeline pumping toxic sewage into innocent homes, giving nightmarish predators access to innocent lives. Individual states began passing laws attempting to prevent this monstrous technology from harming its citizens.

Pennsylvania's law is typical. Passed in 2002, it required all ISPs to block access to sites *accused* of containing child pornography. The state attorney general, or any county district attorney, could ask a local judge to declare that a certain Web site *might* be child pornography, thus requiring any ISP serving Pennsylvania citizens to block it. This would occur with no prior notice to the ISP or Web site owner, with no option of appeal.

The law imposed potential liability on ISPs, even if they had no relationship with the publishers of the allegedly offensive content. *Any ISP doing business in Pennsylvania was therefore potentially liable for content anywhere on the Internet.*

Not satisfied, Pennsylvania's attorney general started issuing orders directly to ISPs himself—over 300—demanding they block certain content. The attorney general has refused to comply with "Right to Know" law requests for the content of these secret orders.

For a year, providing Internet service in Pennsylvania was a dangerous business. Residents never knew which sites they couldn't access due to mere suspicion, or worse, because an innocent Web site was technically entangled with a site that was suspected. Finally, the law was challenged in 2003, and overturned in court a year later.

Pennsylvania's law was technologically impossible and constitutionally unacceptable. But it did make a statement: we are so afraid of child porn that we're willing to shut down the Internet in Pennsylvania.[11]

FILTERING? BLOCKING? CENSORING? YOUR EYES ARE THE BATTLEFIELD

Just as fear of alcohol (particularly of how immigrants, poor people, and minors were using it) 80 years ago led to Prohibition, fear of the Internet (particularly of how perverts, liberals, and minors were using it) led to demands for "filtering" technology.

This was the impetus for developing Internet filtering software, which many private companies made commercially available in the mid-1990s. Installed on a computer, it would prevent the user from accessing Web sites whose address or content were considered "inappropriate"—that is, connected with sexuality. Vendors claimed that their products "protected children" by eliminating "pornographic" content, but the range of sexual references they also eliminated was extraordinarily wide. This included sites about breast cancer, psychology, political debate, art, and even people (Dick Armey) and communities (Middlesex) whose names included certain magic letters.[12] www.MapleSoccer.org was blacklisted by CyberPatrol because it listed teams as "boys under 12," "boys under 10," and so on.

These companies did what any profit-making venture does: they encouraged a demand for their product. Logically, they did so by "alerting" people to the terrible dangers cyberspace posed—mostly for their children, but even for themselves. Note, for example, the headline on this site that sells a variety of filtering products:

> Today's high-tech porn pushers are more aggressive than ever before, making it almost impossible to protect our families from unwanted pornography. Thankfully, with tools like internet filtering software, it's possible to fight back.[13]

Note the language: "porn-pushers" are "aggressive," we need to "protect our families," and now we can "fight back." This site sells fear, need, and a solution in just two sentences.

Thus, these companies were in collusion with others whose agenda is to frighten the public about the sexual uses of the Internet. That has continued to this day, primarily because they have a common goal—to raise alarm about the sexual aspects of the Internet—and also because the institutions of the Right purchase and encourage the use of these products. For example, religious and other conservative groups increasingly urge the use of filtering software as part of the treatment of "porn addiction" and "cybersex addiction." CYBERsitter was once distributed by the antiporn group Focus on the Family. The site FilteringFacts.org, purporting to explain the objective facts supporting filtering, was partly funded by the group Enough is Enough, whose stated mission is protecting children and families from Internet porn.[14]

In selling security products such as burglar alarms and motion detectors, the key to success is persuading potential customers that they are vulnerable. People, of course, are more easily frightened by appeals to emotion than by fact. And so filtering companies, like their antisex collaborators, recklessly tell and retell legends such as, "The average age a child is first exposed to pornography online is 11 years old," and, "Nearly all (90 percent) kids aged 8–16 have viewed porn online, mostly while doing homework."[15]

These numbers are created via categories so broad that they show almost everyone experiencing almost everything. For example, according to www.protectyourkids.info, "More than half of teenagers have visited Internet sites containing pornography, offensive music lyrics, gambling or messages of violence or hate." Only half? With a category that diverse, 99 percent wouldn't be surprising. Looking at scary data just a bit clarifies it a great deal. A 2000 "online victimization" study by the National Center for Missing and Exploited Children (www.ncmec.org) reveals that 96 percent of those who solicit teens are under 25, and nearly half—48 percent—are themselves children under the age of 18. Some 20 percent are female.

Having succeeded in persuading the public that their product is desperately needed, filtering companies sold it, while refusing to tell people exactly what they were buying. What were their algorithms? What words, sites, concepts were blocked? How did they add or delete a site? Every filtering company had the same response: that's proprietary information, and we're not telling.

There's nothing wrong with the manufacturer of Coca-Cola saying that, because no one is forced to buy their product, and Coke isn't needed in order to do your job, get proper health care, acquire an education, or be an effective citizen. But when your employer, library, hospital, city planner, or university is required to use a filtering company's product, or consumers of these institutions are subject to the limitations of filtering products (a doctor can't find out about the health issues involved in anal sex, a library can't provide information about the longevity of nonmonogamous couples, a city planner can't find out about zoning and prostitution, a judge isn't allowed to read Web sites being discussed in a case),[16] "we won't discuss our product" is outrageous and inappropriate.

Private companies enjoying the huge advantages of being used as quasi-public utilities should be required to disclose substantial product information. But presumably, any government that required this transparency wouldn't be requiring Internet filtering in the first place.

Was there really a problem? Morality groups cried yes, although no one could really point to much actual harm. In congressional testimony on November 10, 1998, they told satanic stories of an 11-year-old boy "hooked on pornography" who "left semen samples in his favorite teacher's cup," and a babysitter showing porn to a four-year-old who then wrote "sexually explicit notes to a little girl in his 1st grade class."[17] And unfortunately, their fear drove public policy decisions in Congress. How is it that being frightened is its own credential to discuss sexuality and behavioral science?

Filtering was a solution looking for a problem, according to the federal District Court that overruled the Loudon County (Virginia) library's use of filtering that very year (1998):

> No reasonable trier of fact could conclude that three isolated incidents nationally, one very minor isolated incident in Virginia, no evidence whatsoever of problems in Loudon County, and not a single employee complaint from anywhere in the country establish that the [filtering] policy is necessary to prevent sexual harassment or access to obscenity or child pornography.[18]

Nevertheless, by 1997 the group Family Friendly Libraries identified its top priority as "protecting children from age-inappropriate materials." Chaired by Phil Burress—who went on to promote laws prohibiting same-gender marriage, adult entertainment establishments, and any advertising that "exploited" sexuality—they demanded the installation of filtering systems in public libraries.[19] And did the corporate rationale of "proprietary information" justify the compromise of library patrons' rights? Not according to the federal court that overturned the Loudon County library's filtering policy: "A defendant cannot avoid its constitutional obligation by contracting out its decision-making to a private entity."[20]

The collusion between filtering companies, the Right, and the government reached its zenith in 2000 with the Child Internet Protection Act (CIPA), passed after federal courts overturned two congressional attempts to censor the Internet.[21] CIPA required libraries to install Internet filtering—even for adults—if they wanted to receive federal funds. Undereducated in the meaning of American democracy, ignoring the critical mandate of public schools to encourage curiosity, most city councils and county supervisors thought the funding was more important than whatever material would be excluded. Besides, no elected official wanted to be in the position of sacrificing desperately needed funds so that patrons could "look at porn all day long."

Some libraries didn't even wait for the federal demand to install filters. The Kern County, California, library had to be threatened with legal action in January 1998 if they didn't remove the filtering software. Less than a year later, a federal judge ruled that a library in Loudon County, Virginia, had to reverse its policy of installing filters on its computers.[22]

CIPA exposed any pretense of so-called conservatives of simply wanting to raise their families and live their lives free from government intrusion. Any parent concerned about library computers can take their kids to the library and supervise them, or forbid their kids from going to a library alone. Instead, these "conservatives" brought a system to every town in America in which the government—implementing their personal values—controlled what everyone could see and hear.

They had done it before with adult bookstores, strip clubs, and video shops. But this was the most naked attack on democracy yet—bringing censorship to public libraries. You might as well melt down the Statue of Liberty and use the metal to fashion jail bars, or chastity belts for the mind. To these people, Americans don't deserve their basic rights if they use them in the context of sexuality.

But exactly what criteria these filtering systems would use, what they would block, no one knew—no librarian, no senator, no parent. All anyone knew is that these filtering systems promised to protect children *and* adults from material unsuitable for minors. In reality, there was no category of nonobjectionable sexual references. No health, educational, legal, political, historical, or even religious reference to sexuality could get through the electronic censor. Filtering products attempt to create an Internet in which sexuality doesn't exist, as if there's no such thing as a legitimate or non-dangerous interest in sexuality. And that was an explicit goal of the War on Sex.

Even the court *upholding* CIPA recognized that "a filter set to block pornography may sometimes block other sites that present neither obscene nor pornographic material"—in other words, *legal* material.[23] The Court just didn't think that adults losing access to legal material (called "censorship" when done in countries we don't like) was as important as "protecting" young people from certain words or pictures.

In dissenting, Justice Stevens took the loss of access to legal material seriously—taking as irrelevant the fact that much of it was about sexuality: "The Children's Internet Protection Act (CIPA) operates as a blunt nationwide restraint on adult access to an enormous amount of valuable information that individual librarians cannot possibly review . . . *Most of that information is constitutionally protected speech.* In my view, this restraint is unconstitutional."[24]

So what do filters filter out? As filtering became more popular, thousands of examples of what filtering actually did quickly accumulated. Here's a sample of what some popular programs blocked access to:

- CyberPatrol blocked the book *Sex, Laws and Cyberspace.*
- CYBERsitter blocked the National Organization for Women's Web site.
- SurfControl blocked the "emotional changes" section of www.kotex. com.[25]
- Websense blocked the Web site of A Different Light Bookstore.
- N2H2 blocked the Web site of the Rape Crisis Center of Central Massachusetts.[26]
- Tens of thousands of Web sites with *no* sexual content whatsoever were blocked if their URLS happen to share a numerical Internet protocol address with a pornography site.
- During the 2000 election, numerous candidates' Web sites were blocked, including Jeffrey Pollack's. Running for Congress in Oregon, his site said, "We should demand that all public schools and libraries install and configure Internet Filters"—until he discovered he was filtered, and changed his position.[27]

These are programs being used in public libraries across the United States. They are ammunition in the War on Sex.[28]

According to their 2003 study, says Will Doherty, Executive Director of the Online Policy Group, "For every web page blocked as advertised, there was collateral damage of at least one other page improperly blocked."[29]

It is important to understand that this "collateral damage" is *not* an anomaly—it is the way filtering software works. The question is, is this acceptable? Exactly how much is America willing to pay to protect young eyes from something whose damage hasn't really been studied, and has certainly never been proven? What this tool unintentionally deletes isn't porn or danger or sex, it's information, and it's the freedom to acquire information. This is what the War on Sex is about.

This would be bad enough if that were the extent of it. But it isn't. For starters, you can't know something is filtered out if you don't look for it. You may not realize there's another side to a medical or political story.

And there are a lot of sites that get filtered out for purely political reasons: sites of gay sports clubs, for example, which don't discuss homosexuality; sites involving nuclear disarmament. When filtering company CyberPatrol was confronted with why right-wing hate sites weren't listed as such, they had no good answer. When Peacefire publicized this, CyberPatrol went after *them*. In fact, when Peacefire started posting essays on its Web site critical of filtering software, some software companies such as CYBERsitter reacted by blocking Peacefire's Web site—which clearly posed no threat to minors. And when *Time* magazine criticized CYBERsitter for blocking its critics' sites, CYBERsitter blocked *Time's* site. There has always been a political agenda with blocking software.[30]

If these private companies are living off the quasi-public teat, this is unacceptable. Inserting themselves into the War on Sex because of a profit motive rather than an ideological or psychological one is equally wrong.

Perhaps worst of all is when computer users buy filters unwillingly, or even unknowingly.

One common way this happens is when blocking software is placed on the computer you use by the person or institution that controls it. This can be your employer, city council, hospital, school, or whomever sets policy where you use it. Sites may not come up when you search a topic, or, more generally, they come up but you can't access them. Similarly, if you type in a URL that's blocked by a decision beyond your control, you get an error message, or are told the site is unavailable, when it actually is available—just not to you.

In late 2005, I discovered that both my Web sites (www.SexualIntelligence. org, www.SexEd.org) were blocked on the computers customers rent at Kinko's. I only found this out when I tried to access them there while my own computer was being repaired. Kinko's has 1,200 locations. How many tens of thousands of people across the United States (and world) had searched for words or ideas they could have found on one of my sites—if they hadn't been blocked?

When I inquired about this, I was directed to the company Kinko's had hired to do the blocking. They were very nice, and offered to review my sites. They eventually said my sites had been blocked by "an oversight"—the same thing all producers of non-porn sites are told when they discover their work has been blocked. The vaunted technical capacity and "human review" of filtering products simply cannot do what the companies promise. And since their financial incentive is to overblock rather than underblock, this fundamental inadequacy will not change.

You're probably also a consumer of blocking software through your ISP. AOL, Yahoo, and most others have "user guidelines" or "user agreements" (you did read the miles of fine print, right?) that basically say they'll filter out anything they don't like, and that they're not obligated to tell you what, why, or when. And so AOL has booted the *Triangle News* gay newspaper site. Yahoo closed a variety of sexuality and gender support groups, such as SF Queer Longhairs.[31]

Similarly, MSN Spaces, Microsoft's new blogging tool, censors certain words you might try to include in a blog title or URL. In Xeni Jardin's 2004 experiment, blog titles refused include "Corporate Whore," "Pornography & the Law," and most anything with the traditional "seven dirty words" the Federal Communications Commission won't let you say on network TV.[32] On the other hand, the software allowed "World of Poop" and "Butt Sex is Awesome." It didn't allow "Anal Health for People who Think Buttsex is Awesome," however. All of which shows that filtering software doesn't make kids safer, it just gives them more reasons to disrespect efforts to censor what they read. Which is, ultimately, the effect of all censorship. And as America learned during the drug wars of the 1960s, any government policy whose main effect is creating disrespect for the government is a bad policy.

THE GOVERNMENT'S ATTEMPTS TO CONTROL YOUR ACCESS TO THE NET

From the moment the Internet became a popular medium, local and federal government attempted to limit Americans' access to it—and they've kept at it to this very day. The three most popular charges have been "child pornography" (the definition of which keeps expanding), "obscenity" (a subjective category that can only be defined by a jury which determines the "community standards" allegedly violated), and "harmful to minors" (a completely arbitrary category that has never actually been defined).

Alternately pressured and purchased by conservative, religious, and feminist groups, the government has continuously assumed there is harm posed by the Internet, and has consistently attempted to limit this alleged harm by limiting both adults' and childrens' access to it. Not only has the alleged harm never been proven, the effectiveness of censoring the Internet in limiting this alleged harm has never been demonstrated. Instead, the "common sense" of one part of the community has substituted for the science they don't have and the calmness they don't have or want.

Here are some of the ways government, backed by selected civic groups, has used massive resources in attempting to limit the way Americans can use the Internet to enhance their sexual expression, education, or health:

- 1993: Government entraps Californians Robert and Carleen Thomas, operators of a bulletin board and porn distribution company. Postal Inspector David Dirmeyer orders adult material from a Memphis, Tennessee address, then has them arrested for distribution of obscene material on the Internet. The Court of Appeals, 6th circuit, upholds this in 1996.[33]

- 1995: Congress proposes (but doesn't pass) S.892, "Protection of Children from Computer Pornography Act."
- 1996: Congress passes Communications Decency Act (CDA), criminalizing sending anything "harmful to minors" over the Internet (overturned in 1997).
- 1996: Senators Hatch and Feinstein cosponsor a law criminalizing the use of "morphing" technology (as opposed to actual children) to create computer images that imitate child porn.
- 1998: Congress passes Child Online Protection Act. This establishes the Commission on Online Child Protection, and requires *all* commercial distributors of "material harmful to minors" to prevent minors from accessing their Web sites. "Material harmful to minors" is a much lower standard than "obscenity," and includes female breasts.
- 1999: Court of Appeals upholds injunction against enforcing COPA. The government appeals.
- 2000: Congress passes Child Internet Protection Act, after both CDA and COPA are overturned.[34] This requires libraries and schools receiving federal funds to install filtering software on their computers.
- 2000–2005: various state governments pass "mini-COPAs," criminalizing the use of the Internet to send anything "harmful to minors." These laws are generally overturned by the courts.[35]
- 2000–present: Various states establish that those repairing others' computers, whether employed in the same company or in business as repair shops, are mandated reporters of suspected child pornography— without any training in evaluating this material or protection for those inappropriately reported.
- 2002: Attorney General Ashcroft announces a new "war on porn."
- 2003: Supreme Court upholds CIPA, establishing the constitutionality of requiring mandatory filtering of legal material.
- 2003: Court of Appeals again rules COPA unconstitutional. Government appeals again.
- 2004: Supreme Court upholds block on enforcement of COPA. Government continues looking for ways to enforce it.
- 2005: Department of Justice (DOJ) changes the definition of the "2257"[36] regulations, creating extraordinary record-keeping requirements on all Web sites showing any sexual content, even non-porn content. The requirements are retroactive, punitive, clearly not aimed to accomplish their alleged intention (to prevent minors from performing in adult films, and to give government redundant power to punish child pornography). The law is passed despite clear evidence that minors are not performing in contemporary adult films.
- 2005: Free Speech Coalition sues the DOJ to enjoin the 2257 regulations until they can be challenged in whole in court.

- 2005: Utah is the latest of 15 states passing Internet censorship laws.[37]
- 2005: Attorney General Gonzales announces a war on obscenity, and creates a porn task force in the Federal Bureau of Investigations.
- 2005: The owners of Web sites (e.g., www.RedRose.com, www.ShadesBeyondGray.com) with sexually explicit words, rather than pictures, are arrested, their Web sites shut down as "obscene." Many well-known fetish Web site publishers self-censor or shut down completely to avoid prosecution (e.g., www.BeautyBound.com, www.KinkyGurl.com, www.RealBDSM.com).
- 2006: The DOJ subpoenas Google, Yahoo, and MSN to obtain one million random Web addresses and records of all searches for a week as part of trying to get COPA upheld on appeal. DOJ allegedly does this to prove that blocking and filtering technology doesn't effectively stop children from reaching pornographic Web sites.

SUMMARY

Rather than deal with their fear, rather than recognize the radical potential of the Internet to help fulfill the American promise, those who fear sex have gone the other way—demonizing the Internet, attempting to limit its growth and availability. And they have done this even as they use that same Internet as a tool to undermine the American promises of fact-based public policy, free access to information, and the cherished right to be left alone.

The world is watching. Other countries, such as China, Iran, and North Korea, routinely censor the Internet of political content. Through Voice of America, the United States is helping these countries' dissidents access the Internet—but only after censoring sexually oriented sections of it.

Is our government terrified of sex the way China is of the Falun Gong, or Iran is of moderate Islam? Why? What does this say about our government? Considering the number of Americans who have been jailed, had their businesses seized, or had their children taken from them, is our War on Sex any less gruesome or barbaric than China's war on the Falun Gong?

The sad thing is that Americans today must look to the courts to decide that such restrictions are unconstitutional, rather than expecting our elected representatives to say, "No, revoking Americans' freedoms for *any* reason is just not a wise idea—and it is simply not acceptable."

Because the Internet is pure information, it confronts us with a choice that has become far too common, and is even more stark than usual: which is more dangerous—information, or the consequences of restricting it?

Online predators do pose a threat to a very small number of minors. But revoking even a part of the freedoms of hundreds of millions of Americans, young and old, is a tangible, meaningful threat that should be preceded by a serious, complex social dialogue. That dialogue *must* include the voices of scientists, sexologists, and those who realize that protecting every single child from every potential harm is simply impossible. And it must respect the stubborn, experienced voices of those who know that without real freedom, safety is an illusion.

Chapter Eleven

America Does Not Guarantee Your Right to Be Comfortable: The Lowest Common Erotic Denominator Project

Across America, pictures are coming down and sculpture is being covered; workplaces are being sanitized, as bulletin boards and screen savers are cleared, and e-mail blocking is ever-stricter. College campuses are in the grip of speech codes, as professors are being disciplined for discussing the realities of historical or contemporary gender, intimacy, and, most of all, sexuality.

Now that American culture has decided that sex is the source of virtually all its problems, removing it from the public arena as much as possible is seen as the solution.

The War on Sex is committed to eliminating any public experience that causes *anyone* discomfort around sexuality. This is the Lowest Common Erotic Denominator project. It's stripping us of meaningful art, diminishing our creativity at work, interfering with normal adult relationships, and constraining academic and media discussions of philosophy, social science, the humanities, and politics. But many people apparently feel this is a small price to pay for making sure no one is offended or uncomfortable about sex.

When new regulations outlawed the creation of a "hostile work environment" in the 1980s, they were intended to prevent racial and gender harassment that was repeated, pervasive, and so severe as to obstruct individuals from performing their job.

But now even the most indirect reference to sexuality at work or school can be considered the creation of a hostile employment or learning environment. Given the breadth of sexual influences and expression in human life, this means that any individual can exercise a veto over a huge range of workplace or school issues: dress, language, decor, personal memorabilia, charitable policies, even after-hours recreation. "Hostile environment" law has been perverted to create a right not to be *offended* when one leaves one's home.

While everyone deserves a fair chance to succeed, appealing to the most erotophobic sentiment to create a sexless work or university environment is not about fairness—it's about bleaching eroticism out of society. *This* is patently unfair, and *this* is offensive to many. But sex-positive feelings have no legal standing, because people comfortable with sex are not a protected class like ethnic minorities or women. When can someone sue because short skirts are banned in a private office? Or because a gold cross around someone's neck is acceptable, but a silver vulva isn't?

Patrons of public facilities have also acquired the phony "right" to never be uncomfortable about sexuality, no matter how repressed they are about it. This is used to justify Internet filtering in libraries. People applying for driver licenses or phone service are complaining if municipal clerks show too much cleavage. Art that has civilized, comforted, challenged, and enlightened people for 500 years is being taken down from city halls across America.

So whose standard of discomfort shall we use—the person whose threshold of discomfort is lowest? No one says to an employer or city government, "By the way, I'm cool with the thought-provoking artwork around here." No one says, "By the way, I'm fine that the person at the next desk, or the clerk who processed my forms, wears an open marriage button on her lapel."

Those *not* offended by sexual words or images are a crucial part of the continuum of the public's values. But the standards and feelings of those *not* obsessed with sex are never taken seriously in this matter.

Historically, democratic countries have focused primarily on controlling behavior, while totalitarian governments have attempted to control speech and thought as well. American laws of the last 20 years are changing that, however. Public art, company e-mail, and casual speech are increasingly monitored and restricted, as the "feelings" of coworkers, classmates, customers, and neighbors are seen as sufficient reason for government intervention.

Removing a perfectly legal statue or classical play from public view because its sexual aspects make someone uncomfortable is increasingly common. The workplace, college campus, and public square are now places where some are entitled to the comfort of not having their sensibilities challenged, while the rest of us suffer arbitrary censorship. In such an inhibited, anxious environment, no one grows, and everyone ultimately loses.

We need laws protecting the rights of people offended by the neurotic stripping of human eroticism from workplaces and civic spaces across America.

Wrestling with eroticism has been one of humanity's most glorious, productive, albeit troubling, challenges throughout history. Every culture that interrupts this adult project pays for it in violence or stagnation; that's the lesson of the Spanish Inquisition, the Salem Witch Trials, the Soviet Union, and "modern" Iran.

It's no coincidence that Attorney General John Ashcroft covered the breast on "The Spirit of Justice" statue before launching a massive assault on Americans' liberty.

Chapter Twelve

Battleground: *The War on "Pornography"*

When Attorney General Alberto Gonzales announced the latest federal war on pornography last year, with increased funding and reassignment of eight full-time FBI agents, one law enforcement veteran snidely expressed what a lot of people were thinking: "I guess we've won the war on terror."[1]

We haven't, of course, so here's a clue to the real payoff: according to the *Washington Post*, "Christian conservatives, long skeptical of Gonzales, greeted the pornography initiative with what the Family Research Council called 'a growing sense of confidence in our new Attorney General.'"[2]

Acquiring the support of the Family Research Council in exchange for simply limiting every American's right to private entertainment must seem like a terrific deal to the Bush administration. (You didn't really think the war on porn was about making America's families safer, did you?)

But restricting the amount and type of sexually explicit material you're allowed to look at in private (and driving its producers and distributors out of business) is only one part of the battle against pornography. The other is a massive disinformation campaign—some of it sincere, much of it manipulative, and too much of it outright lies.

We're not talking about porn that involves kids, or violent material that glamorizes coercion. Although antiporn activists focus obsessively on these two exotic genres, they are, fortunately, a tiny minority of what's actually available and consumed; this preference represents a tiny minority of America's 50 million porn viewers.

That leaves the rest of porn, in which actors portray happy male and female characters doing things they enjoy. Sometimes their fun involves stuff you find pleasurable that someone else might not: oral sex, spanking, anal toys, whatever. Occasionally these characters pursue activities you or your mate might not want to do: exhibitionism, playing with urine, group sex, whatever. Either way, *the vast majority of porn portrays consenting, enthusiastic people doing things they enjoy.* These are activities routinely indulged in by tens of millions of Americans, *sexual activities that couples go to marriage counselors to get more comfortable with.*

So when a discussion about porn turns to "violent porn" or "kiddie porn" or "bestiality," these are not representative of mainstream adult material. Condemning all porn because of these exotic subgenres is like eliminating all TV because "The Three Stooges" is stupid or "The Sopranos" is violent. When you hear or participate in a conversation about pornography, see if the other person can talk without referring to porn "addiction," child porn, brutal porn, or mass murder. If they can't, they're not discussing pornography, or even sex; they're discussing violence, power, sadism, and fear.

A WAR ON PEOPLE

The war on porn is a war on people—people who look at porn. The government and conservative groups talk about "pornographers" and "hard-core smut," but rarely about porn consumers—which totals a staggering 50 million Americans.

When these consumers are mentioned, they're almost always described as porn addicts, psychopaths, and child molesters. But such people constitute only a tiny, tiny fraction of porn consumers—just like violent porn is a tiny, tiny fraction of all porn. That's a common strategy of the antiporn forces—talk only about the most extreme examples, and talk as if they're typical.

This distortion opens the door for an extraordinarily wide range of attacks on pornography. These attacks are in many ways a response to private and sociopolitical issues.

Americans are anxious about their sexual "normality" and competence, and about the impact of modern life on their relationships and their kids. The fact that so many of us are taught to feel guilty about our sexual desires, fantasies, and bodies, and that this shame leads to secrecy, of course, complicates things. There may be no easy answers, but people still want their anxiety and isolation to go away.

We want our kids to be sexually healthy, but we don't know how to talk with them—and the sexualized media scare us. We want our sexual relationships to be enjoyable and nourishing, but we don't know how to talk with our mates, and what we're told about everyone else's sex lives scares us.

In this context of emotional vulnerability, people welcome simple explanations that identify clear villains, and give clear solutions. The clergy, our government, the media, and "morality groups" insist that porn is the villain, and fighting porn is the answer. You've observed that many Americans love this. People in pain love knowing that there's a "them" to blame and an "it" to attack.

The war on porn is a psychologically perfect solution to the confusion, anger, self-criticism, and shame that many Americans feel about sexuality and modern life. It's short-sighted, futile, self-destructive, undignified, and disempowering. But it provides an explanation, a target, and hope. *It's a public policy solution to a private emotional problem.* And it empowers and emboldens leaders and institutions who manipulate the public into thinking that sexuality is the *problem,* when sexual self-acceptance, flexibility, skills, and knowledge are the *answer.*

Pornography is the repository of our culture's ambivalence and negativity about sex (e.g., Americans watch porn, but pretend they don't). Porn is, for the most part, portrayals of conventional (many would say normal) sex—intercourse, oral sex, masturbation, vibrators, anal sex. Nevertheless, our society damns these portrayals, the *record of,* the *acknowledgement of,* our fantasy, desire, participation. Porn is the opposite of the closet, of our culture's shame about sexuality. And so those who speak from ambivalence or negativity angrily confront those who use porn: "It's bad enough that you enjoy lusty sex. If you can't have the decency to feel guilty about your sexuality, you certainly don't have to celebrate it, much less deliberately inflame your desire!"

It's not simply that so many of us are uncomfortable about sexuality. *It's the relationship that individuals and the culture have with that discomfort.* The discomfort does not get discussed honestly, nor do most people feel in any way obligated to resolve these feelings. Instead, the discomfort is considered normal and fixed, and the objects of the discomfort—pornography, along with sexual words, music, art, and expression—are the things considered expendable.

This is one reason that pornography is demonized. It has to be conceptualized and described as being far enough away from what's "normal," so that there's no question about which has to change—the *objects* of the discomfort, not the discomfort *itself.*

The demonization of pornography is a way of ending the dialogue before it really starts. If pornography is horrible, there's no conversation; if there is one, the only position left is, "I'm selfish, ignorant, and perverted, and I defend pornography."

There should be room in America's ongoing discourse for discussing people's pain about pornography, and the negative things that some others do with it. But it is unacceptable to make that the *only* conversation about pornography. The government has taken that position strongly, which is cynical, dishonest, and destructive. It would be like making anorexia and bulimia the center of every discussion about nutrition and weight control.

To put it another way, if we have the wrong conversation about pornography, we end up eliminating a lot of sexual expression, at a social, psychological, and constitutional cost that's unacceptable. It's the equivalent of burning down a house to fumigate it.

THE WAR ON PORN

Here are some of the ways government and antiporn forces are warring on pornography *and those who view it.* Most of the following have been done; others have been recently tried, or are about to be attempted.

- Limiting what can be downloaded/uploaded from/to the Internet, and what can be e-mailed. The federal government has been attempting to legislate this since 1996; Arizona, New York, and Michigan have also tried. The federal case is still pending.
- Local groups picketing stores that sell porn DVDs; they often photograph patrons or their license plates to discourage them from entering. The latest campaign like this is being instigated by actor Stephen Baldwin in Nyack, New York.
- Limiting sales of popular magazines like *Cosmopolitan* and *Glamour* in 7–Eleven stores and supermarkets. The nation's 7–Elevens stopped selling *Playboy*, *Penthouse*, and other soft-core magazines in 1986 when the Meese Commission threatened to list the parent Southland Corporation (and two dozen other convenience store chains) as a "distributor of pornography" in its report. Although the threat was clearly illegal (and was declared so by a federal judge), the censorship was accomplished; to this day, such magazines are unavailable at 7–Eleven.[3]
- Internet filtering—now mandatory for public libraries that want federal funds; encouraged by nervous lawyers in universities, hospitals, businesses, and other institutions; demanded by "morality groups" afraid of sexual information; and marketed to parents across the United States concerned about Internet predators and the destructive power of the F word or a naked female breast.
- Expanding the definition of "obscenity" in order to criminalize more depictions and activities—despite everyone's agreement that American sexual mores are getting looser and more inclusive.
- Expecting computer repair shops, photo developing shops, and other businesses to report "suspicious" material to police. Not surprisingly, grandmothers have been arrested for bathtub photos of their grandchildren, and computers have been confiscated by untrained people.
- Demanding that pay-for-porn channels be removed from hotel room televisions. In 2000, the Omni hotel chain discontinued in-room porn, and in 2002, several Cincinnati hotels, including the Marriott, withdrew their adult movies. The domestic erotic terror group Citizens for Community Values then organized a coalition to urge the Justice Department to eliminate all hotel porn in the United States.
- Pressuring Visa and MasterCard to stop accepting payments from porn transactions.
- "2257 Regulations," which require that anyone who exhibits sexually explicit pictures, even of performers who are elderly or deceased, be able to prove that each performer is over 18. This would apply to even the smallest amateur Web sites and publications as well as to large commercial outfits.
- Using zoning laws to eliminate places where stores that sell porn or offer video booths can legally operate.

- Congressional hearings that start with the assumption that pornography is bad for individuals and society. Testimony from antiporn ideologues and "morality" groups is solicited to validate this view; sexologists, social scientists, and consumers are specifically excluded.
- Churches around the country are offering "porn recovery" programs to congregations. Hundreds of $400 kits to help them do this have been sold.
- For people trying to quit watching porn, XXXchurch.com offers "accountability software," which will send a biweekly listing of Web sites one has accessed to a chosen accountability partner. The software has been downloaded over 150,000 times.[4]
- The invention of "porn addiction," which was a logical extension of the ridiculous invention of "sex addiction," by prison addictionologist Patrick Carnes. Various psychologists, clergy, and "morality leaders" claim that men become addicted to porn and have to be cured by discontinuing use altogether.
- Establishing "Victims of Pornography Month" (each May). President Bush himself endorsed it, saying that "pornography is now instantly available to any child who has a computer. And in the hands of incredibly wicked people, the Internet is a tool that lures children into real danger." And the relevance of this to adult porn creation and use is . . . what?[5]
- The myth of activist judges: The idea that porn could be limited or banned "if only" certain judges would stop "creating" law to tolerate porn. This completely misses the point that America has two centuries of laws protecting free expression (even if it offends someone), which judges are supposed to enforce when legislators or police break them. The Traditional Values Coalition even has a "battle plan to take back the courts from the ACLU and the anti-God Left."[6]
- Legislators pass laws they know are not allowed under the American system, trusting courts to challenge them. But then they get to tell constituents and financial backers, "Look, I tried."
- The lack of training for marriage counselors, psychologists, physicians, social workers, and others who counsel those who view adult material. Without training, these clinicians can only fall back on the antiporn myths saturating the media and their professions' sex-negative traditions. Unfortunately, many professionals believe that being trained to treat "porn addiction" is the same as learning about porn use in the general population.
- When the government decides to bust a store that sells adult material, it typically seizes a large percentage or even all of the store's inventory so the defendant can't pay the legal costs of fighting the arrest. Remember, authorities cannot simply declare this inventory obscene—that is, potentially illegal. Only a jury can do that.[7]

- Increasing the number of laws restricting where you can view sexually explicit material—for example, private cars. Six different states have criminalized viewing sexually explicit material in a car. In Virginia, it's even against the law to play material that is "harmful to minors" (a *deliberately* vague expression) if it can be seen outside the vehicle.
- Establishing a porn tax: singling out sexually oriented products for special, very high (10%–25%) taxes. Enabling legislation is currently being reviewed by courts in at least three states (Utah, Washington, Kansas). The idea is to discourage consumption of what can't be legally banned.

A federal porn tax bill was introduced by Senator Blanche Lincoln (D-AR) in 2005. Cosponsored by nine Democrats, it's making little progress in the Republican-controlled Senate. A Republican-sponsored version, however, is now coalescing.

A tax on private recreation is galling enough (how about a comparable tax on guns?). But the proceeds of proposed porn taxes go to sex offender or victim programs, implying that there's a connection between porn and sexual coercion. Every porn consumer (and every victim of a sex offender who can't get treatment because tax money is wasted fighting porn) should be insulted.

WHAT ABOUT KIDDIE PORN?

The American porn industry neither makes nor distributes erotic material featuring underage performers. The underage material available today is either (1) amateur stuff made by individuals and distributed surreptitiously, or (2) made by foreign producers in Russia, Eastern Europe, and Asia, with no affiliation to American businesses. Thus, further regulating the American adult industry will have no effect whatsoever on the amount of underage porn available in the United States It may make legislators look good and constituents feel good, but it will not decrease the availability of, nor the appetite for, the material that everyone agrees is illegal and unconscionable.

In fact, in 1996, the American adult industry established the Association of Sites Advocating Child Protection (ASACP), a nonprofit organization dedicated to eliminating child pornography from the Internet. ASACP's efforts include a reporting hotline for websurfers and webmasters, rewards for accurate reporting/conviction of those responsible for child porn, strict standards for American adult Web sites, and proactive educational campaigns about age verification and other topics. Over the last two years, ASACP has received over 150,000 reports of suspected child pornography sites. Virtually all (99.9%) of these reports can be attributed to non-adult webmasters or pedophiles, not professional adult companies.[8]

Given today's political and economic realities, no one could be more interested in the elimination of child porn than the U.S. adult industry. It is fascinating to observe how the most ridiculous rumors to the contrary are so persistent, for example, that porn is marketed to children. Since children have no credit cards with which to purchase porn, why on earth would marketing target them?

THE PUBLIC HEALTH MODEL— A CLEVER MANIPULATION

Those who wish to limit or ban pornography have cleverly positioned it (and thus, fighting it) as a public health issue. We hear, for example, about its supposed comorbidities (fear of intimacy, low self-esteem, perversion); supposed effects on consumers (addiction, depression, isolation, disrespect for women); supposed impact on communities (increased violence, divorce, tumbling morals)—and the ultimate health issue, that it's supposedly bad for kids.[9]

It's a familiar model, generally accompanied by a familiar imperative: do what's necessary to clean up the threat and protect our kids and communities, even if it costs a bundle and involves curtailing a few rights. As anthropologist Carole Vance says, "Every right-winger agrees that porn leads to women's inequality—an inequality that doesn't bother him in any other way."[10]

In this context, discussing pornography as a free speech or civil rights issue can sound rather unconvincing and even naïve to many people. In some ways, this reflects a deeper problem with our society; while health and safety problems easily acquire special public policy cachet, many Americans seem to feel that free expression and civil rights are less important than almost anything else under discussion.[11]

For starters, the manipulative, extreme claims of the public health model should be challenged. Instead of apologizing or rolling our eyes, we must loudly say that for the most part, adult material *does not cause* these awful consequences. In the same way that coffee often *accompanies* divorce, it's true that many personal and community difficulties *coexist* with adult material. That's because the use of adult material is so widespread, not because it typically causes problems.

And just like there's healthy food and unhealthy food, safe beaches and beaches dangerous for inexperienced swimmers, there's healthy porn and porn that might not be good for someone. Of course, a lot depends on the consumer; just like green peppers are hard for a few people to digest and easy for most everyone else, most porn consumers have no trouble "digesting" what they view. The fact that a very small percentage of viewers have personality disorders is no more reason to banish porn from everyone than the fact that some people can't digest dairy products is good enough reason to remove half-and-half and Häagen-Dazs from supermarkets.

We need to remind everyone that just like there's such a thing as moderate drinking, there's such a thing as moderate porn use. And while some people can't handle even one or two drinks, most adults can—and we let them. We must challenge the idea that all use of porn is abuse of porn (and therefore dangerous). It isn't.

Having said that firmly, even the staunchest anticensorship activist should be sympathetic about people's fear of porn. The American public of non-porn viewers has been traumatized by repetitive, lurid stories of children molested at psychotic orgies; women raped, enslaved, and trafficked; normal men who become drooling, unproductive idiots; loving families destroyed—all because somebody watched an X-rated video. Let's agree that such stories, although untrue, are scary, and that the fear they engender naturally demands action. Let's appreciate the psychological and citizenship skills it would take to resist that demand—from oneself, one's neighbors, or one's civic or religious leaders.

Realistically, only after that can we expect that a conversation about rights will be taken seriously. We must say over and over that we're talking about *our* rights, not just "pornographers' rights"; that the right to look at porn is directly related to the right to criticize the government, choose your own religion, and raise your kids free of interference, and how the wrong approach to porn will inevitably undermine everyone's *non-porn* rights. We've already seen this with attempts to censor network TV airings of *Schindler's List* and *Saving Private Ryan,* and with attempts to remove Harry Potter books from public school libraries because of their so-called satanic influence.

In India, people starve while cows roam the streets. It isn't because they think steak is unhealthy, it's because their religion forbids them to kill or consume animals they consider sacred. We may make fun of this. But at least they don't pretend it's a public health issue.

Continuing with the public health model, we do have limits on consumer product availability: expiration dates on milk, inspection of meat, warning labels on fish. Certain foreign products don't meet our standards, and so are denied entry. All of this depends on science—not consumer discomfort, not vague "holistic" or political ideas. When everyone was miffed at the French a few years ago (remember Freedom Fries?), no one proposed that French cuisine be banned, only boycotted. And that only lasted a few weeks, and it was mostly tongue-in-cheek.

Framing the war on porn as a health issue makes it easy to drive people to near-hysteria about this alleged dangerous epidemic. The government (supported by conservative feminists and the Religious Right) can then deflect attention from *how* it limits porn's "bad effects" (i.e., how it limits porn), because "nothing's too good for our kids," and "we need to do whatever it takes to secure the health of America."

While this alleged epidemic rages, and frightened, angry people work overtime to keep it away from our precious children, we should remind ourselves that there is *still* no evidence that seeing pictures of naked smiling people, or depictions of adult sex, or words like dick have a harmful effect on children. The government and Religious Right are determined that there never *will* be any data about this—because, they say, the effect of sexual imagery on kids is too dangerous to *study*. That's what Socrates, Galileo, Freud, and virtually every professor in Pol Pot's Cambodia were told—that what they wished to study was too dangerous.

Teaching kids to fear sex, to be ashamed of their bodies, to be secretive about masturbation, to believe men and women are from different planets, to focus on avoiding disease instead of creating pleasure and understanding

---

REALLY—IS PORN HARMFUL?

The links between pornography and any changes in perceptions, attitudes, and behaviors are "circumscribed, few in number and generally laboratory-based."[a]

Surgeon General C. Everett Koop report, part of
Ronald Reagan-appointed Meese Commission report, 1985.

No evidence of a relationship between popular sex magazines and violence against women.[b]

Dr. Cynthia Gentry, Wake Forest University.
"Pornography and Rape: An Empirical Analysis."

There is no systematic research evidence available which suggests a causal relationship between pornography and morality. There is no systematic research which suggests that increases in specific forms of deviant behavior, reflected in crime trend statistics (e.g., rape) are causally related to pornography. There is no persuasive evidence that the viewing of pornography causes harm to the average adult, or that exposure caused the average adult to harm others. . .or that exposure causes the average adult to alter established sex practices.[c]

H. B. McKay and D. J. Dolff, "The Impact of Pornography:
An Analysis of Research and Summary of Findings."

In European countries where restrictions on porn have been lifted, incidence of rape over the last 20 years has stayed constant or declined. Between 1965–1982, after Denmark made pornography more accessible to the public, sex crimes against female children dropped by 80%.[d]

Berl Kutchinsky, "Pornography and Rape: Theory and Practice? Evidence from Crime
Data in Four Countries Where Pornography Is Easily Available."

(continued)

(continued)

The aggregate data on rape and other violent or sexual offenses from four countries where pornography, including aggressive varieties, has become widely and easily available during the period we have dealt with would seem to exclude, beyond any reasonable doubt, that this availability has had any detrimental effects in the form of increased sexual violence.[c]

Berl Kutchinsky, "Pornography, Sex Crime, and Public Policy".

Participants exposed to explicit sexual content without accompanying violence did not become desensitized.

Linz, Donnerstein, and Adams, in Measuring the Effects of Sexual Content in the Media: A Report to the Kaiser Family Foundation.

In West Germany, rape rates declined once bans on pornography were lifted in 1973.

Philip D. Harvey, The Government vs. Erotica: The Siege of Adam & Eve.

After a three-year inquiry into the effects of pornography, the Committee found that non-violent sexually explicit material does not cause violence or aggression.

Australian Joint Select Committee on Video Material, 1988.

It is certainly clear from the data reviewed that a massive increase in available pornography in Japan has been correlated with a dramatic decrease in sexual crimes, and most so among youngsters as perpetrators or victims—despite the wide increase in availability of pornography to children.

Between 1975 and 1995, reported rapes declined by more than half.

Milton Diamond, "The Effects of Pornography: An International Perspective."[f]

---

[a]U.S. Department of Justice, Attorney General's Commission on Pornography, by Edwin Meese (Washington, DC: Government Printing Office, 1986).

[b]Deviant Behavior: An Interdisciplinary Journal 12 (1991): 277–288.

[c]In Working Papers on Pornography and Prostitution Report No. 3 (Canada: Department of Justice, Canada, in Joint Select Committee Report, 1988).

[d]International Journal of Law and Psychiatry 14, no. 1 and 2 (1991): 47–64.

(paper presented to the Australian Institute of Criminology Conference, "The Sex Industry and Public Policy," Sydney, May 6–8, 1991).

[e]Aletha C. Huston Ph.D., Ellen Wartella Ph.D., Edward Donnerstein Ph.D. April 30, 1998. (Amherst, NY: Prometheus Books, 2001), 273.

[f]In Porn 101: Eroticism, Pornography, and the First Amendment, eds. James Elias et al. (Amherst, NY: Prometheus Books, 1999)

intimacy—every one of these is more dangerous than catching a glimpse of pubic hair. And all of these together—what some people consider normal childrearing—that's a recipe for heartbreak, dysfunction, and erotic guilt.

You can prevent mad cow disease by banning beef altogether; bird flu by banning all poultry; and reduce anaphylactic shock episodes by banning penicillin and Peanut M & Ms. But the American public wouldn't stand for it if it were framed that way (i.e., "it's bad for some people, so let's ban it all").

A NEW GOVERNMENT STRATEGY—FEELING GOOD WHILE ACCOMPLISHING NOTHING

In 2005, the government introduced a new strategy for controlling the production and distribution of sexually explicit material. The 2257 Regulations, as they are known, require extraordinarily onerous record-keeping, with enormous penalties for failure to comply. They resemble, for all the world, a Soviet-style bureaucratic obstacle to free expression.

Ostensibly to eliminate underage performers from the business, the government demands that anyone producing Web sites, magazines, DVDs, or other sexual material collect and archive photo identification (indexing and cross-referencing every name each performer has ever used) for every nude photo disseminated. "Even if a couple is in their 60s, you have to prove they're over 18," says Robert McGinley, President of Lifestyles Organization. "Since they can't just criminalize all sexy pictures, the government has created a new category of crime involving record-keeping." Will the rules apply to a swinger's Web site where members post racy pictures of themselves? "It still isn't clear," says McGinley. "But web companies will be moving offshore," he predicts, subject to much less regulation, easily defeating the alleged goal of the new law.[12]

The regulations extend backward to 1995. Can you get records from every single person you've met for the last 12 years? What a sneaky, undignified way around the rights of free expression.

The 2257 Regulations are the subject of multiple lawsuits. "The statute imposes heavy burdens on a broad category of protected speech, namely sexually explicit images, based solely on the basis of the content of that speech," wrote the attorneys (including Louis Sirkin and Paul Cambria) who represent the plaintiffs in *Free Speech Coalition v. Gonzales.*[13] The regulations "reach a vast amount of protected speech that not even arguably involve children, and which are outside the Government's interest in controlling child pornography."

The 2257 Regulations pretend to solve a problem that doesn't exist—underage performers in commercial porn—in a way that just happens to create enormous operating burdens for the adult industry. The government shrugs and falls back on a favorite justification: eliminating child porn. Since virtually everyone supports this goal, those who challenge the law look like creeps. Even if that's all 2257 accomplishes, the government wins. But of course, the logistical nightmare of the regulations will force many smaller producers and distributors out of business (achieving the government's primary, though unstated goal), and it gives the government the unlimited right to examine and challenge the detailed operations of the rest. During the eight years that the government obsessively stalked retailer Adam & Eve (*PHE, Inc. v. United States Department of Justice*, 1990, *United States v. PHE*, 1992),[14] it admitted that it saw harassment as a legitimate law enforcement tool when porn is involved. 2257 is the latest flavor of harassment.

"The government has the same data as ASACP. They must know that 99.9% of child porn has nothing to do with the professional adult industry," says Joan Irvine, ASACP executive director. "The new 2257 rules will not stop the production or distribution of child pornography. Adult companies already comply with the current laws; the criminals involved in child porn don't and never will. I wish the government would focus their time and financial resources on apprehending the real criminals, and truly saving children."[15]

2257 and other attempts to curtail porn use are pointless, says University of California, Los Angeles, Law School professor Eugene Volokh. No matter how much the U.S. government can curtail domestic porn distribution, foreign sites will take up the slack. "It's not like Americans have some great irreproducible national skills in smut-making. And even if overall world production of porn somehow improbably falls by 75 percent, will that seriously affect the typical porn consumer's diet? Does it matter whether you have, say, 100,000 porn titles to choose from, or just 25,000? The investment of major prosecutorial resources yields a net practical benefit of roughly zero." 2257 won't change that, but it will create plenty of dangerous constitutional precedents.

Of course the government, continues Volokh, can go after porn consumers. Set up phony sites to entrap American users, then arrest, prosecute, and lock them up. Seize their houses on the theory that it's a forfeitable asset. Make each one register as a sex offender. That would reduce porn consumption. Is America ready to acknowledge what it would take to dramatically change the viewing habits of one-fifth of the adult population?[16]

WARRING ON PORN AND TERROR

There's an increasing—and creepy—association between America's war on porn and its war on terrorism.

During 2005, Chris Wilson operated a Web site from his Florida home, www.nowthatsfuckedup.com. It offered pleasant amateur porn (and many discussion groups) for a small fee. One interesting feature was that American soldiers received free entry if they sent photos of themselves from Iraq. They did. These weren't always pretty, and the government didn't like this.

So Wilson was busted for obscenity, for hosting a Web site of "free" Americans back home showing off their bodies and having consensual sex in front of the camera. He faced felony charges and 300 misdemeanor counts. He sat in jail two different times, went through two Pentagon investigations (his personal and business computers shipped to Washington for a forensic examination), and had his home searched.

Facing possible new racketeering (!) forfeiture threats and serious prison time, he plea-bargained. His probation requires he close the site, and shun nudity or sex on any future Web site. Wilson and his attorneys agree that the obscenity bust was used to disrupt the soldiers' posting of photos, and to punish Wilson for inviting it.

In early 2006, the Department of Justice asked the four largest Internet search engines in America—Google, AOL, Yahoo, and MSN—for "a random sample of one million URLs" and the text of every search made over a one-week period.[17] The government wanted the information to help it impose tougher laws on Web sites with information believed to be harmful to minors. In the old days, this was known as prior restraint, which of course is illegal. At least in theory.

When Google refused to comply, the Department of Justice sought a court order to force them. What gives the government the right to ask for this information? Why, the Patriot Act and other Homeland Security laws.[18]

On February 9, 2006, uniformed officers of Montgomery County's Department of Homeland Security marched into a public library in Bethesda, Maryland, and announced that it was forbidden to use library computers to view pornography. They then challenged a patron about the Web site he was visiting and asked him to step outside. A courageous librarian intervened, the police came, and the Homeland defenders had to withdraw, clearly operating outside their authority.[19]

The unannounced, unrecorded "sneak-and-peak" searches of our homes and personal data (phone, travel, computer, etc.) that will continue under the Patriot Act require no prior justification. Our government has a history of feeling politically threatened by a broad range of sexual interests; the sexuality of Martin Luther King, Jr., John Lennon, Emma Goldman, Lenny Bruce, and Paul Robeson, among others, has been investigated.

POLYSEMICITY AND DECIPHERING PORN[20]

Polysemicity is the concept that no text or visual image has only a single meaning. Meaning is supplied by the reader or viewer, and so texts and pictures can have as many meanings as beholders. Said another way, the same thing can mean very different things to different people. In fact, the same experience isn't really the same experience to two different people. And offense is generated in the beholder and directed to the material, not the other way around.[21]

To John, ice cream is a treat to be enjoyed; if he eats it, he's OK. To overweight, self-critical Sam, it's a seductive adversary to be avoided; if he eats it, he's a pig. To Sue, wearing a mini skirt is a desperate bid for attention; to

Maria, it's a statement of pride in her looks; to Linda, it's a declaration of independence from her husband; to Joann, it's a way to thumb her nose at the church; to Sarah, it's a way to let men know she's sexually available.

The vast majority of porn's critics say they don't watch or read porn. So how can they know what it portrays, much less how viewers interpret what they see or read? True, porn's critics include a number of self-described ex-porn addicts. Are the reports of these self-described sick, compulsive, spiritually dead, self-destructive people the source of all the antiporn movement's information?

People who don't view porn (who typically know very little about it) assume that the experience of viewers is the same as the experience a nonviewer would have. It's easy to imagine a nonviewer—say, someone who's never seen two women kissing, or done anal sex, or been ejaculated on, or had sex with the lights on—imagining that looking at porn is uncomfortable, gross, or perverse. It's easy for that person to imagine that anyone acting in such a film is feeling humiliated or being coerced or hurt. And it's easy for that person to imagine that anyone who enjoys looking at porn is emotionally troubled, angry at his wife, or sexually perverse—willing to be violent, coercive, exploitive, or worse.[22]

One reason the concept of "porn addiction" is so appealing is that it explains behavior—"I'm out of control"—that is otherwise hard for nonviewers to understand, or for viewers themselves to fully accept.

Antiporn forces continually pontificate about porn viewers and the porn viewing experience. They tell us porn viewers are addicted, immature, antiwoman, intimacy-fearing, selfish, gullible, and of course, dangerous to children.

Perhaps these are the qualities nonviewers would have if they viewed porn. But characterizing America's 50 million porn consumers this way is just nuts. What's even crazier is the way this has become accepted as truth.

THE TRUTHS THAT PORN TELLS

Pornography is not a love story, but it does tell *some* truths. Not literal truths—few of us look like porn actors—but more philosophical, eternal truths. Politically relevant truths. That's why porn is ultimately subversive, a key reason that it's under siege.

Although American media and culture obsess about sex, most of us live with simplistic, superstitious, anhedonic, fear- and danger-based concepts of eroticism. Many obvious sexual facts are denied, tabooed, and distorted. Examples include: virtually all children masturbate, virtually everyone has sexual interests, most people fantasize sexually, primarily about "inappropriate" partners or activities, and most people are curious about others' bodies and sex lives.

Pornography tells a variety of truths about sex and gender to viewers who decipher what they're seeing (that is, the vast majority of consumers). These truths are far more important than the surgically enhanced breasts, abnormally big penises, and casual group sex that are staples of the genre (which, when taken literally, are misleading). These truths include:

- Anyone can feel (and thus be) sexy.
- Nothing is inherently nonsexual or non-erotic.
- The only rules in sex are arbitrary.
- Many, many people love sex.
- The erotically "nasty" can be life-affirming.
- Even "nice" people enjoy "nasty" fantasies and games.
- Neither intercourse nor orgasm are the center of sexuality.
- Focusing on sexuality for its own sake is legitimate.
- Women and men who feel secure in their dignity and admit that they love sex can enthusiastically submit erotically, because they don't fear judgment (others' or their own).

These truths, of course, defy America's dominant paradigm about sexuality. In the traditional view external rules are important; body parts are clearly either sexual or nonsexual; "nice" and "nasty" eroticism are clearly distinguishable from each other; different, non-overlapping groups of people indulge in each; and eroticism is dangerous if people don't control their arousal.

Consumers of pornography regularly visit an erotic world quite different than this.

The truth that porn tells is that all people have the option of conceptualizing their sexuality any way they like. Social norms regarding age and beauty, religious norms about godly and ungodly sex, personal fears about acceptance, cultural myths about the human body, all of these are ignorable; none are inevitable. Each of us can triumph over the ways social institutions attempt to control our sexual experience.

Ironically, this paradigm of pornography's truths is what sex therapists try to get couples to understand and install in their own lives. These professionals know that the keys to satisfying sexual relationships are self-acceptance and self-empowerment, not losing a few pounds, buying flowers, going away on vacation, or wild positions.

Porn's subtexts of abundance and validation are as responsible for contemporary cultural resistance—that is, the war on porn—as its explicit presentations of sexual activity.

AMATEUR PORNOGRAPHY AS TRUTH

A new way in which pornography tells the truth even more radically is amateur porn, which has exploded via the democratic frenzy of the Internet. Several million people across the globe are now photographing themselves during various sexual activities, uploading these photos onto personal and commercial Web sites, and inviting the entire computerized world to enjoy them.[23]

In contrast to most commercial pornography, common features of amateur porn include:

- a wide range of bodies, including ordinary and even conventionally unattractive ones;
- a wide range of ages, including adults conventionally considered way past the prime of their attractiveness or sexuality;
- a mostly unproduced physical environment (poor lighting, composition, etc);
- a heightened sense of mundane reality (shots with unkempt kitchens or kids' toys in the background, scenes filmed in Motel 6, etc.);
- a sense of humor and even parody.

Conventional criticism of pornography would not predict amateur porn's meteoric popularity. These criticisms assert that the supernatural beauty of actresses is central, that the desultory domination of actress by actor is crucial, that spectacular genital friction is what viewers most envy and desire.

Amateur pornography turns these assumptions upside down. There are no actresses, only real women. These women aren't pretending to be excited, they *are* excited. They aren't flaunting impossibly perfect bodies, they are enjoying their bodies as they are—some of them gorgeous, most of them imperfect and attractive, some appealing only insofar as they are enthusiastic. Virtually all the women in amateur porn share that quality—enthusiasm. They are actually enjoying themselves: the activities, the violation of taboos, the exhibitionism. Clearly, there's no coercion here.

In contrast to the typically grim, ideological antiporn critique, our analysis of porn's attraction and value *would* predict and *can* explain why amateur porn is such a rapidly growing genre. If the keys to porn's popularity are validation of the viewer's vision of erotic abundance, female lust, and the reasonableness of erotic focus, a viewer can experience those even more intensely when this validation comes not from actors but from real people. Rather than actors *implying* that the viewer isn't alone, amateur photos and video show real people *proving* the viewer isn't alone.

So what does the viewer of amateur porn see? Everyday folks being lusty, exhibiting themselves, and participating in an erotic community. It's a community where sexuality is understood as wholesome even when it's expressed in taboo ways.

PORNOGRAPHY'S TRUTHS AS SUBVERSIVE

And why does our culture resist these truths? Because the revolutionary implications of empowering people sexually challenge the cultural status quo. Pornography does this without even portraying sex exactly as most people experience it.

Pornography is an admission that human beings feel, imagine, and do what they do. In a culture committed to both hiding and pathologizing (and therefore shaming) sex as it really is, this admission isn't polite. It's subversive.

Ultimately, pornography's truths are subversive because they claim that we can empower ourselves and create our own erotic norms. Political structures just hate when ideas or cultural products empower people. This is the recurring lesson of Copernicus, Guttenberg, Margaret Sanger, Lenny Bruce, Timothy Leary, and Martin Luther King, Jr.

In the conventional fear/danger model, the genders are adversaries. Pornography shows a reconciliation of the war of the sexes, as it contains no adversaries. In most of it, everyone shares the same interests: passion, unselfconsciousness, self-acceptance, pleasure, and mutuality. Porn undermines the conventional scarcity-themed sexual economy and gender hierarchy; this is one of its most radical features, and is a big reason it attracts political opposition.

The massive popularity of pornography, and its consistent themes of female lust and male-female mutuality, testify to our pain about the conventional sexual economy. Taking porn on its own terms would require society to acknowledge this pain; such a cultural challenge makes pornography subversive.

Porn is subversive because it says that sex is not dangerous.

AMERICA'S CONVERSATION ABOUT PORN: ONE HAND CLAPPING

The format of America's cultural conversation about pornography reveals a great deal.

- It focuses almost exclusively on negativity.
- It depends on misinformation and mythology.
- Critics claim they don't use the product, but claim expertise on the product's content (and its effects on users and the community).
- Almost no one will stand up for mainstream pornography.
- People who do stand up for it are perceived as immoral, antifamily, antichild, and antiwoman.

What does this mean? Doesn't anyone notice that there is an activity done by 50 million people that practically no one will stand up and defend? And that anyone who does defend it is personally attacked? Gun ownership is controversial, but its practitioners defend it passionately—they actually proselytize, hoping to convert nonowners. Drinking alcohol is demonstrably harmful for a percentage of drinkers and for innocent bystanders, yet alcohol distributors extol their product enthusiastically, no one ever suggests banning it for adults, and all but the most destructive drinkers are considered normal or even cool.

So what does the current one-sided "dialogue" *mean?* What does it mean when one part of society discusses the behavior (and consciousness) of the other, and the voice of that other is missing?

It means that we hear only about porn's "victims." It means antiporn activists can maintain the illusion that porn is a pathetic activity for marginalized people. This isn't healthy for our Republic's integrity.

Every antiporn fundraising appeal, every government hearing, every op-ed piece shouts that porn is everywhere, that it's taken over, that it's a multi-billion dollar industry. Then they say porn is "attempting" to be mainstream—as if it isn't. They say porn is on the margins of our culture trying to get in and infect "normal" society. They say we have to stop it.

But to say that it's everywhere and that it's marginalized is a willfully distorted interpretation of the reality they themselves describe. With 50 million viewers, half of all Internet searches, $12 billion spent annually (more than all the tickets to professional baseball, basketball, and football combined), porn is the mainstream entertainment choice of America. The fact that most people won't talk about their choice, and that nonviewers damn this choice, doesn't change the fact. Viewing porn is a central American activity.

Why don't porn consumers speak up when they hear themselves mocked, pitied, attacked, feared, dehumanized? When the fury of enraged neighbors is whipped up by the bully pulpits of the ignorant and authoritarian, and supported by the legal machinery of city and state—all arrayed against their choice of entertainment, which they experience as harmless?

It's because people who consume porn have learned to hide it. You mention it to your neighbor, and maybe your kids can't play there anymore. Your neighbor mentions it to his poker buddy, and maybe you lose a customer, or a promotion. If you suggest it to your wife and she watches Oprah, or Maury, Montell, Tyra, Nancy, or Katie, you may regret it for the rest of your life.

Religious training has instilled a tremendous shame in many porn consumers. That doesn't stop them from using it (guilt can actually drive usage),[24] only from feeling comfortable about it—and feeling they have a legitimate right to it.

The unending (and escalating) propaganda about porn leading to violence and child endangerment means that defending the right to use porn (say, in a letter to the editor about a local vigilante group) invites the wrath of a righteous mob that no sane person wants. And with the successful demonization of "pornographers," no one wants to be associated with those subhumans.

Americans have had so many rights of expression, economic choice, and privacy for so long, that most have trouble envisioning their world without them. For people who enjoy a little porn once a week, it's hard to imagine our country's constitutional structure turning on such a seemingly trivial thing. The righteous anger of the Right, enthroned in federal and state government, clearly sees what the average porn consumer still doesn't—the profound connection between the personal and the political.

DEFENDING DEMOCRACY

Finally, we have to say that there's more at stake in the war on porn than the right to look at a friendly lady's nipples. It just so happens that sexuality/pornography is the vehicle of the moment in the eternal tug-of-war about the nature and meaning of the American system. At various times, that vehicle has been race (separate-but-equal; Japanese internment camps); age (child labor law, mandatory education); and private property rights (eminent domain, antidiscrimination law). Similarly, religion is another contemporary vehicle in this tug-of-war (stem cell research, right-to-die, school vouchers, school prayer, Christmas displays).

Pornography might not be the battlefield on which you or I would choose to defend secular pluralism, free expression, and science-based (as opposed to emotion-based) public policy. But as this is the battlefield that has been chosen for us, we must respond with energy and vision, neither apologizing nor acquiescing to manipulative descriptions of what porn is, who porn consumers are, or what the fight over porn is about.

The increasingly aggressive and confident attacks on porn are based on the following assumptions:

- The right to look at porn is trivial.
- The social benefits from limiting/banning porn are huge.
- The social and personal costs of limiting/banning porn are virtually zero.
- Limiting/banning porn doesn't harm the American system.

Resisting the War on Sex requires articulating these assumptions, discussing their importance to all Americans, and then challenging every single one. Those who want to eliminate porn justify their extreme proposals by saying that the stakes are too high for halfway measures or fey concerns about free expression. They're absolutely right—the stakes are very, very high.

Chapter Thirteen

Extreme Religion and Public Policy

I am pro-life. So are you.

So is Osama Bin Laden. So was Hitler.

So were Lincoln and the guy who killed him.

And John Lennon and the guy who killed him.

Every mass murderer is pro-life.

The question is—which life, or lives, does a person mean by "pro-life"?

Who gets to decide? Why? The American system is not allowed to assume that one person's ideas about "life" are more legitimate than anyone else's, even if that person is "religious." The idea that government policy should reflect any religious belief is rejected by our Constitution.

Our system creates a civic paradox that some find uncomfortable:

- The government is forbidden to dictate what you believe, so . . .
- you're allowed to believe anything you want, so . . .
- you can join with your fellow believers and influence public policy, but . . .
- only to the extent that it doesn't intrude on the private beliefs of others—especially their nonreligious beliefs.

That's the genius of America, the feature that has enabled our country to prosper while functioning as a multicultural melting pot: give everyone the same chance, and don't let officials or groups dictate what citizens believe in private. This allows everyone to have dignity and personal power, no matter how poor they are or how idiosyncratic their beliefs. This is exactly what was missing from multicultural societies that imploded in the last 20 years, from Yugoslavia to Iraq.

When Iran issued its infamous 1990 fatwa against Salman Rushdie, many in the West were indignant about a political regime passing a death sentence on someone simply for articulating a "blasphemous" thought.[1]

Western Europe is now struggling with the early breakdown of their social contract of pluralism and tolerance. The 2004 assassination of Dutch filmmaker Theo van Gogh for criticizing Islam's treatment of women was a shocking challenge to the principle that people with contradictory religious ideas can coexist in civil society. Early in 2006, Denmark grappled with its Islamic community's reaction to newspaper cartoons they said insulted the Prophet Muhammad. Local Muslims said they were "mentally tortured" by the images, and wanted the public expression of certain ideas forbidden. The newspaper, of course, was well within the West's normal rights of free expression, but the artist received death threats. In subsequent months, over a million Muslims in dozens of countries marched in protest, almost always resulting in violence and, to date, hundreds of deaths.[2]

Islamic preachers throughout the world are now explicitly calling for the destruction of the Western political system. They do not want those who believe differently to have the rights that they do. In February 2006, Sheikh Hassan Nasrallah told hundreds of thousands of Shia followers in Beirut that, "We want the European parliament to draft laws that ban newspapers from insulting the Prophet."[3] The stark irony that it is precisely in the West that Muslims may express their ideas more fully than in any Muslim country on earth, of course, completely escapes these religious zealots.

It seems clear that more assassinations, accompanied by increasing numbers of people inhibiting what they say, write, and draw will surely follow. *While pluralism makes room for religious fundamentalism, religious fundamentalism wishes to destroy pluralism.* This asymmetry is an enormous political advantage for religious fundamentalism.

Similarly, zealous American Christians believe they are called upon to shape the public policy of the country in which they live. They believe that everyone should follow the word of the Christian god, even those who don't believe in that god, or who interpret that god's word differently. They might be called the Christian-American Taliban.

The ferocity, the lying, the emotional and physical violence in which these people are willing to engage make it clear that they are involved in a fundamentally different struggle than the daily civic strife of healthy democracy. Indeed, political animosity in America goes all the way back to Founders such as Thomas Jefferson, Alexander Hamilton, and Thomas Paine, who passionately and publicly hated their rivals' positions. But they all agreed on the rules of the game, and sought to manifest the same American dream for their countrymen.

American Christianity is extremely heterogeneous. Many Christians celebrate pluralism and the reality of different beliefs—including non-belief—in their communities and the world. But today's religious zealots, like James Dobson, Phyllis Schlafly, Brent Bozell, Pat Robertson, Rick Santorum, Sam Brownback, and yes, George W. Bush, do not agree with their opponents on the rules of the game. They do not want to govern a pluralistic, secular democracy; they want to govern a country whose goals are fundamentally different than America's have ever been, whose citizens have fundamentally different rights than we have today.

They see a powerful connection between non-believers' sexuality and their own. They believe their world is being polluted by the sexuality of nonbelievers. Conceptualizing their world as being vulnerable to others' sexual sin almost inevitably leads to warring on the sexuality of nonbelievers in order to take care of themselves.

And most importantly, they see this battle as far bigger than mere earthly issues of pluralism, democracy, and individual rights. And so legal, cultural, social, even spiritual appeals to traditional American pluralism can't succeed, because they don't live in a world in which they can be safe if others are not like them. And so Randall Terry will go to jail 40 times, James Kopp will murder physicians, and other religious terrorists—individually, in groups, or as elected officials—will pursue an America equally theocratic (no more, no less) than Iran.

Americans can no longer count on elected officials to uphold the single most important principle of American government and society—that everyone has the right to their own opinion, and has the right to live their own nonviolent life as they please. This war is no metaphor. The struggle is tangible, and sexual expression is a key battlefield on which the war for the American covenant is being fought.

If these people did not claim to be devoutly religious—if, say, they were inspired by alcoholism, or visions of King Tut, or a desire to return the Louisiana Purchase to France—their demands would receive little serious consideration (and wouldn't be tax-exempt). But because they say their program is driven by religious considerations, they get a seat at America's public policy table. And so their bizarre demand that, for example, every American be prevented from using contraceptives or having abortions is taken seriously, included as a legitimate voice in public debate—because they claim this is the demand of their god.

The very idea that sexuality is a religious issue, that public policy about sexuality requires the input of religious leaders, that religious leaders have special expertise about sexuality and public policy (because it involves what they call morality), is just an opinion—primarily the opinion of religious believers. The fact that so many people now accept the pragmatic inevitability of this linkage is itself another antisex victory in the War on Sex. (Once again validating the peculiar idea that "morality" is about limiting sexual expression.)

Given the high visibility and political influence afforded religious leaders today, which voices will be heard in the public square? For two decades, it has primarily been the least tolerant, most antisex figures. If moderate or sex-positive religious leaders and laypeople cannot recapture their organizations from radicals

BREAKING THE LAW TO PROTECT GOD

The following has been summarized from Joshua Green's fine article in *The Atlantic*, which appeared in October 2005.

Soon after taking office as chief justice of the Alabama Supreme Court in 2001, Roy Moore caused a national uproar by commissioning and installing a granite monument of the Ten Commandments in the state Supreme Court building and refusing to remove it. In the summer of 2003, "Roy's Rock" was the focus of intense debate about the government's proper relationship to religion. When Moore defied a federal court order to remove the monument, supporters from across the country descended on Montgomery, living on the steps of the Supreme Court building, and praying, singing, threatening, blowing ram's horns—all to protect God from the government's latest assault. After the conflict went to the U.S. Supreme Court, Moore was removed from office for disobeying the federal court order.

Here's the climax of Attorney General Bill Pryor's 2003 cross-examination of Alabama Chief Justice Roy Moore, on trial for disregarding a federal court order preventing him from displaying a 5,000-pound religious sculpture of the Ten Commandments in his courthouse:

PRYOR: And your understanding is that the federal court ordered that you could not acknowledge God; isn't that right?

MOORE: Yes.

PRYOR: And if you resume your duties as chief justice after this proceeding, you will continue to acknowledge God as you have testified that you would today?

MOORE: That's right.

PRYOR: No matter what any other official says?

MOORE: Absolutely. Let me clarify that. Without an acknowledgment of God, I cannot do my duties. I must acknowledge God...

PRYOR: If you do resume your duties as chief justice, you will continue to do that without regard to what any other official says. Isn't that right?

MOORE: ...I think you must.[a]

---

[a]Joshua Green, "Roy and His Rock," *The Atlantic Online*, October 2005, http://www.theatlantic.com/doc/200510/roy-moores-ten-commandments.

who threaten our democracy, secular, pluralistically minded people will have to protect our democracy from them. This terrifying struggle is giving all American religion a bad name. The mass media is complicit in this, giving religious radicals far more exposure than moderates because their extreme, divisive opinions make for dramatic, conflict-oriented shows and stories.

In *Planned Parenthood v. Casey* (1992), the Supreme Court declared it is up to each individual to determine "the concept of existence, of meaning, of the universe, and of the mystery of human life."[4] This summarizes what makes America different from Saudi Arabia, North Korea, and other totalitarian societies. Every American is expected to agree to tolerate his neighbors' wacky ideas about the meaning of life in exchange for tolerance of his own ideas. The lack of this single idea led to hundreds of years of brutal religious warfare in Western Europe.

In contrast, Pope John Paul II warned against this very "alliance between democracy and ethical relativism." *Christianity Today* says, "This means that when truth itself is democratized—when truth is no more than the will of each individual or a majority of individuals—democracy is deprived of the claim to truth and stands naked to its enemies."[5]

By "truth," they and the Pope mean religious truth—that is, belief. By "truth," the Supreme Court means scientific truth—that is, facts. This truth is not up for referendum. Gravity exists whether people believe in it or not. Racism and sexism have real, measurable consequences. Similarly, belief is not up for referendum. People believe what they believe, no matter how little grounded in fact or possibility. Truth is eternal, and belief is eternal. But they are not the same thing. When belief is elevated above truth, when religion and "morality" are taken as some ultimate, factual measure for law, democracy is deprived of the claim to truth and does stand naked to its enemies. We all hate that this enslaves a hundred million people in Iran and its neighbors. We must prevent it from taking over here as well.[6]

BELIEF VERSUS ACTION

No matter how misplaced, many of the battles to control and limit Americans' sexual expression have a heartfelt component. In addition to (ill-informed) practical concerns (porn causes rape, sex on TV hurts kids, contraception causes sterility), people often invoke "moral" considerations (teens shouldn't be sexual, pornography enables infidelity). These "moral" concerns are particularly common in the battle over reproductive rights/abortion.

Abortion can be located in morality (both the autonomy of the woman and the value of fetal life), complete subjectivity (when does life begin), a tiny bit of science (ditto), and some (mostly recent) religious doctrine. Thus, those opposing abortion can sound like they're on solid ground—that at the very least, their argument is as legitimate as any other. But it's a familiar, multifaceted program—attempting to control everyone's sexuality, saying anything necessary to justify it, even referring to an alleged "culture of life" (which is ad hoc nonsense, given their other public policy positions).

Some people claim a religious doctrinaire approach to oppose abortion and contraception. History shows that this argument is an artifact of political, very human decision-making. No less than St. Augustine (fifth century),

Pope Innocent (thirteenth century), and St. Thomas Aquinas (thirteenth century) believed abortion in the first trimester was at times acceptable. Pope Sixtus (sixteenth century) said abortion at any stage was murder and should be punishable by death; only three years later, Pope Gregory reversed this, accepting abortion through 16½ weeks of pregnancy. So today's Christian who screams that all abortion is murder would be condemning several cherished saints and popes.

In 1869, Pope Pius IX once again reversed the Catholic church's tolerant stance on abortion, where it has remained for 137 years—just a mere coffee break in the 20 centuries of Church time.

The construct of Limbo was adopted almost a thousand years ago as the destination of unbaptized infants' souls; last year Pope Benedict started eliminating it, wanting it replaced by a more "compassionate" doctrine.[7]

No American is prevented from believing what he or she wants about abortion or Limbo. But when the Church changes its position on abortion or Limbo again in a decade, a century, or a millennium, presumably the rights it will support for nonbelievers will change again. Will believers then apologize for how they have forced, or tried to force, nonbelievers to live?

YEARNING FOR THE SIMPLE, YEARNING FOR THE DIVINE

Complex times such as ours demand a great deal of self-direction and confidence from individuals. The wish for a simple morality to help one through complex times is understandable. Some people also yearn to connect with the Divine, and, of course, that's a key promise of religious observance. Americans who want this, though, typically want it now, not after a lifetime of meditation and prayer. So for those who want to connect with the Divine now, acquiring ritual purity has far more appeal than painstakingly developing actual ("moral") purity. For many people, that's what religion is for: to tell them what they can do to have certifiable contact with the Divine.

Many Christian spiritual leaders have said that the key is doing good works. Jesus himself proposed that getting to heaven involved, more than anything else, helping others in tangible ways (see Matthew 25). But for some Christian fundamentalists, the modern route to heaven isn't so much what you do, it's what you believe—which is a lot easier. It can be done without any sacrifice of position or comfort, and almost none of time.

So for many fundamentalist Christians these days, the way to experience the Divine is to believe. And how do you show that you really believe? By attempting to force others to act the way you think is right. Wanting other people to forego behavior you think is immoral is a very low-cost way to feel religiously intact. Write a check, vote for an antichoice candidate, go to church and commune with those who also believe. No sacrifice—just force others to sacrifice.

In some Christian sects, being against unauthorized sex is a certifiable way to contact the Divine. Conceptualizing "unauthorized sex," of course, is the first step. Attacking sex is a way to live in the modern world and feel spiritual, without foregoing the comforts of technology or material goods.

Most Western religions have problematized the body (e.g., early influential Christian philosophers, such as Tertullian and Anicius Boethius, called woman "a temple built over a sewer").[8] At various times, Judaism has been obsessed with seminal emissions and menstrual impurity.

Believers, therefore, have to "solve" this "problem." Seeing sex as the representative of the body calls for a philosophical policy about it, and seeing sexuality in a highly limited way makes this project much easier. Conceptualizing sexuality as impure then simply presents the religious community the task of purifying it. That means giving those who would be pure two choices: authorized sex or no sex.

With the two most revered figures in Christian history (Jesus and the Virgin Mary) both considered celibate (and she celebrated for that far beyond other qualities such as compassion or wisdom—it's her name!), there's a limit to how much believers can embrace sexuality and still feel spiritual. Eschewing eroticism (however that is intellectually justified) is a far more internally coherent solution to this Christian dilemma. And so any rationalizations that conceptualize and then condemn "uncontrolled" or "unspiritual" sex are very convenient.

In fact, today's fundamentalist Christians are often pietistic; they observe or profess beyond what's required as a way of making a statement about themselves to themselves. Piety reinforces one's self-identification as spiritual. It is always symbolic at its core, which makes it easier to profess than to actually live Jesus' project of empowering the powerless. Jesus never said, "Fighting abortion is more important than feeding the poor." But it is easier, cleaner, more exciting, and it doesn't upset the neighborhood. Similarly, Jesus never said, "Since your time is limited, and you can't rescue everyone, care about the unborn more than the born. Way more."

But somehow, that's what millions of Christians are choosing to rescue—the unborn, rather than the born—and choosing to adopt—frozen embryos instead of warm foster children. How are they choosing their projects? Apparently, to maximize their political impact. Not coincidentally, they keep selecting projects that limit others' sexual choices. Their War on Sex around reproduction helps them feel holy, although it doesn't help (and demonstrably harms) the disadvantaged already living.

It isn't that the Right has no heart, it's that it applies its heart to causes that pay off in controlling sexuality. So it claims it cares for "degraded" porn actresses, "vulnerable" prostitutes, and heartbroken teenagers. It doesn't show the same concern for poor women who need day care, immigrant women who need English classes, or single women who need contraception to avoid pregnancies that will damage or destroy their families.

Many leaders of the Religious Right explicitly say its goal is installing a moral, Christ-centered government in the United States. That is, they want a government that will abandon America's 200-year-long tradition of pluralism. That is, they want to change the most fundamental rules of America. And if 51 percent of America votes for this, or if 99 percent of America votes for this, it will still be wrong. It certainly won't be "traditionally" American.

GOVERNMENTAL COLLUSION

America's religiously themed antisex program couldn't succeed without active, enthusiastic government action. So why have America's federal and state governments fallen in with these repressive elements?

There are presumably a variety of reasons, but they are primarily the twin evils of politics—money and power, along with something rarely found in American government—personal belief. And the impact of the irrational belief is enhanced because of the piety factor described above.

President George Bush describes himself as ardently "pro-life," and has said he believes the laws of America should reflect his religious beliefs as much as possible. In 2002, he declared January 18 the first annual "Sanctity of Life Day," describing America's "essential moral duties, including . . . caring for children born and unborn." And when he signed a 2004 bill recognizing that fetuses have rights separate from the mothers carrying them, he said, "We reaffirm that the United States of America is building a culture of life."[9]

Thousands of other American politicians explicitly say they are attempting to inject Christian values into American governance. And former Alabama Chief Justice Roy Moore says God is the basis of American government—his vision amounting, according to *The Atlantic*, to "a theocracy." "Let every soul be subject unto the higher powers," says Moore. "Separation of church and state does not mean separation of God and government! We must return God to our public life and restore the moral foundation of our law."[10]

In 2000, presidential candidate Pat Buchanan said that RU-486 is an abomination to God, and therefore, if elected, "I would use all the power of my office, including FDA appointments, to prevent RU-486 from being put on the market."[11] Note the logic: Buchanan's decision that his god disapproves of RU-486 is the reason that all Americans, including those who don't believe that Buchanan's god exists, should be denied access to this medication. How different is this from saying that since Elvis would disapprove, no one should have access to the drug?

This idealism is horribly misguided, a fundamental misunderstanding of the American system. But it is idealism nevertheless. Unfortunately, that means that not even a high-quality civics lesson would be enough to change such at-titudes about the role of belief in democratic government. There is no difference between President Bush and Judge Moore saying 'the law must conform to my religious beliefs,' and Ayatollah Khomeini and President Ahmadinejad saying 'the law must conform to my religious beliefs.'

Money and power are the more sinister reasons that politicians are at-tempting to destroy Americans' reproductive rights—and their influence, of course, is everywhere. Churches and religious organizations are giving more money to political candidates and officials than ever before. And in return, the government is giving churches and religious groups more money than ever before.

President Bush's 2001 "faith-based initiative" was an honest declaration of his intention to do so, and he has been extremely effective. Under this plan, tens of millions of federal tax dollars are distributed to religious (i.e., Chris-tian) ministries to provide social services that have historically been provided by government agencies or secular grantees, including health care "counsel-ing," abstinence education, after-school programs, job training, drug treat-ment, prison rehabilitation, and pregnancy "counseling."

For example, Herb Lusk is a Philadelphia preacher with a long history of partisan activity on behalf of Republicans. In January 2006, his Greater Exo-dus Baptist Church hosted a nationally broadcast rally to support the confir-mation of Supreme Court nominee Samuel Alito, Jr. Sponsored by the Fam-ily Research Council, speakers included Jerry Falwell, Tony Perkins, James Dobson, and Senator Rick Santorum (R-PA, who's facing a tight reelection campaign).[12]

Reverend Lusk has been awarded $1.4 million of taxpayers' money in faith-based grants by the Bush administration—and despite his work's obviously partisan nature, he can administer the funds through tax-exempt organiza-tions. Is his passion for Alito or for money and power? According to *The New York Times,* Lusk said, "I don't know enough about him to actually think he's the right man to do the job."[13]

Another personal cause of President Bush is so-called embryo adoption. At a 2005 press conference on stem cell research, he introduced a (now feder-ally funded) agency, Nightlight Christian Adoption. He spoke of the value of human life and that there is no such thing as a "spare embryo." Twenty-one children born from adopted embryos ("snowflake children") were paraded on stage to, as the agency director put it, "put a face to these embryos under discussion."[14]

This pattern is repeated in abstinence programs, crisis pregnancy centers, and other tax-exempt religious institutions across America—state and federal officials funnel money to local and national groups, which support these of-ficials and elect others. These groups now brazenly boast of their influence in destroying Americans' reproductive rights: Concerned Women for America,

RELIGIOUS PLURALISM

Fortunately, not all religious believers are intent on controlling others' behavior, whether through forced conversions, or by changing the laws to criminalize that which they consider sinful and requiring that which their god demands.

There has always been a tolerant side to the American religious tradition, expressed variously by Quakers, the civil rights movement, social justice theology, and the antiwar movement. Now that sexuality is the focus of so much hostile and dangerous religious input into public policy, America desperately needs that religious tolerance applied to it as well.

And so, the Religious Institute on Sexual Morality, Justice, and Healing, was founded in 2001. Now directed by Reverend Debra Haffner, it advocates for sexual health, education, and justice in faith communities and society. It supports religious leaders and congregations in creating sexually healthy faith communities.

The Institute has published an historical declaration, now endorsed by more than 2,500 religious leaders from dozens of traditions. As a reminder of how religion and sexual health can passionately coexist, and as a way of honoring the Institute's life-affirming work in a sexually hostile world, the declaration is reproduced here in full. Readers are encouraged to find out more at http://www.religiousinstitute.org.

Religious Declaration on Sexual Morality, Justice, and Healing

Sexuality is God's life-giving and life-fulfilling gift. We come from diverse religious communities to recognize sexuality as central to our humanity and as integral to our spirituality. We are speaking out against the pain, brokenness, oppression, and loss of meaning that many experience about their sexuality.

Our faith traditions celebrate the goodness of creation, including our bodies and our sexuality. We sin when this sacred gift is abused or exploited. However, the great promise of our traditions is love, healing, and restored relationships.

Our culture needs a sexual ethic focused on personal relationships and social justice rather than particular sexual acts. All persons have the right and responsibility to lead sexual lives that express love, justice, mutuality, commitment, consent, and pleasure. Grounded in respect for the body and for the vulnerability that intimacy brings, this ethic fosters physical, emotional, and spiritual health. It accepts no double standards and applies to all persons, without regard to sex, gender, color, age, bodily condition, marital status, or sexual orientation.

(continued)

(continued)

God hears the cries of those who suffer from the failure of religious communities to address sexuality. We are called today to see, hear, and respond to the suffering caused by violence against women and sexual minorities, the HIV pandemic, unsustainable population growth and over-consumption, and the commercial exploitation of sexuality.

Faith communities must therefore be truth-seeking, courageous, and just. We call for:

- Theological reflection that integrates the wisdom of excluded, often silenced peoples, and insights about sexuality from medicine, social science, the arts and humanities.
- Full inclusion of women and sexual minorities in congregational life, including their ordination and the blessing of same sex unions.
- Sexuality counseling and education throughout the lifespan from trained religious leaders.
- Support for those who challenge sexual oppression and who work for justice within their congregations and denomination.

Faith communities must also advocate for sexual and spiritual wholeness in society. We call for:

- Lifelong, age appropriate sexuality education in schools, seminaries, and community settings.
- A faith-based commitment to sexual and reproductive rights, including access to voluntary contraception, abortion, and HIV/STD prevention and treatment.
- Religious leadership in movements to end sexual and social injustice.

God rejoices when we celebrate our sexuality with holiness and integrity. We, the undersigned, invite our colleagues and faith communities to join us in promoting sexual morality, justice, and healing.

for example, lists thwarting over-the-counter sales of the morning-after pill as one of its 2005 accomplishments.[15]

CHALLENGING AMERICA'S COVENANT

The U.S. Constitution guarantees each of us the freedom to practice any religion. This freedom does not extend to challenging the fundamental principle of the United States, that your freedom ends where my nose (or uterus) begins. Regardless of the majority's wishes, fundamental principles like these can never be put up for referendum.

Somehow, those against the public's access to contraceptive technology have put this access up for referendum. Each side continues scrambling for adherents. This means that those opposed to the unlimited availability of contraceptives have already won a crucial victory in the War on Sex. Wouldn't we say the same thing if slavery were put up for a vote? Regardless of who won such a vote, the forces of freedom and democracy would have lost.

Chapter Fourteen

<u>Battleground:</u> *Sexual Privacy and Sexual Minorities—Civil Rights or Immoral Privileges?*

I t's hard to believe, but in America today, who you make love with, and how, actually determines what your rights are—both in and out of your bedroom.

Yes, the government uses your sexual preferences and orientation to help decide if you should get custody of your kids, remain in the military, or get a security clearance at your job. And if the government doesn't approve of your private sexual interests, you won't be allowed to buy the toys you want, gather with strangers to have sex, or flirt with your partner in public. Your sexual preferences even help determine whether or not you get fully competent services from a physician, attorney, or therapist.

For decades, a variety of Christian groups have demanded that America pursue this prejudice more energetically and punitively. They were behind the nineteenth-century Comstock ban on selling or mailing contraceptives, the 1930s Hays code that censored Hollywood films, and J. Edgar Hoover's postwar FBI drive to identify and punish homosexuals in the government and public life. You can see it in the thousand dollars the First Baptist Church in Huntingburg, Indiana, donated to Spencer County to help county commissioners get rid of the local Love Boutique. Separation of (tax-exempt) church and state, anyone?[1]

The central question, almost beyond belief in a modern country, is: Do all Americans have to have sex the same way in order to claim their fair share of the American dream, or of American justice? To people obsessed with "normal" sex, the answer is yes.

You may think this has nothing to do with you. "I'm not gay and I'm not kinky," you might say. "I'm sympathetic to people who get busted for being either one, but that's just the way it is. And it's not my problem."

Wrong.

Because once the government can pathologize any kind of sex, it can pathologize any kind of sex—even yours.

Impossible? Well, now that the right of states to criminalize the sale of sex toys such as vibrators has been affirmed, what if your state decides to do so? Don't say it can't happen, because it already has—in six states. Since millions of Americans use sex toys, you or someone you care for may be a target.

And although your sexual interests may currently be perfectly legal (the very idea that private sex has to be declared "legal" is itself chilling), what if you experiment with something new and like it? Or you get involved with a new partner who likes something you never thought about? Or some local group decides that what you now enjoy is dangerous for the community? You could find yourself a sexual fugitive faster than you think. Because like all wars do, the War on Sex is creating refugees everywhere.

Today, some 30 million tax-paying, otherwise law-abiding Americans are in danger—not because they hurt others or others' property, but because they enjoy certain kinds of sex in private. Whether they're gay, or into S/M, or they swing with their spouse, they have fewer rights than others do. Despite their enormous numbers, they live as part of a sexual minority.

The creation of sexual minorities—groups who are disenfranchised or in danger because their sexual interests are disapproved of—is dangerous not just for people in those groups. It's also dangerous for those who are not part of a sexual minority.

The sex under attack doesn't have to be extreme sex, doesn't have to hurt anyone, doesn't even have to generate any complaints. It can be as innocuous as riding the glass elevator at the Hyatt Regency without panties. Or your professor overhearing your girlfriend talk about the rough sex you both like. That's why you should care.

To give you a bird's-eye view, laws that were recently passed by America's state or local governments have punished citizens who:

- played an X-rated videotape in a moving car;
- paid to get an erotic spanking at a strip club;
- had rough sex with a consenting adult;
- went to a private swing club and watched his wife give a friend a blow job;
- sold sex toys at a party of adults who invited her.

And don't forget the general who lost his job for having sex with someone who wasn't his wife—even though they're in the middle of an amicable divorce and neither woman complained.

The prevailing Big Lie is that "giving" sexual minorities civil rights somehow undermines the rights of everyone else—and, of course, sends the "wrong message" (of tolerance, how ugly). We should consider the other side—how, ironically, depriving sexual minorities of their civil rights undermines the freedom of all Americans.

WHY PUBLIC-IZE SEXUALITY? (Pronounced "public eyes.")

Remember, "sexuality" is much more than intercourse or genital stimulation.
So is private sex in America, um, private?
It depends on whom you ask.
Those who fear sex conceptualize all sex as public. They have a well-worn list of ways that private, consensual, adult sexual behavior supposedly affects the community, and is therefore not really private. If your private sexual behavior doesn't meet their criteria for "normal," they believe that it:

- hurts children (always the number one reason for restricting sexual rights);
- undermines other people's conventional marriages;
- encourages "sex addiction" (to vibrators, S/M, or whatever individuals do);
- exploits women (always a great reason for restricting any sexual rights);
- disrespects the God-fearing community;
- encourages masturbation (which is presumed a bad thing).

People who believe this think your sexuality is their business. Many of them want to use the law to establish moral norms and express social disapproval. This was Justice Antonin Scalia's reason that the Supreme Court should keep anal sex illegal when he dissented in *Lawrence v. Texas* in 2004. Such people are public-izing your private sexuality.

And there's a deep, more personal concern, which may not even be conscious.

Many people who fear sex in general learn, in childhood, to fear their own sexuality. More than any other Western country, America is filled with family, religious, and community environments that teach children that their sexuality is bad. Growing up, they project this internalized erotophobia outward, onto others. The simple unconscious logic is, "If my sexuality is dangerous, so is my neighbor's."

For people caught in such a bind, the easiest way to reduce anxiety about their own sexuality is to repress others'—that is, *yours*. They then rationalize their anxiety-reduction strategy of controlling your sexuality: "I owe it to my family/community/God." Your private sexuality then becomes everybody's business.

Thus, public-izing private sexuality is an effective way of addressing one's fear of others' sexuality. This explains the desire for censorship, even of oneself—eliminating sexual opportunities for others, because one's own self can't be trusted.

A lot of public policy is unconsciously formulated and consciously presented as a response to public need, when it's really a response to personal need. This explains why some people are so obsessed with regulating others' sexual behavior and decision-making. And it's absolutely predictable that they would see sex everywhere, providing a never-ending source of energy to repress it.

Since these frightened people conceptualize all sex as public, they feel entitled to demand that the government control everyone's sexual behavior. That was the justification for criminalizing sex between people of different races, contraception for single people, and anal sex. And why it's still illegal in much of America to lie on a beach nude even when no one's complaining, or to gather behind the closed doors of a private club and have sex with strangers.

Many of these frightened people also say they are called by their religion to set the rules for everyone's sexual expression, regardless of the rights our secular government ensures each of us. And they think that because they are thus called, they actually have the right to do so! Whether they phrase this gently ("We want everyone to enjoy the advantages of our way of life") or harshly ("We must prevent others from living differently from us"), their intention is the same.

And so religious conservatives are no better than any other radical pressure group that threatens American pluralism and tolerance. Why should swing club owners be considered just a self-interested lobby, while a group trying to eliminate a town's swing clubs is considered the "community voice" or "community activists"? Similarly, why are those who aren't prejudiced against gays adopting kids considered "the gay lobby," while those who oppose it are considered "the public" or "the voice of America's families?"

The idea that "all sex ultimately accrues to the community" must be met with the psychological and political truth that "the *results* of public-izing all sex accrues to the community." When sexual expression is repressed, when individuals' rights are routinely violated and they are made to feel guilty, everyone suffers. Consciously or not, most people struggle with "normality anxiety."[2] The community must cope with the anger, acting out (sexual and nonsexual), secrecy, and even addictions provoked by the resulting guilt and restrictions. Society can't repress something as fundamental as sexual orientation or sexual expression without paying a price in reduced mental health and community safety.

SEX, CLEAN AND DIRTY

With sex in America firmly public-ized, how are "clean" and "dirty" sex to be differentiated? That's the principal conceit behind criminalizing certain sexual expression. It's commonplace to note that nonreproductive sex is often considered dirty, but the issue goes beyond that. Attached to reproduction or not, antisex people feel that passion is dirty, lust is dirty, pleasure itself is suspect, even within the context of monogamous, heterosexual intercourse. This is even more true for other erotic configurations. Sexual intensity, then, is the enemy, and virtually anything done to increase the intensity of sexual arousal or experience is problematic. For those afraid of sex, in fact, that's the definition of kinky: anything that attempts to heighten the intensity of so-called normal sex. As recently as 50 years ago, many Americans considered oral sex kinky, done only by prostitutes and other taboo subcultures.[3]

For such people, there are layers of clean/dirty sex. Some relationships can't be clean, so it doesn't matter what you do within them (e.g., a same-gender couple). Other relationships are clean, but the activities in them can be dirty (e.g., a monogamous wife playing the "oops I forgot my panties game" at a gas station). Some relationships and activities are clean—unless you're too lusty, which tarnishes the activity (e.g., monogamous intercourse in which the wife asks the husband to ejaculate on her face).

The public-izing of sex attempts to mobilize the community to protect the American hearth, to contain the power of sexuality. The antisex community fears this power can spread from one home to another like a contagion. Like witchcraft did. Like heresy did. Like the 1960s did. That's one reason they're so committed to maintaining the myth of kids' sexual innocence—kids are seen as the generational firewall that helps contain the contagion.

In reality, sexuality encompasses a broad range of our self: what we think and feel, do with our bodies, fantasize, how we choose partners, and express ourselves. More pragmatically, it involves what we wear, contraceptive choices, role-playing, toys, and more. Public-izing our sexuality attempts to limit or eliminate a broad swath of these options, which is a lot of our human heritage to lose. And Americans are not safe from further losses: as you read this, churches, morality groups, legislators, and prosecutors are busy narrowing your sexual choices even more.

Americans deserve to reclaim the intrinsic privacy of private sex. Fulfilling the American promise demands it. To do so, we need to reestablish the comprehensive concept of private sex. Outside of sex, this principle is already established throughout our culture: personal activity is considered private unless it involves coercion, fraud, or the forced, disruptive participation of the public. Playing soccer during rush hour in the center of Times Square is, rightly, prohibited. Making love there should be, too—for exactly the same reason, no more, no less. The sex part is irrelevant.

But "There is no fixed consensus on privacy and sexuality, in spite of the fact that most people feel their bodies are private," says Kinsey Institute Executive Director, Dr. Julia Heiman.[4]

Antisex forces have found many ways to create a gray zone between private and public sexual expression. The War on Sex pursues that gray zone with legal, economic, and political pressure. Zoning laws, morality crusades, powerful but meaningless anecdotes, and undocumented claims of secondary effects transform private activity into gray zone activity, and gray zone activity into public activity. And so Phoenix, Arizona, was able to close private swingers' clubs by declaring them places offering "live public sex acts," and an Arkansas strip club has been forced to stop offering erotic "birthday spankings" because "people can get hurt." Texas has actually made it illegal to educate customers while selling sex toys; the seller has to state "these are novelty items only." When "passion consultant" Joanne Webb refused to pretend that in 2003, she was arrested.

WHO'S ALLOWED TO PRACTICE SEX UNRESTRICTED?

Throughout history, legal or religious codes have restricted various people in expressing their sexuality: the unmarried, elderly, adolescent, mentally ill, physically handicapped, terminally ill, warriors in training, menstruating women. And, in many cultures, anyone having sex with someone of the same gender.

In most modern societies, those restrictions are either gone or facing challenges. In their place, however, Americans now face other restrictions. They're based on the discomfort and superstitions of those who legislate, and the vocal minority that alternately critiques and supports them. Whether it's a zoning board, city council, district attorney, family mediator, or police chief, the story is almost always the same: Adults shouldn't be allowed to do just any sexual thing they want, even when everyone involved consents and no one complains. Certain activities, relationships, and equipment are judged both bad for participants, and bad for the community.

Or to put it more honestly, "That stuff seems weird and it scares me," or, "That stuff seems exotic and exciting and it scares me," or, "If that's allowed, then other stuff that's even scarier might be allowed, and it scares me."

As New York City prosecutor (Special Victims Unit) Linda Fairstein said in 2001 when describing why she was prosecuting S/M activity that she knew was consensual, she doesn't believe that "one human being should be allowed to do that to another, even if it is consensual."[5] And as Robert Peters, President of Morality in Media says, "Conclusive scientific data is not necessary" when restricting sexual activity.[6] A bunch of people being scared or disgusted is apparently all that is. It works in Iran, it worked for the Taliban, so I guess there's no reason it can't work here.

There's a word that accurately describes this policy: discrimination. Discrimination against those who enjoy inflaming their own passion (lustism?), and against those who enjoy sexual activity of which others disapprove (kinkophobia?). When people are denied rights simply because society disapproves of who they are or what they do, it's called discrimination. Kinkophobia and lustism are like racism and sexism. Remember when jobs were advertised according to gender? And houses were rented according to race? Now access to jobs and housing (and to sexual expression) is available according to sexual preference/orientation: "House for rent: no swingers, please." "Job promotion available: no gays, please." "Sex allowed: nothing kinky, please."

WHAT'S A SEXUAL MINORITY?

As we look at this question, do keep in mind your experience with whatever minority you're most familiar: racial, ethnic, religious, and so forth. You'll see that "sexual minority" fits the familiar model of ethnic minority almost perfectly.

During three centuries of American history, "minorities" have included immigrants, Jews, African Americans, "Orientals," Mexicans, Quakers, Mormons, and Catholics. The designated "other" against which the majority defines itself, ethnic minorities have typically been described as:

- a homogeneous group;
- less than adult, perhaps even less than human;
- not "normal";
- proselytizing or seducing "normal" people;
- dangerous and therefore needing to be controlled;
- practitioners of secret, exotic rituals;
- impulsive and/or compulsive.

American society has historically maintained myths about minority groups, their activities, and the consequences of allowing minorities to follow their "nature." At the same time, society often lacks awareness about the extent to which minorities are deprived or in pain.

This is what it's like to be gay or bisexual in America, or to prefer sex that involves variations such as swinging, S/M, exhibitionism, cross-dressing, sex toys, or adult entertainment. The tens of millions of people in one or more of these categories know that their activities could cost them their job, their apartment, their physical safety, or their freedom at any time. They also know that anything that involves their sexuality may be met with ignorance, hostility, or both.

The way professionals are trained, and the services they provide us, are an example. To protect consumers by guaranteeing a minimum level of competence, all states credential professionals such as physicians, attorneys, and psychologists. Thus, everyone has the right to expect their doctor, lawyer, marriage counselor, social worker, and physical therapist to understand a variety of clients; lawyers are expected to understand that some children are cut out of their parents' wills. Physical therapists know that not everyone is right-handed.

When it comes to sexuality, training in all professions is limited, and many sexual minorities cannot expect expert or non-judgmental services. Because of lack of training and cultural ignorance/prejudice, a physician might misdiagnose an S/M-playing patient with bruises as an abuse victim (and be legally required to file a police report). A marriage counselor who doesn't understand open relationships might assume that a swinging couple coming for communication skills are afraid of intimacy. Many psychologists would mishandle a bisexual patient ambivalent about committing to marriage. Even Oprah's therapy guru, Dr. Phil, responded to a question about swinging with derision and ignorance. Calling a caller's boyfriend "a loser" and "slime," he cautioned her not to "whore yourself and screw his friends."[7]

The 1999 National Coalition for Sexual Freedom survey of those in alternate sexual lifestyles, for example, found that 30 percent of the respondents experienced discrimination, while 36 percent suffered violence or harassment (including losing jobs or custody of children).[8] Similarly, Dr. Joseph Marzucco's 2004 study of 786 people regularly involved in sadomasochism showed that men and women were significantly concerned about getting adequate medical care if physicians saw the physical results of their sexual play.[9] The majority remain unknown to their physicians. With millions of Americans practicing S/M regularly or occasionally, studies like these reflect a serious public health problem.

Similarly, a majority of women who self-identify as lesbians do not disclose their sexual behavior or orientation to their physicians. This can prevent them from receiving appropriate medical and psychological information and services.[10]

Let's turn now to some of the ways that sexual minorities—millions and millions of tax-paying, mind-their-own-business Americans—are facing legal and economic violence from judges, prosecutors, and other authorities.

"But blacks can't help being black," you might say, "while sexual expression is a choice, so a democratic society can pathologize any sexual choices it wishes." Actually, much sexual expression is inborn the same way race is. Sexual orientation—same-gender or other-gender—is, for almost everyone, fixed at birth or very early childhood. Millions of other people experience sexual preferences so strong that they function as an orientation. These can include sadomasochism, cross-dressing, exhibitionism, and a rigid erotic attachment to objects such as leather or rubber garments.

More to the point, America has also outlawed discrimination in employment and public accommodation against a person's religion—which is adopted, not inborn. The right to wear a turban or cross in public is protected no matter how uncomfortable it makes others. There is no reason that someone's choice to go to a swing club can't be as protected as his or her choice to go to church (and yes, lots of Americans do both, swinging on Saturday night, praying on Sunday morning).[11]

CASE STUDY: CRIMINALIZING YOUR RIGHT TO SWING

Swingers' clubs—private places where couples and individuals can congregate and have sex with each other in a safe environment—have quietly existed in most major metropolitan areas since the 1970s. Fueled by the aging of the baby boomer generation and their belief in personal liberty and sexual expression, the phenomenon has grown every decade since. By most estimates, there are now at least 5,000,000 swingers in the United States.[12]

By 1966, the military had some 50,000 swingers in its ranks under investigation, intending to court martial and discharge all of them.[13] When civilian aerospace engineer Robert McGinley was identified as one of these "sexual deviants," he lost his Air Force security clearance (and therefore his job). In 1975, McGinley founded the Lifestyles Organization (LSO); in less than five years, LSO was hosting weekend conventions attended by 500 or more couples. Soon, hotels and resorts throughout southern California were bidding for their lucrative convention business. They had learned that these thousands of couples were relatively affluent, well-behaved, and often returned—with their friends. They were perfect customers.

But in 1996, some California state officials decided to discourage swinging, and to "run LSO out of the state of California."[14] Since swingers weren't doing anything illegal, how could this be arranged? By declaring that their sexual behavior was dangerous: that it was immoral, which led to the breakdown of family values, and therefore bred crime. The police had no authority to stop this *legal* behavior, but the state did have an agency mandated to protect the "public morals" in places it licensed: the Department of Alcoholic Beverage Control (ABC).

And so, in October 1996, the ABC told the Seaport Marina Hotel in Long Beach that their liquor license could be revoked if they hosted the Lifestyles Halloween Banquet and Ball. Six weeks later, the ABC temporarily suspended the liquor license of the Town and Country Hotel in San Diego that had hosted the lifestyles convention that August. In response, the hotel cancelled the contracts it had signed with LSO for the next three years.

A few months later, the ABC warned that any California hotel hosting the 1997 LSO convention (of 4,000 swingers) could lose its license. ABC District Supervisor Dave Gill declared that their morality rules applied even at events at which no alcohol was served. Even more astonishing, he added that the ABC rules applied even to hotel sleeping rooms, since they were on the premises of license holders: "The regulations apply at all times to their facilities regardless of whether the activity is private or public in nature." The ABC was declaring that adults could not swing in their own locked hotel rooms. Frightened hotels and convention centers were breaking contracts with LSO left and right, creating financial havoc.[15]

In subsequent court hearings, the American Civil Liberties Union described the ABC as "drunk with its own power." Robert Burke, president of the University of California, Los Angeles, Law School, accused the agency of practicing "state Gestapo-ism."[16] Ultimately, a 9th Circuit judge ruled that the ABC was aggressively misusing its authority in order to suppress expression, and invalidated the regulations that prevented "any depiction of sex in any manner" at licensed venues. In addition, the ABC had paid the city of Long Beach to uncover dirt about LSO; the city was fined when it was discovered its police officers had lied about the debauchery they supposedly found while undercover at an LSO event.[17]

"From 1996–99, there were over 30,000 swing club gatherings in North America," reports multiple–award-winning investigative journalist, Terry Gould. "They were verifiably peaceful...I couldn't document a single 911 call placed from a club. But local police nationwide persisted in raiding these private clubs, arresting and humiliating couples inside. Sometimes tipping off TV stations ahead of time, police would drive people out into the glare of waiting cameras," he revealed in his landmark study, *The Lifestyle*. "Swinging is peaceful activity that the government insists on treating like criminal behavior."[18]

But the nationwide crackdown was just getting rolling.

You couldn't describe Phoenix as sleepy when the fuss there started, and you certainly wouldn't now—with a million and a half people, it's America's fifth largest city. By 1998, it had an active community of tens of thousands of swingers, with gay bathhouses, mixed-gender clubs, and regularly scheduled house parties. Lots of people got laid, and no one complained.

But then the Phoenix City Council adopted the Live Sex Act Business ordinance. Drafted primarily by the Christian-based National Family Legal Foundation, it declared that sex at a private swing club was a "live sex act," and that clubs are "detrimental to the health, safety and morals" of residents. It was adopted as an emergency ordinance, so the city could *declare* a problem rather than having to *prove* it. And so the city could ignore the vocal input of "the community"—swingers.

The first U.S. law specifically banning swingers' clubs, the city's reasons for it were phony from the start:

- Eliminating prostitution, although not one complaint or arrest was ever made;
- Limiting overuse of police services, although no unusual level of calls was ever noted, and no one was ever arrested prior to the ordinance;
- Preventing STDs, although all clubs required safer sex practices, although no one has ever shown higher rates of STDs among swingers than non-swingers. Not only did all clubs provide condoms, the gay club The Chute offered free HIV testing, often at their own expense;[19]
- Preventing blight, although the clubs were in industrial and other non-glamorous neighborhoods. The building that housed The Chute was eventually sold for three times its original cost. Wouldn't you love to suffer such blight?
- Zoning infractions: The relentless, discriminatory inspections required club bathrooms to be cleaner than a restaurant's. Some inspectors promised to return daily. Clubs were cited for missing lightbulbs.

Other problems the city's swing clubs and bathhouses never experienced were drunkenness, violence, guns, sexual assault, gambling, safety problems, financial irresponsibility, corruption, illegal drugs, or underage people. This is a record of public decorum unmatched by the Phoenix 7–Elevens or the Arizona State University football program.

And yet, ordinance in place, the Phoenix police hounded swing clubs. At a cost of millions of taxpayer dollars, they sent in undercover officers week after week (hazardous duty, to be sure—"Honey, it was all in the line of duty. I swear I didn't enjoy it."). When the busts came, it was by cops in riot gear, with guns drawn. Did they imagine the swingers had concealed weapons? It's hard to imagine a bunch of naked 40-year-olds in the middle of kissing, sucking, licking, and screwing becoming a dangerous mob.

The night that police raided Flex, there were 10 felonies in the area, including car theft. It was a great example of how Phoenix's obsession with sex clubs distorted their public safety priorities.

Club owners spent hundreds of thousands of dollars in legal fees simply for the right to stay in business. They met with the city and attempted to compromise; the response was everything from bizarre applications of arcane hotel regulations ("no more than six in a bed") to falsified police reports. Courts disallowed documented facts while relying on the "common sense" of city and church officials, anonymous zoning inspectors, and reports by cops who perjured themselves. Phoenix City Attorney James Hays says he was instructed to do whatever was necessary to close down the clubs, especially the most elegant, Club Chameleon.

In 2002, a federal court ruled "there is no First Amendment protection for the physical sexual conduct."

By 2005, the owners and staffs of six different clubs had been arrested and booked on charges ranging from facilitating live sex acts to "moral turpitude" (yes, really). They were told to expect serious jail time and large, punitive fines. Chute co-owner Donnel McDonnel was threatened with having to register as a sex offender for life. To lighten their sentences, most owners agreed to close their clubs (forfeiting their right to make a living). The very few that remained open were reduced to a desultory, cheap motel blandness, nothing like the vibrant joyfulness once enjoyed by so many. The sophisticated, nonviolent, nonproblematic Phoenix swing scene and bathhouse scene was destroyed.

And now, eight years after the ordinance's enactment? Couples still swing, and gay men still cruise. Except both groups do it in settings far less safe, less controlled, less healthy, and less dignified than they used to. "Some of the sex has moved to public parks," says McDonnel bitterly, "probably with fewer condoms used. The Vice Squad says they're going after that next—having chased it there, from when it was safely behind our closed doors." "People are not going to stop what they are doing because there is no Club Chameleon," agrees former club owner Milo Fencl. "They'll find other ways to do what they want, even if they feel less comfortable with it."[20]

Legitimate business owners like the Fencls have learned that religious bigotry, not due process or ethical government, runs Phoenix. Current city council members who helped push the discriminatory ordinance, like Peggy Bilstein, refuse to discuss the matter today.

It's not just a bunch of gathering places that Bilstein, police Lieutenant Larry Jacobs, and others shut down. An established community—with safety norms, etiquette, education, and mutual support, where people know and care for each other—was deliberately destroyed. "It was a place where women felt absolutely safe—they knew they were surrounded by people who would be respectful," laments Nancy Fencl, co-owner of the now-closed Club Chameleon.[21]

Phoenix didn't wipe out swinging. It just made swinging less safe, less predictable, less sober, less contained. All the things those in city government and the Community Defense Council sanctimoniously claimed they were worried about.

"The Phoenix ordinance is the first of its kind in this country," reported the *Phoenix New Times* in 1999, "and appears primed to spark a monumental battle in the legal war over the business of sex in America." How prescient. Cities that criminalized swing clubs for consenting adults since 2004 include Philadelphia, Indianapolis, and St. Paul. The Community Defense Counsel (which is what the National Family Legal Foundation became) predicts many more cities will be cleansed.[22]

Says Mayor Bart Peterson of Indianapolis, "Our zoning laws exist for a reason: to protect families and children from being exposed to the negative effects that adult businesses can have on a community. Illegal adult establishments like Reel One are a detriment to strong, healthy neighborhoods and simply will not be tolerated in Indianapolis."[23]

It isn't only swinger's gatherings that are attacked. S/M conventions have been harassed and disrupted by authorities around the country. Just a sample from the last five years:

- After "Nawlins in November" met in New Orleans annually without incident, police inform the host hotel that if it hosts the event this year, they'll get busted.
- When hotels in Maryland and Virginia notify police they'll be hosting S/M events, alcohol control authorities threaten to suspend the hotels' licenses, even though no alcohol will be served there.
- San Diego, Baltimore, Washington, DC, and Attleboro, Massachusetts selectively enforce zoning and public indecency laws against local S/M communities.
- From February to May 2002, S/M conventions are blocked by Concerned Women for America, American Family Association, and the American Decency Association. The coordinated media and civic attacks take place in Chicago, Michigan, Oklahoma, and St. Louis.[24]

CASE STUDY: S/M

According to national surveys, 12 percent of American adults have engaged in consensual sadomasochism, erotic power play, or bondage-and-discipline games (S/M).[25] These sexual activities may or may not involve toys, equipment, and role-playing. They often involve physical stimulation that produces pain ranging from mild to intense. These games are always consensual, always negotiated ahead of time, and are always accompanied by good communication skills and the ability to change or stop what's happening whenever desired.

Practitioners of alternative sexual lifestyles have not fared well in child custody hearings. Because America's family court system is often biased against sexual minorities, parties in divorce proceedings sometimes try to gain legal advantage by exposing a former partner's sexual history. Parental fitness has been questioned, for example, because one spouse has committed adultery, been "promiscuous," is gay, or participates in "unusual" sexual activity. Courts often agree, typically without evidence, that a child would be endangered because a parent engages in non-approved sexual behavior.

Over the years, I have been professionally involved in many custody proceedings that involved sexual issues. One of these was recently described in a peer-reviewed journal.[26] The article convincingly demonstrates how family courts can be prejudiced against sexual variations. It is noteworthy that this case took place in California, often considered the most sexually liberal and sexually educated state in the country.

When Mr. Smith and Ms. Smith divorced in the late 90s, they shared custody of their son, Ed. The boy lived with his father; his mother had liberal visitation rights and alimony. Mr. Jones eventually became the mother's live-in boyfriend, whom everyone agreed soon had an excellent stepparenting relationship with Ed.

During an investigation about the boy's health (which was soon completed) when he was 11, Ms. Smith volunteered that she and Mr. Jones had an intense S/M relationship. This triggered an investigation about the fitness of the mother and the possible danger posed by the live-in boyfriend. The investigation (by court-appointed Dr. Blair) confirmed that:

- no child abuse had occurred;
- the child was unaware of the mother's sexual interests;
- the child never saw any incidents or suggestions of inappropriate sexual activity;
- the child was doing well emotionally and in school.

Nevertheless, Dr. Blair was concerned that the couple's interest in S/M would lead to dangerous or illegal activities. He attempted to show that Mr. Jones had a sexual interest in children, but admitted that there was no evidence to support this belief. Despite this, he said Mr. Jones could pose a risk to Ed in the future. Dr. Blair admitted there was no evidence that the couple were ignorant or careless, but he worried about "the effects on the child if Ms. Smith were to die or become impaired during sexual activity."[27]

Worse still, Dr. Blair decided that the couple's consensual sexual activities constituted domestic violence. And while noting that "the child has not observed it," Dr. Blair wildly speculated that "he is exposed to the after-effects," even though "I don't have enough information to understand what the effects on the child might be."[28]

As a result of Dr. Blair's alarm and recommendations, the court severely limited the mother's visitation and custody rights, ended her alimony, and required her to attend psychotherapy for almost a year—specifically focusing on domestic violence. The court ended Ed's relationship with Mr. Jones, even though all parties agreed Ed had a better relationship with him than with his biological father. All of this, despite Dr. Blair's opinion that the boy was well-adjusted and healthy.

It is heartbreakingly ironic that, although victims of domestic violence rarely have their children taken from them, the court's insistence on treating Ms. Smith as a victim of domestic violence provided the rationale for limiting her contact with her own child.

According to the National Coalition for Sexual Freedom, there are hundreds of tragic cases like this every year. Says national forensic expert Dr. Charles Moser, "We know of no cases where the parent admitting to S/M interests obtained or retained custody of the minor."[29] America's family courts are directed to act in the best interests of the children they see. Ignorance about sexual behavior, whether S/M, bisexuality, nonmonogamy, or anything else, can make it impossible for courts to fulfill this mandate.

Compassionate Americans look back in shame at the distorted rulings that historically mar our otherwise proud legal system. Decisions involving runaway slave Dred Scott, the Japanese internment camps, and the denial of women's right to vote fill us with wonder: "What were those judges thinking?" The time will come when our descendents look back on the routine denial of child custody to capable, caring parents who happen to make love the "wrong" way or to the "wrong" gender, and they will wonder the same thing about us.

GAY AMERICANS

According to every study of American sexual behavior, some 30 or 40 million heterosexual men and women have same-gender sex one or more times in their lives. Of course, they remain straight. They're straight.

About 10 million Americans have sex with people of the same gender throughout their adult lives. Like everyone else, most of these Americans fall in love at some point. Like everyone else, they want to be left alone to go to work, raise their kids, pay their bills, and watch TV. They're not looking for approval, just the chance to live a decent life. And they want their basic rights—visiting their partner in the hospital, handling their kids' school stuff, keeping their job even though their boss hates "fags."

That's it. That's the whole gay thing.

But some people are obsessed with homosexuality, seeing it as a poison that must be stopped. They talk about protecting themselves and their loved ones from the evil Gay Agenda. Here, for example, is the guiding principle behind the American Family Association's (AFA) opposition to this Gay Agenda:

> We oppose the efforts of the gay movement to force its agenda in educa-
> tion, government, business and the workplace through law, public policy
> and the media . . . We oppose the effort to convince our culture that be-
> cause individuals participate in homosexual behavior, they have earned
> the right to be protected like racial and other minority groups.[30]

But the AFA has it wrong. It isn't having gay sex that earns you protection in America. It's being American. That's why blacks and Mormons and the handicapped are "protected"—because they're American. That's all that gays want—the normal protections of all Americans.

So besides wanting "protection," what is this Gay Agenda?

"Middle America better take note. Last night Hollywood exposed its own corrupt agenda. [It] is no doubt on a mission to homosexualise America," said Stephen Bennett of Straight Talk Radio, after the 2006 Golden Globe Awards honored films like *Brokeback Mountain* and *Capote*.[31]

What does that even mean? If Bennett thinks gays are lined up around the block to have sex with him, he's flattering himself. Are gays determined to seduce straights? Of course not. Do they want to destroy marriage? No, they cherish it so much, they want to join it! But not because they want the cake, the dress, or the flowers. They want the civil rights. Yes, every state is in the marriage business, and it awards financial, legal, and parenting rights to mar-ried people. That's what gay Americans want—the "special rights" the govern-ment gives the people it marries.

How would this affect anyone else's marriage? In Massachusetts, the only state that allows same-sex marriage, the heterosexual divorce rate has *gone down.* Some would chide that gay marriage helps *protect* "traditional" marriage. No one's marriage is threatened by same-sex marriage any more than your friendships are threatened by mine.

But 29 U.S. senators took time out from fighting global terrorism, our de-clining education system, and skyrocketing health care costs this summer to sponsor an amendment to our sacred Constitution. It would prevent any state from allowing same-gender marriage "or the legal incidents thereof" (those "special rights" gay people want).[32]

The Republican Party would soil our beautiful Constitution by pandering to some of its constituents' worst fears. "When America's values are under attack, we need to act," said Senate Majority Leader Bill Frist (R-TN). Yes, we must maintain the American value of discrimination, enshrining it in our beloved Constitution.

This legal discrimination already exists in a range of parenting arenas, such as child custody (gays lose it) and adoption (difficult or against the law).[33] Referring to the fact that some states allow same-sex couples to adopt children, radio host Janet Parshall told Larry King, "[I] think what you have in many respects is state-sanctioned child abuse."[34] Would Larry King have sat there quietly if she had said this about adoption by black or Jewish parents?

Not that it will change any minds, but there are dozens of published psychological and sociological studies showing that children of gay parents do just as well as children of heterosexual parents.[35]

Christian conservatives say that homosexuality offends God (They mean, of course, *their* god). I am perfectly willing to believe that—but so what? Lots of what we do in the United States offends their God: working on the Sabbath, heterosexual adultery, drinking alcohol, blasphemy. None of these is illegal in the United States, because "offending God" isn't a crime.

So why should homosexuality be legally disadvantaged, just because some people don't like who they have sex with? The fundamental agreement in America is that just doing something that offends others' beliefs will never be illegal. That's rule number one in America, remember? "Life, liberty, and the pursuit of happiness."

The Family Research Council (FRC) says that once people are allowed to marry someone of the same gender, they will want the right to marry animals. Yes, they really said that. They can't really believe that, but it's part of the systematic lies and distortions of the Religious Right. Along with Focus on the Family, Concerned Women for America, and other groups, FRC's goal is to scare people.[36]

The real story is that the Republican Party has decided to mobilize Christian believers. Since communism is dead, and terrorism apparently doesn't scare people enough, homosexuality is the most frightening thing they can think of. Karl Rove predicted that putting an antigay measure on the 2004 Ohio ballot would bring millions of new evangelical voters to the polls, and it worked perfectly, reelecting George Bush. Blaming liberal, urban, young, sex-crazed homosexuals for the fear, alienation, depression, and powerlessness that average Americans feel (as the result of the President's policies) is bad karma, but very smart politics. Having persuaded conservative Christians that gays want to steal their country, Republicans are promising to protect them from this insidious threat.

And since the government and Religious Right are already waging a War on Sex, the civil rights of gays and other sexual minorities can be just one more front, one more casualty-strewn battleground.

This is one way in which the War on Sex is part of something bigger and far more sinister.

SEXUAL RIGHTS AS HUMAN RIGHTS

Communities throughout the United States feel free—no, feel compelled—to discriminate against sexual minorities. Cities, counties, and states are zoning their clubs out of existence, disrupting their erotic activities, destroying their families, and undermining their health. This process is weakening respect for the law, disenfranchising millions of citizens, and building anger and shame in them.

Since no one actively thanks government for leaving them alone, the only time government hears from a constituency about sexuality is when they complain. There is no organized constituency of sexual people (who have learned to remain as invisible to the authorities as possible), so there's no effective way to repudiate unfair accusations or challenge the resulting laws. Sexual minorities are essentially sitting ducks for whatever opposition to their activities gathers steam.

For better or worse, the American government is famous for its human rights agendas. Between 2002 and 2005, for example, the Bush Administration urged that:

- China let people pursue any religious belief they want;
- Russia let people read what they want;
- Iran stop executing gay people;
- North Korea let people access the Internet;
- Afghanistan let women and men mingle socially;
- Pakistan and Nigeria prevent the torture and execution of women who engage in non-approved sexual conduct.

These are fine ideas. And we should start implementing them in America.

Chapter Fifteen

Revolutionizing American Government—Bad News for Democracy

If adult entertainment has so many customers, why is there so little outcry when these businesses are harassed, chased out of town, or closed? Why don't customers hold elected city councils, state assemblies, and local judges accountable? Why don't they challenge uninformed local churches, hostile civic groups, and biased media?

Adult entertainment is a textbook example of the limits of democracy, and the tyranny of the loud. Since local institutions do typically respond to pressure, a vocal minority can shut down what a majority won't speak up about. That's why it's so crucial that everyone agree on the basic rules of fair governance, an agreement that does *not* exist in America when it comes to sexuality. Certain rights are so fundamental that they must *not* be put up for a vote. A majority should not have the right to strip the minority of its rights, a danger that both Alexis de Tocqueville and John Stuart Mill foresaw almost two centuries ago.

Most people aren't shy about revealing the kind of car they drive; if Toyotas were banned, satisfied Toyota owners would make a fuss. Similarly, most people will tell you their favorite food, and if it were suddenly subject to a huge tax or limits on availability, its devotees would squawk.

But despite the size of its audience, adult entertainment patrons are not eager to reveal their interests. We live in such a sex-negative environment that adult customers around the country are shamed and demonized; few Americans are willing to lose their job or marriage simply to keep the local strip club open. Since patronizing adult businesses is typically a hidden activity, no one can support it in the normal open way that true democracy requires. Customers won't write letters to the editor, complain to their city councilman, educate their clergy. And so, realistically, supporting the rights of adult entertainment can only be done (1) in principle, and (2) by outside organizations. Opponents of adult businesses exploit this by claiming *they* speak for the community, pretending that they don't know that the community is full of customers and supporters who feel intimidated about speaking out—upstanding taxpayers and parents like us.

Opponents of adult entertainment typically focus on denying a *business's* right to function, to "just make money" and "degrade" sexuality. They rarely mention their *neighbors'* rights to consume this entertainment. Citizens for Community Values, for example, says adult businesses "prey upon unsuspecting towns, cities, and counties that don't have [preventive] legislation in place, in order to open their 'sex-for-sale' establishments."[1] You'd think these businesses were kidnapping unwilling townspeople and forcing them to watch the "sex for sale." This is the same manipulative strategy that focusses on denying "pornographers'" rights without discussing *consumers'* rights, and attempting to limit broadcasters' rights without discussing *viewers'* rights.

A naïf might imagine that if only the consumers of adult material would reach a critical mass, they would become a political force, but if that were true, it would have happened already. Millions of Americans already go to swing clubs, and tens of millions more patronize strip clubs, massage parlors, adult bookstores, nude beaches, home sex toy parties, X-rated DVDs, and other forms of adult entertainment. But the social sanction against such activities is so strong that almost no one will stand up and defend what he or she does, much less assert its wholesomeness.

Democracy isn't working, because one side (anti-pluralism and pro-censorship) represents cultural (although not behavioral) normativity, while the other side (consumers of adult materials) suffers with cultural dystonia (typically involving shame, guilt, and silence). In an environment so ambivalent and negative about sexuality, the typical individual will deny and fear his or her eroticism. So when the civic subject is in any way related to sexuality, any pro-sex voice dies in the throat. This civic paralysis means that sex-positive individuals will always be dramatically marginalized. It will be almost impossible to gather the momentum needed to reach the threshold of political influence—of *civic visibility*.

And so, one group, the Parents Television Council (PTC), can generate over 98 percent of all indecency complaints to the Federal Communications Commission (FCC) over the past two years (and via a mechanical e-mail blaster, at that). As the Cato Institute's Adam Thierer notes, the PTC is quickly acquiring a "heckler's veto" over programming in America, as many of the shows they complain about receive significant fines or are even driven off the air.[2]

But virtually no one writes to the FCC outraged that same-gender kissing is forbidden on network television 24 hours per day; no one complains when shows are tortured with bleeps and electronic gauze. The FCC received very few complaints that the Rolling Stones were muzzled on their 2006 Super Bowl halftime performance—exactly as they had been on the *Ed Sullivan Show* 40 years ago. And when something with sexual integrity sneaks in—Chris Rock on Comedy Central, a condom machine in a nightclub bathroom, the cleavage parade on Oscar night, a pharmacy that carries emergency contraception without a fuss—sex-positive people are pleased to remain invisible, rather than enjoying a moment out of the closet and telling *someone,* "Yes, this works for me. I like living in this world. Thank you."

Seventy years after its founding, America was torn by one of the bloodiest civil wars the world had ever seen. Both sides fought like they understood it was a war for the soul of the nation. One hundred forty years after that, we again face a profound conflict about the soul of our nation. Will it be a secular, pluralist democracy as the Founders envisioned, or a theocratic, authoritarian one like the land they left behind?

Those who war on sex often remind us that the Founders wanted everyone to worship as he or she desired. They leave out a crucial detail—the Founders wanted no institution forcing or shaping that worship. Today's War on Sex is a struggle over whether or not institutions will have the right to force Americans to worship—to conform to a single vision of "morality," "chastity," "decency," "family values," even "faith."

When the Civil War ended in 1865, boys and men from each side wearily embraced and shared what little food there was. They stopped to worship their common God, and talked about planting their common crops. In years to come, these former enemies would gather together on the Gettysburg battlefield and embrace again, marveling at how they had changed each others' lives forever.

I don't see us doing this for many generations, if ever. Those who war on sex mistrust my vision of individual autonomy, sexual integrity, faith in pluralism, and tolerance of differences. They hate what they perceive as our arrogance, narcissism, hubris, and dependence on reason rather than fear. They particularly resent living in a world that will not let them completely run away from their sexual impulses and crippling guilt.

Democracy, secularism, and pluralism are messy, scary, and inefficient—unlike theocracy or totalitarianism. This radical system requires people to accept being periodically uncomfortable as the price for the benefits they get from it (benefits that start with one's own choices being tolerated by everyone else). When people are no longer willing to manage their discomfort about others' choices, our entire system breaks down.

We are looking at the early stages of this in America today, where some people don't believe they have to accept their own discomfort about others' choices. They frame their rejection of this civic requirement as their religious obligation, *but they are breaking the democratic covenant.* And we're all in trouble as a result.

What, then, will be the basis for public policy: fact, science, and personal autonomy, or faith, a single morality, and anxiety reduction? This is *the* central question in world politics today. The fact that the vehicle for America's internal discourse is sexuality shouldn't lull us into thinking we're dealing with something trivial.

We're not.

Appendix:
Declaration for Human Rights Day—
How about Sex?

December 12 is International Human Rights Day. Each year, organizations and governments around the world issue statements and resolutions. I'm in favor of just about all of them.

What we don't hear much about is sexual rights. I don't just mean freedom from rape and an end to clitoridectomies, although those goals are laudable. I mean the concept that the expression of consensual sexuality is a fundamental human right—and that every one of us deserves that right without government interference or social hysteria.

I wrote the following for the Woodhull Freedom Foundation, the national organization devoted to comprehensive sexual liberty for adults. You can explore their fascinating work at http://www.woodhullfoundation.org.

Let it be resolved in honor of International Human Rights Day:

Whereas between 2002–2005, the Bush Administration urged that:

- China allow people to pursue any religious belief they want;
- Russia allow people to read what they want;
- Iran stop executing gay people;
- North Korea let people access the Internet;
- Afghanistan let women and men mingle socially;
- Pakistan and Nigeria prevent the torture and execution of women who engage in non-approved sexual conduct;

In this same spirit, all Americans should call on our governments, from the White House down to the smallest locale, to repeal laws and reject tactics restricting our human sexual rights. We should:

- call on the federal government to stop all discrimination against gay people in the military and national security matters, including job clearances;

- call on county and state courts to adjudicate custody and other parenting cases fairly and rationally, seeking out expertise and scientific evidence rather than relying on prejudice;
- call on local jurisdictions to accept the legitimacy of a broad range of consensual sexual behavior, ending inflammatory rhetoric about not being "the kind of community that tolerates such things;"
- call on zoning boards to stop using their power discriminatorily to eliminate venues for consensual sexual expression;
- call on alcohol control boards to stop their threats to close down venues hosting law-abiding sexually-oriented events;
- call on police departments to stop sending undercover officers to observe consenting sexual behavior.

Like Western Civilization, Sexual Rights is an idea worth trying. Let's start in America.

Afterword

I've known Marty Klein for more than a quarter of a century. I have interviewed him for many of my television reports because I always thought his voice should be widely heard on our century's critical issues. That voice is on display here with these essays, courageously taking on the major issues of our day related to sex.

It is no easy task to confront sexual repression, or those who would silence others who speak out for freedom of speech about sex. Klein does this, in compelling chapters full of examples, both historical and contemporary. I know this role, as I have so often been invited on television shows, over many years, to engage in such debates. In such settings, it is common for those who want to silence others to speak over their opponents' point of view, in a literal display of attempted repression using emotional appeals instead of facts.

In his book, *America's War on Sex,* Klein is clearly waging his own war—against the repression and demonization of sex. But when he takes on topics such as abstinence-only programs, pornography, and cybersex, he should by no means be taken as promoting sexual acting out or endorsing irresponsibility. Instead, he demands facts, making us think and challenging extremists' points of view. For example, he highlights the lack of peer-reviewed studies that would support the popular but inaccurate assertion that abstinence-only education works. When Klein corrects the common myth that 'talking about sex makes kids go out and do it,' research proves that point; a study on my radio show callers has shown that not only does open talk not encourage kids to have more sex, but those who are already engaging in the act are motivated to be more careful and more aware of making smarter decisions.

Klein's e-newsletter is called *Sexual Intelligence*. In this book, he encourages us to use our intelligence instead of emotion. He bolsters us with factual examples to evaluate issues related to sexuality today from a social and political perspective. He discusses how economics drives sexual repression campaigns, and how fear is used as its fuel. Almost every aspect of sexual life, including words that are biological in nature, have been targets of attack. I remember all too well Senator Proxmire's Golden Fleece Awards protesting government funding for a study about the nature of love, and when television investigative reporter John Stossel, in a story about fertility, had to replace the word "ejaculate" in a jar, with "deposit sperm."

As Klein points out, even homespun Minnesota sage and Prairie Home Companion broadcaster Garrison Keillor was taken off the air by a Kentucky (where I grew up) radio station general manager for fear of an FCC indecency fine for twice using the word "breast." Only recently, the state of Alabama outlawed the use of vibrators—body massagers proven to help women's and couples' sexual functioning.

While America is often regarded as a role model for other countries, this does not apply when it comes to sex. For example, many delegates at United Nations conferences oppose America's policies regarding reproductive rights. Recently, the World Association of Sexology proposed its 11-point Declaration of Sexual Rights, stating that the full development of sexuality is essential for individual, interpersonal, and societal well-being, and that sexual rights are universal human rights based on the inherent freedom, dignity, and equality of all human beings. These rights include the right to sexual freedom (to express one's full sexual potential), sexual autonomy (to make autonomous decisions about one's sexual life), sexual equality, making responsible reproductive choices, sexual information based upon scientific inquiry, comprehensive sexuality education, and even sexual pleasure. Klein's thesis is consistent with these principles.

Fear is responsible for the extent of sexual problems in individuals and couples today, and must be lifted for sexual health, prevention of disease, and promotion of healthy families. Klein makes us face that fear, as well as the facts and the feelings about sexual freedoms today.

Dr. Judy Kuriansky
Series Editor, Sex, Love, and Psychology

Notes

FOREWORD

1. See *Loving v. Virginia*, 388 U.S. 1 (1967). (The Court struck down, in a lawsuit brought by the ACLU, anti-miscegenation laws that were still on the statute books in 16 states.)

2. Lindsey Gruson, "Second Thoughts on Moments of Silence in the Schools," *The New York Times*, March 4, 1984, sec. 6E.

3. See for example, Thomas Jefferson, "Eternal vigilance . . . ," *QuoteDB*, http://www.quotedb.com/quotes/2283 (April 13, 2006).

4. *Lawrence v. Texas*, 539 U.S. 558 (2003); *Romer v. Evans*, 517 U.S. 620 (1996).

5. See, for example, *Ashcroft v. American Civil Liberties Union*, 542 U.S. 656 (2004); *Ashcroft v. American Civil Liberties Union*, 535 U.S. 564 (2002); *Ashcroft v. Free Speech Coalition*, 535 U.S. 234 (2002); *United States v. Playboy Entertainment Group*, 529 U.S. 803 (2000); *Reno v. American Civil Liberties Union*, 521 U.S. 844 (1997).

6. *Lawrence v. Texas*, 539 U.S. 558 (2003).

7. *Bowers v. Hardwick*, 478 U.S. 186 (1986).

8. John Bartlett, *Bartlett's Familiar Quotations*, ed. Justin Kaplan (Boston: Little, Brown, and Company, 1992), 643.

9. John Stuart Mill, *On Liberty* (Indianapolis: Hackett, 1978 [1859]), 73.

10. See note 6 above, 562.

11. See, for example, *Nebraska Press Ass'n v. Stuart*, 427 U.S. 539, 582 (1976); *Smith v. California*, 361 U.S. 147, 169 (1959).

12. See note 6 above.

13. See note 6 above, 590.

14. *Brown v. Board of Education*, 347 U.S. 483, 74s.ct. 686 (1954).

15. *Planned Parenthood v. Casey*, 505 U.S. 833 (1992).

16. See note 15 above, 851.

17. President, American Civil Liberties Union; Professor of Law, New York Law School. For research assistance with this Foreword, Professor Strossen gratefully acknowledges Steven Cunningham (NYLS '99) and Brenna Sharp (NYLS '07).

CHAPTER TWO

1. Hannah Brückner and Peter Bearman, "After the Promise: The STD Conse-quences of Adolescent Virginity Pledges," *Journal of Adolescent Health* 36, no. 4 (2005): 271–78.

2. www.religioustolerance.org/abonbr.htm.

3. Judith Levine, *Harmful to Minors: The Perils of Protecting Children from Sex* (Minneapolis: University of Minnesota Press, 2002), 90.

4. John Moore, "Former POW, Senator Accused Kerry of Treason," *Useful Fools,* March 10, 2004, http://www.tinyvital.com/BlogArchives/000751.html.

5. Lectures in various locales, 1980–2000.

6. Debra Hauser, "Five Years of Abstinence-Only-Until-Marriage Education: Assessing the Impact," *Advocates for Youth,* http://www.advocatesforyouth.org/PUB-LICATIONS/stateevaluations.pdf, 5.

7. Scott Williams, "Abstinence Becomes a Business," *Milwaukee Journal Sentinel,* October 9, 2000. sec. 510(B) (abstinence-only program funding alone supports more than 700 programs nationwide); See also, Peggy Burch, "Just Say 'Not Yet' Lecturer Pushes 'Sexual Revolution'—Abstinence," *The Commercial Appeal,* October 14, 2000, sec. G1 (describing "Aim for Success" abstinence-only program, a family business that runs abstinence-only education programs in schools in eight states).

8. The World Health Organization and other researchers agree that, over a pe-riod of a year, about 99 percent of the uninfected partners of "always" condom users remained HIV negative. BBC News, "Condoms: The Science," *BBC News,* June 27, 2004, http://news.bbc.co.uk/1/hi/programmes/panorama/3845011.stm.

9. National Center for HIV, STD and TB Prevention, Division of HIV/AIDS Prevention, "HIV/AIDS among Men Who Have Sex with Men, " July 2005. *Depart-ment of Health and Human Services, Centers for Disease Control and Prevention,* July 2005, http://www.cdc.gov/hiv/PUBS/Facts/msm.htm.

10. Abstinence Clearinghouse, "Take the Condom Quiz," brochure available from http://www.abstinence.net.

11. Matt Apuzzo, "Study: Abstinence May Lead to Risky Acts," *SFGate.com,* March 18, 2005, http://sfgate.com/cgi-bin/article.cgi?file=/news/archive/2005/03/18/na-tional/a115514S47.DTL.

12. See http://www.silverringthing.com.

13. "The Pledge," in *60 Minutes.* First broadcast May 22, 2005 by CBS.

14. Sexuality Information and Education Council of the United States, "SIECUS State Profiles: A Portrait of Sexuality Education and Abstinence-Only-Until-Mar-riage Programs in the States Released Today," *SIECUS,* March 23, 2005, http://www.siecus.org/media/press/press0095.html.

15. Professional Data Analysts, Inc. and Professional Evaluation Services, "Min-nesota Education Now and Babies Later Evaluation Report 1998–2002," as prepared for the Minnesota Department of Health, January 2004.

16. Peter Bearman and Hannah Brückner, "Promising the Future: Virginity Pledges and the Transition to First Intercourse," *American Journal of Sociology* 106, no. 4 (2001): 859–912.

17. See note 1 above.

18. Marty Klein, "Virginity Pledges >>STDs," *Sexual Intelligence,* April 2005, http://www.sexualintelligence.org/newsletters/issue62.html#four.

19. "For Many, Abstinence Doesn't Work," *Sexual Intelligence,* August 2003, http://www.sexualintelligence.org/.

20. United States House of Representatives, Committee on Government Reform, Minority Staff, Special Investigations Division. *The Content of Federally Funded Abstinence-Only Education Programs,* prepared for Representative Henry A. Waxman (Washington, DC: Government Printing Office, 2004), http://www.democrats.reform.house.gov/Documents/20041201102153–50247.pdf.

21. Clara S. Haignere, Rachel Gold, and Heather J. McDaniel, "Adolescent Use of Condoms and Abstinence: Are We Sure We Are Teaching What Is Safe?" *Health Education and Behavior* 26, no. 1 (1999): 43–54.

22. Marty Klein, "Government Report: Abstinence Programs Lie," *Sexual Intelligence,* January 2005, http://www.sexualintelligence.org/.

23. Of course, the whole Bush administration is antiscience: global warming, pollution, overfishing, Plan B, and so forth. In 2004, the government's own CDC website ignited a firestorm with its deliberate inaccuracies about sexual health. In 2005, it even tried to appoint a veterinarian to head the Women's Health Division of the FDA.

24. Bill Frist, speech at the Health Legacy Partnership (HELP) conference, Washington, DC (October 22, 2003).

25. See note 1 above.

26. See note 13 above.

27. Committee on Economic, Social and Cultural Rights, 22nd session. *General Comment 14. The Right to the Highest Attainable Standard of Health,* Paras. 12(B), 16 and Note 8, 2000, http://hrw.org/reports/2002/usa0902/USA0902–07.htm#P729_181328.

28. Ibid, *General Comment 24(52), General Comment on Issues Relating to Reservations Made Upon Ratification or Accession to the Covenant or the Optional Protocols Thereto, or in Relation to Declarations Under Article 41 of the Covenant,* U.N. Human Rights Committee, 52nd sess., 1989, para. 11; and *General Comment 14. The Right to the Highest Attainable Standard of Health,* Committee on Economic, Social and Cultural Rights, para. 12(b) and note 8.

29. See *General Comment 14. The Right to the Highest Attainable Standard of Health,* Committee on Economic, Social and Cultural Rights, paras. 12(b), 16 and note 8.

30. *General Comment 24(52), General Comment on Issues Relating to Reservations Made Upon Ratification or Accession to the Covenant or the Optional Protocols Thereto, or in Relation to Declarations Under Article 41 of the Covenant,* U.N. Human Rights Committee, 52nd sess., 1989, para. 11.

31. Office of the United Nations High Commissioner for Human Rights and the Joint United Nations Programme on HIV/AIDS, "HIV/AIDS and Human Rights-International Guidelines" (from the Second International Consultation on HIV/AIDS and Human Rights, Geneva, September 23–25, 1996), U.N. Doc. HR/PUB/98/1, Geneva, 1998, para. 38(h).

32. "Conclusion, " in *Ignorance Only: HIV/AIDS, Human Rights and Federally Funded Abstinence-Only Programs in the United States, Human Rights Watch* 14, no. 5 (September 2002), http://hrw.org/reports/2002/usa0902/USA0902–08.htm#P796_199849.

33. Report on Web site of Human Rights Watch, http://hrw.org/reports/2002/usa0902/USA0902–07.htm#P697_173261.

34. "Protocol Additional to the Geneva Conventions of August 12, 1949, and Relating to the Protection of Victims of Non-International Armed Conflicts (Protocol II). Adopted on June 8, 1977 by the Diplomatic Conference on the Reaffirmation and Development of International Humanitarian Law Applicable in Armed Conflicts," *Office of the United Nations High Commissioner for Human Rights,* http://www.unhchr.ch/html/menu3/b/94.htm.

CHAPTER FOUR

1. The Planned Parenthood Federation of America, "The Assault on Birth Control and Family Planning: Executive Summary" (New York: The Planned Parenthood Federation of America, 2003), 2.

2. Senator Richard Durbin speaking on the floor of the Senate on the Partial-Birth Abortion Ban Act of 2003, March 11, 2003, S3469.

3. As Pope Benedict said in his first encyclical, "Monogamous marriage" is on a par with "the image of a monotheistic God." The pope notes that "marriage based on exclusive and definitive love becomes the icon of the relationship between God and his people and vice versa." Heterosexual romantic love is described as "the one in particular [that] stands out [from all other love] . . . where body and soul are inseparably joined and human beings glimpse an apparently irresistible promise of happiness."; See, Rocco Palmo, "The Surprising Message Behind 'God Is Love,'" *Beliefnet,* 2006, http://beliefnet.com/story/184/story_18403_1.html.

4. "Evangelicals and STD's," *SexInfo,* http://www.soc.ucsb.edu/sexinfo/?article=stds&refid=039.

5. It also raises the standard of living for entire countries. See the ongoing work of International Planned Parenthood Federation (http://www.plannedparenthood.org) and the Alan Guttmacher Institute (http://www.guttmacher.org/).

6. Shulamith Firestone, *The Dialectic of Sex: The Case for Feminist Revolution* (New York: Morrow, 1970).

7. Although the Catholic hierarchy had trouble accepting test-tube babies at first, and the most conservative still reject artificial insemination.

8. K. Greenwood, and L. King, "Contraception and Abortion," in *Women in Society,* ed. Cambridge Women's Studies Group (London: Virago, 1981).

9. Patricia Spallone, "Reproductive Technology and the State: The Warnock Report and its Clones," in *Made to Order: The Myth of Reproductive and Genetic Progress,* ed. Patricia Spallone and Deborah Lynn Steinberg (Oxford: Pergamon), 173-174.

10. Ann Friedman, "Over-the-Counter Insurgency," *Mother Jones,* November 29, 2005, http://www.motherjones.com/news/update/2005/11/planb_timeline.html.

11. Ibid.

12. James Dobson, "HPV Epidemic Plagues Young People," *Focus on the Family,* uExpress, January 12, 2003, http://www.uexpress.com/focusonthefamily/index.html?uc_full_date=20060108.

13. Ibid.

14. Debora MacKenzie, "Will Cancer Vaccine Get to All Women?" *New Scientist.com,* April 18, 2005, http://www.newscientist.com/channel/sex/mg18624954.500.

15. Marty Klein, "FDA Bad-Mouths Condoms," *Sexual Intelligence,* December 2005, http://www.sexualintelligence.org/newsletters/issue70.html#four.

16. Associated Press, "Debate Ranges over Condom Labeling," *FOXNews. com,* June 29, 2005, http://www.foxnews.com/story/0,2933,160981,00.htm.

17. Henry J. Kaiser Family Foundation, "Vatican Continues to Debate Condom Use to Prevent HIV Transmission, Church Leaders, Theologians Say," *The Body: The Complete HIV/AIDS Resource,* March 22, 2004, http://www.thebody.com/kaiser/2004/mar22_04/vatican_condoms.html.

18. According to studies by the FDA and the National Abortion Federation, there are no known long-term risks associated with using mifepristone and miso-prostol. Feminist Women's Health Center, "The Abortion Pill: Mifepristone and Misoprostol for Early Abortion," *Feminist Women's Health Center,* October 25, 2005, http://www.fwhc.org/abortion/medical-ab.htm.

19. The Planned Parenthood Federation of America, "Planned Parenthood Sues to Protect South Dakota Women," *Planned Parenthood,* June 6, 2005, http://www.plannedparenthood.org/pp2/portal/media/pressreleases/pr-050606-abortion.xml.

20. Guttmacher Institute, State Policies in Brief, "Mandatory Counseling and Waiting Periods for Abortion," *Guttmacher Institute,* May 1, 2006, http://www.guttmacher.org/statecenter/spibs/spib_MWPA.pdf.

21. Guttmacher Institute, State Policies in Brief, "'Choose Life' License Plates," *Guttmacher Institute,* May 1, 2006, http://www.agi-usa.org/statecenter/spibs/spib_CLLP.pdf.

22. Center for Reproductive Rights, "2005 Mid-Year Report," *Center for Reproductive Rights,* 2005, http://www.crlp.org/st_leg_summ_midyear_05.html.

23. National Abortion Federation, "Bush's Strategy to Restrict Reproductive Freedom: A Chronology," *National Abortion Federation,* 2005, http://www.prochoice.org/policy/national/bush_strategy.html.

24. Guttmacher Institute, "State Focused on Reproductive Health in 2005," *Guttmacher Institute,* January 12, 2006, http://www.guttmacher.org/media/inthe-news/2006/01/12/index.html; National Abortion Federation, "Threats to Abortion Rights," *National Abortion Federation,* http://www.prochoice.org/policy/states/states_threats.html.

25. Evelyn Nieves, "S.D. Abortion Bill Takes Aim at 'Roe': Senate Ban Does Not except Rape, Incest," *washingtonpost.com,* February 23, 2006, http://www.washingtonpost.com/wp-dyn/content/article/2006/02/22/AR2006022202424.html.

26. Dahlia Lithwick, "Smells Like Teen Snogging: Kansas' Wacky Attorney General Smells Sex Everywhere," *Slate,* February 2, 2006, http://www.slate.com/id/2135328.

27. Kline has already attempted to subpoena the abortion records of adult women on the pretext of fighting child abuse, and has filed suit to terminate state funding of abortions for Medicaid beneficiaries. Ibid.

28. The Henry J. Kaiser Family Foundation, "Pregnancy & Childbirth: Women in U.S. Having More 'Unwanted' Pregnancies, Study Says; Reasons for Shift Unknown," *Kaisernetwork.org,* December 20, 2005, http://www.kaisernetwork.org/daily_reports/rep_index.cfm?DR_ID=34414.

29. The Abortion Access Project, "Fact Sheet: The Shortage of Abortion Providers," *The Abortion Access Project,* http://www.abortionaccess.org/newpages.php?id=63.

30. Ibid.

31. Megan Cooley, "Catholic Hospitals Refuse Patients Contraception," *Women's eNews,* February 4, 2003, http://www.womensenews.org/article.cfm/dyn/aid/1209.

32. B. A. Robinson, "Abortion and Roman Catholic Hospital Mergers," *Religious Tolerance.org*, December 8, 2000, http://www.religioustolerance.org/abo_rcc.htm.

33. http://www.stlouisreview.com, August 30, 2002.

34. Gary Heinlein, "Bill Would Ban Over-Counter Sales of Morning-After Pill: As FDA Examines Nonprescription Sales of Drug, a State Lawmaker Aims to Ward Off Its Widened Use," *Detroit News Online*, November 25, 2005, http://www.detnews.com/apps/pbcs.dll/article?AID=/20051125/POLITICS/511250337/1003/METRO.

35. The Unborn Victims of Violence Act (also known as "Laci and Conner's Law"), signed into law by President George W. Bush on April 1, 2004.

36. See note 18 above.

37. Lynn M. Paltrow, "Prison or Rehab: What Is the Best Place for a Pregnant Woman Using Illicit Drugs?" *ReconsiDer: Forum on Drug Policy*, http://www.reconsider.org/asp/biography.asp?SpeakerID = 1501; *Ferguson v. City of Charleston*, 532 U.S. 67 (2001).

38. Guttmacher Institute, State Policies in Brief, "Refusing to Provide Health Services," *Guttmacher Institute*, February 1, 2006, http://www.guttmacher.org/statecenter/spibs/spib_RPHS.pdf.

39. Adam Sonfield, "New Refusal Clauses Shatter Balance between Provider 'Conscience,' Patient Needs," *The Guttmacher Report on Public Policy* 7, no. 3 (August 2004), http://www.guttmacher.org/pubs/tgr/07/3/gr070301.html.

40. Ibid.

CHAPTER SIX

1. Brent Bozell, Parents Television Council, http://www.parentstv.org/ptc/community/speech.htm.

2. "Dick Cavett and Comedy on the Streets," *San Jose Mercury News*, May 4, 1994. Also at http://www.bookreporter.com/community/quote/02-09.asp, at September 1.

3. Advocates for Youth, "European Approaches to Adolescent Sexual Behavior & Responsibility," *Advocates for Youth*, 2006, http://www.advocatesforyouth.org/news/events/stdytour.htm.

4. The Parents Television Council, "Comedy Central Roast Brings Unspeakable Vulgarity into Two-Thirds of American Homes," *PTC Insider* 7, no. 10 (October 2005) http://www.parentstv.org/ptc/publications/insider/2005/October.pdf.

5. *The 60th Annual Golden Globe Awards*, first broadcast January 19, 2003 by CBS. Directed by Chris Donovan and Al Schwartz.

6. See Timothy Taylor, *The Prehistory of Sex* (New York: Bantam, 1997).

7. Mary Calderone, conversation with author, spring 1987.

8. Michael Scherer, "The FCC's Cable Crackdown," *Salon.com*, August 30, 2005, http://archive.salon.com/news/feature/2005/08/30/fcc_indecency/index_np.html.

9. Robert Corn-Revere, "Can Broadcast Indecency Regulations Be Extended to Cable Television and Satellite Radio?" *Progress on Point* 12, no. 8 (May 2005), http://www.pff.org/issues-pubs/pops/pop12.8indecency.pdf.

10. Censorship crusader Senator Ted Stevens (R-AK), among others, is using the same justification to restrict programming on cable TV. See his Congressional "decency"

hearings, for example, March 11, 2005, http://www.sfgate.com/cgi-bin/article.cgi?file=/n/a/2005/03/01/national/w141707S29.DTL.

11. Motion Picture Production Code of 1930, articles 1, 2, and 3, www.artsreformation.com/a001/hays-code.html.

12. James R.W. Bayes, Kathleen A. Kirby, and Martha E. Heller, "Third Circuit Court of Appeals Revisits Earlier Decision on Media Ownership Rules," Wiley Rein & Fielding LLP, October 2004, http://www.wrf.com/publication_newsletters.cfm?ID=11&year=2004&publication_ID=9525&keyword=].

13. Marjorie Heins, personal email to author, April 17, 2006. See also her media democracy fact sheet at http://www.fepproject.org/factsheets/mediademocracy.html.

14. Kevin J. Martin, Letter to Parents Television Council concerning f-word decision, December 5, 2003, http://www.parentstv.org/PTC/fcc/2003/martin-letter2.htm.

15. See note 8 above.

16. http://www.theorator.com/bills108/hr3717.html.

17. Michael Hayes, "Bush Signs Indecency Bill, Fines for Broadcasters Increase Tenfold," *Xbiz News*, June 16, 2006, http://xbiz.com/news_piece.php?id=15545.

18. Notable exceptions are Emancipation, Prohibition, and criminalizing contraception.

19. James Poniewozik, "The Decency Police," *Time Archive*, March 28, 2005, http://www.time.com/time/archive/preview/0,10987,1039700,00.html.

20. Jeff Jarvis, "The Shocking Truth About the FCC: Censorship by the Tyranny of the Few," *BuzzMachine*, November 15, 2004, http://www.buzzmachine.com/archives/2004_11_15.html.

21. Todd Shields, "FCC Hires Conservative Indecency Critic," *Mediaweek*, August 8, 2005, http://www.mediaweek.com/mw/news/recent_display.jsp?vnu_content_id=1001010563.

22. Kids First Coalition, home page, http://www.kidsfirstcoalition.org.

23. Penny Nance, on Fox News Live with Bob Sellers, July 19, 2004. See http://www.mediamatters.org/items/200407200005.

24. See note 21 above.

25. Ibid.

26. Jeff Jarvis, "The Daily Stern," *Buzz Machine*, March 7, 2004, http://www.buzzmachine.com/archives/2004_03_07.html#006461.

27. Jim Dyke, http://www.televisionwatch.org.

28. Ben Scott, http://www.americanprogress.org/site/pp.asc?c=biJRJ80VF&b=480225.

29. *New York Times*, December 30, 1969.

30. Ben Charney, "Janet Jackson Still Holds TiVo Title," *CNET News.com*, September 29, 2004, http://news.com.com/Janet+Jackson+still+holds+TiVo+title/2100-1041_3-5388626.html.

31. *New York Times*, November 28, 2004.

32. CNN Newsnight Aaron Brown, "Debate over FCC Guidelines," *CNN.com*, November 17, 2004, http://transcripts.cnn.com/TRANSCRIPTS/0411/17/asb.01.html.

33. For example, see the mission statement of Morality in Media, at http://www.moralityinmedia.org/.

34. Carole Jenny, T.A. Roesler, and K.L. Poyer, "Are Children at Risk for Sexual Abuse by Homosexuals," *Pediatrics* 94, no. 1 (1994): 41-44.

35. See, for example, Alfred Kinsey, *Sexual Behavior in the Human Male* (Philadelphia: WB Saunders, 1948); and Alfred Kinsey, *Sexual Behavior in the Human Female* (Philadelphia: WB Saunders, 1953); also various SIECUS publications.

36. See, for example, Focus on the Family's annual ex-gay conference, Love Won Out, "A dynamic one-day conference addressing, understanding and preventing homosexuality" in which gays and their families are told that homosexuality is "preventable and treatable." http://www.lovewonout.com/.

37. The video is produced by We Are Family Foundation. http://www.wearefamilyfoundation.org/; "SpongeBob, Barney Promote 'Gay' Agenda? 61,000 Schools to Receive 'We Are Family' Video with Lesson Plan," *WorldNetDaily,* January 6, 2005, http://www.worldnetdaily.com/news/article.asp?ARTICLE_ID=42253.

38. Geneva Collins, "Buster to Visit Gay Moms on Some pubTV Channels," *Current.org,* January 31, 2005, http://www.current.org/ch/ch0502buster.shtml.

39. "Tinky Winky Comes out of the Closet," *Jerry Falwell's National Liberty Journal,* February 1999, http://www.nljonline.com/index.php?option=com_content&task=view&id=269&Itemid=0.

40. Jerry Falwell, "Children's Television Programming," *Jerry Falwell Ministries,* February 10, 1999, http://www.falwell.com/?a=news&news=prstubb.

41. Nicholas A. Jackson, "Public Libraries, the Left, and the Corruption of Children," *The Conservative Voice,* August 8, 2005, http://www.theconservativevoice.com/articles/article.html?id=7377.

42. See note 8 above.

CHAPTER SEVEN

1. Rob Garver, "The Family Research Council Says Anti-clerical Judges Pose a Greater Danger Than Al-Qaeda," *The American Prospect Online Edition,* April 13, 2005, http://www.prospect.org/web/page.ww?section=root&name=ViewWeb&articleId=9499.

2. "Chapter VII. Discrimination Based on Gender and Sexual Orientation," in *Ignorance Only: HIV/AIDS, Human Rights and Federally Funded Abstinence-Only Programs in the United States, Human Rights Watch* 14, no. 5 (September 2002), http://hrw.org/reports/2002/usa0902/USA0902-06.htm.

3. National Abortion Federation, "Bush's Strategy to Restrict Reproductive Freedom: A Chronology," *National Abortion Federation,* 2005, http://www.prochoice.org/policy/national/bush_strategy.html.

4. Advocates for Youth, "Will the Politics of Teen Sex Stop a Cancer Vaccine?" *Advocates for Youth,* 2005, http://www.advocatesforyouth.org/publications/cancervaccine.htm.

5. Tad Walch, "Family Group Draws BYU into Porn Fray," *deseretnews.com,* September 25, 2003, http://deseretnews.com/dn/view/0,1249,515034237,00.html.

6. Steven Ertelt, "Planned Parenthood Abortions Increase, Now 20 Percent of U.S. Total," *LifeNews.com,* December 12, 2005, http://www.lifenews.com/nat1900.html.

7. See note 1 above.

8. *Lawrence v. Texas,* 539 U.S. 558, 27 (2003).

9. Ken Tucker, "Station Pulls Keillor for 'Offensive Content'," *Billboard Radio Monitor,* August 12, 2005, http://billboardradiomonitor.com/radiomonitor/news/business/net_syn/article_display.jsp?vnu_content_id=1001014255.

10. George Washington, "Labor to Keep Alive...," *QuoteDB,* http://www.quotedb.com/quotes/1271.

11. Parents Television Council, "Frequently Asked Questions," *Parents Television Council,* 2004, http://www.parentstv.org/PTC/faqs/main.asp#Arent%20you%20violating%20First%20Amendment%20freedoms%20by%20censoring%20TV%20shows.

12. Daniel Weiss, "Porn Feeds Human Trafficking," *DenverPost.com,* January 27, 2006.

13. Jerry Falwell, "The Moral Majority Coalition," *Jerry Falwell Ministries,* http://www.falwellsecure.com/libertyalliance/otgh/.

14. House Government Reform Committee, Subcommittee on Criminal Justice, Drug Policy and Human Resources, *CDC's Human Papillomavirus (HPV) and Cervical Cancer Prevention Activities,* March 11, 2004.

15. "Hollywood Sinks to New, All-Time Moral Low to 'Homosexualize' America," *Straight Talk Radio,* January 17, 2006, http://www.earnedmedia.org/sbm0117.htm.

16. Brian Skoloff, "Ave Maria Co-Founder Backs Off Moral Stance," *HeraldToday. com,* March 5, 2006, http://www.bradenton.com/mld/bradenton/news/local/14019307.htm?source=rss&channel=bradenton_local.

17. J. Bennett Guess, "CBS, NBC Refuse to Air Church's Television Advertisement: United Church of Christ Ad Highlighting Jesus' Extravagant Welcome Called 'Too Controversial'," *The United Church of Christ,* November 30, 2004, http://www.ucc.org/news/u113004a.htm.

18. Ron Suskind, "Without a Doubt," *NYTimes.com,* October 17, 2004.

19. Jeremiah Denton, "Who's Kerry?" *WorldTribune.com,* April 4, 2004, http://www.worldtribune.com/worldtribune/WTARC/2004/guest_denton_4_04.html.

20. Nicholas A. Jackson, "Public Libraries, the Left, and the Corruption of Children," *The Conservative Voice,* August 8, 2005, http://www.theconservativevoice.com/articles/article.html?id=7377.

21. "President Bush Signs Unborn Victims of Violence Act of 2004: Remarks by the President at Signing of the Unborn Victims of Violence Act of 2004," *The White House,* April 1, 2004, http://www.whitehouse.gov/news/releases/2004/04/20040401–3.html.

22. CNN Larry King Live, "Debate over Gay Marriage," *CNN.com,* January 17, 2006, http://transcripts.cnn.com/TRANSCRIPTS/0601/17/lkl.01.html.

23. "U.S. Senate Judiciary Committee Hearing on Judge Samuel Alito's Nomination to the Supreme Court, Part II of II," *washingtonpost.com,* January 9, 2006, http://www.washingtonpost.com/wp-dyn/content/article/2006/01/09/AR2006010901016.html.

24. Nick Farrell, "Watching Web Porn Is 'Cheating'," *vnunet.com,* June 12, 2002, http://www.vnunet.com/vnunet/news/2119054/watching-web-porn-cheating.

25. Kevin J. Martin, Letter to Parents Television Council concerning f-word decision, December 5, 2003, http://www.parentstv.org/PTC/fcc/2003/martinletter2.htm.

26. Abstinence Clearinghouse, "First Lady Laura Bush Endorses Abstinence," *Abstinence Clearinghouse,* January 18, 2006, http://www.abstinence.net/library/index.php?entryid=2480.

27. Eric Schlosser, "The American Sex Industry," unpublished work, 1997.

28. Diane, "Culture of Fear, Culture of Death," *ToughEnough.org*, May 22, 2005, http://toughenough.org/2005/05/culture-of-fear-culture-of-death.html.

29. See note 12 above.

30. Morality in Media, et al., Letter to President George W. Bush re Supreme Court nominee, July 14, 2005, http://www.obscenitycrimes.org/news/Bush_letter_re_Sup_Ct_nominee_(Jul05).pdf.

31. Tom Strode, "Life Digest: Mass. To Promote Destructive Stem Cell Research; Calif. Reconsiders Assisted Suicide; S.D. Pro-Life Bills Now Law," *BPNews.net*, April 4, 2005, http://www.bpnews.net/bpnews.asp?ID = 20511.

32. See note 13 above.

33. "Is Sex Ever Really 'Safe,'" Focus on the Family, http://www.troubledwith.com/stellent/groups/public/@fotf_troubledwith/documents/articles/twi_013892.cfm?channel=Parenting%20Teens&topic=Sexual%Activity&sssct=Background%20Info.

34. Oppose Censorship in Omaha, "Censorship in Omaha," *Oppose Censorship in Omaha*, January 2005, http://www.omaha-neb.com/censorship.html.

35. See note 20 above.

36. "Bush Added to the Nuremberg Files," *The Christian Gallery*, 2001, http://www.christiangallery.com/bushnuremberg.html.

37. Aubree Bowling, "Worst TV Show of the Week: Crossing Jordan," *Parents Television Council Publications*, January 16, 2005, http://www.parentstv.org/PTC/publications/bw/2005/0116worst.asp.

38. Jane Lampman, "Churches Confront an 'Elephant in the Pews'," *The Christian Science Monitor*, August 25, 2005, http://www.csmonitor.com/2005/0825/p14s01-lire.html.

39. "The Pledge," in *60 Minutes*, first broadcast May 22, 2005 by CBS.

40. Peter Lattman, "Justice Alito's Thank-You Note to James Dobson," *The Wall Street Journal Online*, March 2, 2006, http://blogs.wsj.com/law/2006/03/02/justice-alitos-thank-you-note-to-james-dobson/.

CHAPTER EIGHT

1. The federal government also spent *multi-millions* of dollars on such operations in 2005; for example, on pursuing and prosecuting Edward Wedelstedt of Littleton, Colorado, for operating a chain of adult video arcades. See http://www.freespeechcoalition.com/wedlestedtsentenced1.htm.

2. Larry Walters, personal phone call to author, February 3, 2006.

3. *City of Erie v. Pap's A.M.*, 529 U.S. 277 (2000).

4. Officials in San Bernardino, CA are trying to blur the distinction between prostitution and erotic dancing in an obvious attempt to close local strip clubs. The local district attorney alleges that women dancers are having sex with each other in front of men who pay to watch, which he says is prostitution. Since the California Penal Code describes prostitution as "any lewd act between persons for monies or other considerations," this legal strategy could actually succeed; Marty Klein, "Carpal Tunnel Censorship?" *Sexual Intelligence*, August 2000, http://www.sexualintelligence.org/newsletters/issue06.html#carpal.

Christies Cabaret in Greensboro, North Carolina, is a typical case. They were involved in court for five years after challenging the law preventing performers from touching their breasts while dancing (see Association of Club Executives, http://www.acenational.org/). The *Déjà Vu* case in Cincinnati lasted six years. The *Pap's A.M.* case in Erie lasted ten years.

5. San Antonio, TX. See Marty Klein, *Sexual Intelligence: An Electronic Newsletter,* Issue 59, January 2005, www.SexualIntelligence.org/newsletters/issue59.html#five, January, 2005.

6. *Renton v. Playtime Theatres,* 457 U.S. 41 (1986).

7. Dissenting in *Boos v Berry,* 485 U.S. 312 (1988).

8. Three years later, Antonin Scalia said the same thing in attempting to uphold Texas's ban on sodomy in *Lawrence v Texas,* 539 U.S. 558 (2003).

9. The Free Expression Policy Project, "Fact Sheet on Sex and Censorship," *The Free Expression Policy Project,* http://www.fepproject.org/factsheets/sexandcensorship.html.

10. *Flanigan's Enterprises, Inc. v. Fulton County, GA,* 00-11152, 11th circuit, February 20, 2001.

11. *City of Los Angeles v. Alameda Books,* 535 U.S. 425 (2002).

12. S.B. No. 27 Sec. 4301.25 Section 3, http://www.legislature.state.oh.us/bills.cfm?ID=126_SB_27.

13. Judith Lynne Hanna, "Exotic Dance Adult Entertainment: A Guide for Planners and Policy Makers," *Journal of Planning Literature* 20, no. 2 (2005): 116–134.

14. Ibid., "Undressing the First Amendment and Corsetting the Striptease Dancer," The Drama Review 42, no. 2 (Summer 1998): 38–69; Ibid., "Exotic Dance Adult Entertainment: Ethnography Challenges False Mythology," *City and Society* 15, no. 2 (2003): 165–193.

15. Mark Kernes, "The Myth of Secondary Effects," Free Speech Coalition, http://www.freespeechcoalition.com/Myth_of_Secondary_Effects.htm.

16. October, 2005

17. "Canadian Court Lifts Ban on 'Swingers' Clubs," MSNBC.com, http://www.msnbc.msn.com/id/10561253.

18. Matt O'Conner "Adult Businesses Prepare to Challenge Georgia Law," *XBiz,* December 19, 2005, http://www.xbiz.com/news_piece.php?cat=2&id=12274.

19. And about 6,000,000 used, according to the study: Michael Castleman and Amy Levinson, "Toys in the Sheets: The First Survey of Americans Who Use Sexual Enhancement Products," San Francisco, CA: Lawrence Research Foundation, 1997.

20. *Williams v. Pryor,* see http://www.atheism.about.com/library/decisions/privacy/bldec_WilliamsPryor.htm.

21. Marty Klein, "Heads Spin over Vibrator Sales Ban," *Sexual Intelligence,* August 2004, http://www.sexualintelligence.org/newsletters/issue54.html#two.

22. See Philip D. Harvey, *The Government vs. Erotica: The Siege of Adam and Eve* (Amherst, NY: Prometheus Books, 2001).

23. E-mails released by federal investigators in June 2005 suggest that Reed secretly accepted payments from Jack Abramoff to lobby against Indian casino gambling and oppose an Alabama education lottery at the same time that Abramoff was being paid to promote Indian casino gambling. Additional e-mails released in November 2005 show that Reed also worked for another Abramoff client seeking to block a congressional ban on Internet gambling. Reed has said he did not know the funds came from pro-gambling sources. http://www.washingtonpost.com/wp-dyn/content/custom/2005/12/23/CU2005122300939.html#reed.

24. http://www.uaprogressiveaction.com/archives/2006/02/irs_delivers_wa.html.

25. Richard Enrico, personal conversation with author, Fall 1989.

26. *City of Erie v. Pap's A.M.*, 529 U.S. 277 (2000).

27. http://www.ccv.org/About_CCV.htm.

28. Citizens for Community Values website/promotion.

29. Val Walton, "ABC, Club Square Off over Topless Dancer Ban," *al.com*, November 1, 2005, http://www.al.com/news/birminghamnews/index.ssf?/base/news/113084029965690.xml&coll=2.

CHAPTER NINE

1. George Lakoff, *Don't Think of an Elephant* (New York: Chelsea Green Publishing Company, 2004).

2. Marty Klein, *Sexual Intelligence*, Issue 30, August 2002, http://www.sexualintelligence.org/newsletters/issue30.html#five.

3. Nicholas A. Jackson, "Public Libraries, the Left, and the Corruption of Children," *The Conservative Voice*, August 8, 2005, http://www.theconservativevoice.com/articles/article.html?id=7377.

4. Jan LaRue, "Let's End 'Victims of Pornography Month'," *Morality in Media, Inc.,* 2004, http://www.moralityinmedia.org/index.htm?obscenityEnforcement/EndVOP-Month.htm.

5. Alan Leshner, personal conversation with author, June 3, 2003.

6. Robert Rector and Kirk A. Johnson, "Teenage Sexual Abstinence and Academic Achievement," *The Heritage Foundation*, October 27, 2005, http://www.heritage.org/Research/Welfare/whitepaper10272005-1.cfm, at footnote 1.

7. Steven Ertelt, "Planned Parenthood Abortions Increase, Now 20 Percent of U.S. Total," *LifeNews.com*, December 12, 2005, http://www.lifenews.com/nat1900.html; The Alan Guttmacher Institute, "Trends in Abortion in the United States, 1973–2002," The Alan Guttmacher Institute, January 2003, http://www.guttmacher.org/presentations/trends.pdf; Ceci Connolly, "Number of Abortion Providers at Its Lowest in Three Decades," *The Tech*, January 22, 2003, http://www-tech.mit.edu/V122/N65/Abortion.65w.html.

8. Daniel Patrick Moynihan, "Everyone has a right to...," BrainyQuote, http://www.brainyquote.com/quotes/authors/d/daniel_patrick_moynihan.html.

CHAPTER TEN

1. We'll see this happen again in a few years when porn is common on cell phones and iPods, and satellite radio becomes standard in middle-class homes.

2. See Timothy Taylor, *The Prehistory of Sex* (New York: Bantam Books, 1996); and James Petersen and Hugh Hefner, *The Century of Sex* (New York: Grove Press, 1999).

3. Source for this list, unless noted, is Cindy Kuzma, "Sex and Technology: A Brief History" Planned Parenthood Federation of America, May 13, 2005, http://www.ppfa.org/pp2/portal/files/portal/webzine/artsculture/art-050513-sex-technology.xml.

4. Peter Johnson, "Pornography Drives Technology: Why Not to Censor the Internet" *Indiana Law*, 1997, http://www.law.indiana.edu/fclj/pubs/v49/no1/johnson.html.

5. See note 3, discussed in a phone call with *LibidoMag* editor Jack Hafferkamp, December 29, 2006.

6. WorldScreen.com, "TV Data: North America," WorldScreen.com, 2002, http://www.worldscreen.com/northamerica.php; see also note 4 above.

7. Oblivious to how these sexual uses made the now-valuable technology feasible for mass adoption in the first place.

8. David Sobel, "Internet Filters and Public Libraries," *First Amendment Center Publication* 4, no. 2 (October 2003), 14, http://www.firstamendmentcenter.org/PDF/Internetfilters.pdf.

9. Antonio Gulli and Alessio Signorini, "The Indexable Web Is More Than 11.5 Billion Pages," The University of Iowa Department of Computer Science, 2005, http://www.cs.uiowa.edu/~asignori/web-size/.

10. Sobel, 11.

11. Center for Democracy & Technology, "Pennsylvania Web Blocking," Center for Democracy & Technology, 2004, http://www.cdt.org/speech/pennwebblock/.

12. For more information, see Bennett Haselton, *Peacefire.Org,* 2006, http://www.peacefire.org/.

13. "Internet Filter Review," *TopTenREVIEWS,* 2006, http://internet-filter-review.toptenreviews.com/.

14. Bennett Haselton, email to author, January 15, 2006.

15. Robyn Greenspan, "Porn Pages Reach 260 Million," eSecurityPlanet.com, September 25, 2003, http://www.esecurityplanet.com/trends/article.php/3083001.

16. Jonathan Wallace, "Federal Courts Use Censorware; Free Speech Advocates Object," The Censorware Project, 1998, http://censorware.net/reports/courtcen.html.

17. Karen Jo Gounaud, "Kids and the Internet: The Promise and Perils," *Testimony to the U.S. National Commission of Libraries and Information Science, Family Friendly Libraries,* http://www.nclis.gov/about/November-1988.pdf, page 105.

18. Sobel, 10.

19. Sobel, 9. According to their Web site, Family Friendly Libraries is affiliated with Focus on the Family and the Family Research Council.

20. Sobel, 10.

21. "A Briefing on Public Policy Issues Affecting Civil Liberties Online,". *Center for Democracy & Technology Policy Post* 9, no. 12 (June 23, 2003), http://www.cdt.org/publications/pp_9.12.shtml.

22. Only California, New York, and Maine reject this federal money—specifically because they don't want Washington controlling their libraries.

23. *U.S. v. ALA,* 539 U.S. 194 (2003).

24. *U.S. v. ALA,* 539 U.S. 194, No. 02–361 (2003).

25. Will Doherty, "Sex and the Internet" (presentation to the Society for Scientific Study of Sexuality, San Jose, CA, April 12, 2003).

26. Doherty, "Sex and the Internet."

27. Bennett Haselton and Jamie McCarthy, "Blind Ballots: Web Sites of U.S. Political Candidates Censored by Censorware," *Peacefire.org,* November 7, 2000, http://www.peacefire.org/blind-ballots/.

28. See note 16 above.

29. Doherty, "Sex and the Internet."

30. Greg Lindsay, "Cybersitter Decides to Take a Time Out," *TIME Digital*, August 8, 1997, http://web.archive.org/web/20000830022313/http://www.time.com/time/digital/daily/0,2822,12392,00.html.

31. Doherty, "Sex and the Internet."

32. Xeni Jardin, "MSN Spaces: Seven Dirty Blogs," *Boing Boing*, December 2, 2004, http://www.boingboing.net/2004/12/02/msn_spaces_seven_dir.html.

33. *United States of America V. Robert Alan Thomas and Carleen Thomas*, F. App. 0032P (6th Cir.), Nos. 94-6648/6649 (1996), *Electronic Privacy Information Center*, http://www.epic.org/free_speech/censorship/us_v_thomas.html.

34. See note 21 above.

35. "A Briefing on Public Policy Issues Affecting Civil Liberties Online," *Center for Democracy & Technology Policy Post* 10, no. 14 (September 10, 2004), http://www.cdt.org/publications/pp_10.14.shtml.

36. 18 U.S.C. §2257.

37. See note 35 above.

CHAPTER TWELVE

1. Barton Gellman, "FBI Forms Anti-Porn Squad 'I Guess This Means We've Won the War on Terror,' One Agent Says," *SFGate.com*, September 21, 2005, http://www.sfgate.com/cgi-bin/article.cgi?file=/c/a/2005/09/21/MNGRSER4141.DTL&type=printable.

2. Ibid.

3. A key informant in this illegal bullying was Donald Wildmon, head of the then-new Religious Right pressure group, National Federation of Decency, which is now known as the powerful American Family Association. See Marjorie Heins, *Sex, Sin, and Blasphemy: A Guide to America's Censorship Wars* (New York: New Press, 1998), 70.

4. Jane Lampman, "Churches Confront an 'Elephant in the Pews'," *Christian Science Monitor*, August 25, 2005, http://www.csmonitor.com/2005/0825/p14s01-lire.html.

5. Jan LaRue, "What Are the U.S. Attorneys Doing for Victims of Pornography?" *Victims of Pornography*, 2004, http://www.victimsofpornography.org/Articles%20in%20The%20News/Articles%20in%20the%20News.htm.

6. Traditional Values Coalition, "The Plan to Win over Judicial Tyranny," *Our Battle Plan to Take Back Our Courts*, 2006, http://www.ourbattleplan.com/plan.php.

7. For example, on February 6, 2006, police seized more than *700* adult DVDs from Dr. John's Lingerie in Omaha, Nebraska, claiming they had *reason to believe* that *some* of the store's inventory violated state obscenity laws. "Dr. John" Haltom himself was victimized by a number of raids at his store in Omaha, resulting in him serving several jail terms. See "Censorship in Omaha," *Oppose Censorship in Omaha*, January 2005, http://www.omaha-neb.com/censorship.html.

8. "ASACP Data Indicates 99.9% of Validated CP Reports Are Not Related to Adult Entertainment Industry," Association of Sites Advocating Child Protection, *ASACP*, June 24, 2005, http://www.asacp.org/press/pr062405.html.

9. As common as these allegations are, not a single one has ever been proven.

10. Nadine Strossen, *Defending Pornography: Free Speech, Sex, and the Fight for Women's Rights* (New York: Anchor Books, 1995), 299.

11. Such as the price of gasoline, the convenience of banking online, the luxury of not feeling uncomfortable at the beach, and the comfort of not being faced with too many questions about sexual things from one's children.

12. Robert McGinley, phone call with author, February 20, 2006.

13. Civil action 05-CV-01126-WDM-BNB.

14. 983 F.2d 248, 250 (DC Cir. 1990); 965 F.2d 8484 (10th Cir. 1992).

15. See note 8 above.

16. Eugene Volokh, "Obscenity Crackdown—What Will the Next Step Be?" *CATO Institute*, April 12, 2004, http://www.cato.org/tech/tk/040412-tk.html.

17. From the government's subpoena, reported in Howard Mintz, "Feds After Google Data," *MercuryNews.com*, January 19, 2006, http://www.siliconvalley.com/mld/siliconvalley/13657386.htm.

18. *Gonzales v. Google, Inc.* (2006), can be found at "The Internet and the Law," *Find Law*, http://news.findlaw.com/hdocs/docs/google/gonzgoog11806m.html.

19. Cameron W. Barr, "Policing Porn Is Not Part of Job Description: Montgomery Homeland Security Officers Reassigned after Library Incident," *washingtonpost.com*, February 17, 2006, http://www.washingtonpost.com/wp-dyn/content/article/2006/02/16/AR2006021602066.html.

20. I am indebted to Alan Soble for a remarkable discussion of this concept in his book. Alan Soble, *Pornography, Sex, and Feminism* (Amherst, NY: Prometheus Books, 2002).

21. See also Marty Klein, "The Meaning of Sex," no. 3, May 15, 1997, http://sexed.org/archive/article03.html.

22. That's one part of what makes obscenity trials so bizarre. A jury of strangers sitting fully clothed in a conference room watches porn to determine what it means to the so-called average person (whoever that is). How can their experience possibly relate to the experience of watching the film at home, in private, naked, playing with a consenting partner or masturbating alone?

23. One amateur site, http://www.voyeurweb.com/, gets over 2 million hits per day. It features new photos from over 100 contributors each day. That's over 30,000 unique individuals or couples each year on this site alone.

24. As sex educator Dr. Sol Gordon says, "guilt can provide the energy for the repetition of behavior people feel conflicted about."

CHAPTER THIRTEEN

1. In America, various indecency statutes still criminalize blasphemy and moral turpitude. At least the punishments involve fines and prison rather than death

2. Dan Bilefsky, "Denmark Is Unlikely Front in Islam-West Culture War," *NYTimes.com*, January 8, 2006, http://select.nytimes.com/search/restricted/article?res=FA0D12FC34540C7B8CDDA80894DE404482.

3. BBC News, "Mass Anti-Cartoon Rally in Beirut: Hundreds of Thousands of Shia Muslims in Lebanon Have Turned a Religious Ceremony into a Protest over Cartons Satirising the Prophet Muhammad," *BBC News*, February 9, 2006, http://news.bbc.co.uk/1/hi/world/middle_east/4697286.stm.

4. *Planned Parenthood v. Casey*, 505 U.S. 833 (1992).

5. Richard John Neuhaus, "A Voice in the Relativistic Wilderness: The Pope Crusaded For "Moral Truth." We Should Welcome His Help," *Christianity Today.com*, April 4, 2005, http://www.christianitytoday.com/ct/2005/109/44.0.html.

6. Ibid.

7. Richard Owen, "Limbo Consigned to History Books," *Times Online*, November 30, 2005, http://www.timesonline.co.uk/article/0,13509–1897480,00.html.

8. Boethus says this in his The Consolation of Philosophy; see Kenneth Humphreys. "Putting the Dark into the Dark Age: 'Wonderful Events That Testify to God's Divine Glory," *Jesus Never Existed*, 2004, http://www.jesusneverexisted.com/dark-age.htm; for Tertullian, see David King, "Chapter 9: Religion," in *A Guide to the Philosophy of Objectivism*, http://rous.redbarn.org/objectivism/Writing/DavidKing/GuideToObjectivism/CHAPTR09.HTM.

9. "President Bush Signs Unborn Victims of Violence Act of 2004: Remarks by the President at Signing of the Unborn Victims of Violence Act of 2004," *The White House*, April 1, 2004, http://www.whitehouse.gov/news/releases/2004/04/20040401–3.html; see also National Abortion Federation, "Bush's Strategy to Restrict Reproductive Freedom: A Chronology," *National Abortion Federation*, 2005, http://www.prochoice.org/policy/national/bush_strategy.html.

10. Joshua Green, "Roy and His Rock," *The Atlantic Online*, October 2005, http://www.theatlantic.com/doc/200510/roy-moores-ten-commandments.

11. Jesse Gordon, "Pat Buchanan on Abortion," *On The Issues: Every Political Leader on Every Issue*, 2000, http://www.issues2000.org/Celeb/Pat_Buchanan_Abortion.htm.

12. Thomas B. Edsall, "Christian Right Mobilizes for Judge: Conservative Tilt Sought on Bench," *washintonpost.com*, January 9, 2006, http://www.washingtonpost.com/wp-dyn/content/article/2006/01/08/AR2006010801069.html.

13. Laurie Goodstein, "Minister, a Bush Ally, Gives Church as Site for Alito Rally," *NY Times.com*, January 5, 2006, http://select.nytimes.com/gst/abstract.html?res=FB0B14F63A540C768CDDA80894DE404482.

14. Ronald Stoddart, director of Nightlight Christian Adoption, Washington, DC, May 24, 2005.

15. http://www.pfaw.org/pfaw/general/default.aspx?oid=17625.

CHAPTER FOURTEEN

1. "Church Passes the Plate for County Fight," Free Speech X-Press, February 10, 2006, http://www.freespeechcoalition.com/FSCview.asp?coid=301.

2. See, Marty Klein, *Your Sexual Secrets: When to Keep Them, When and How to Tell* (New York: Dutton, 1988).

3. Many commentators were shocked, *shocked* that men and women told Kinsey they enjoyed such "perversions" as oral sex, premarital sex, and anal sex. One of the main reasons his two best-selling volumes were damned after publication in the late 1940s and 1950s—*and continue to be damned*—is that some people don't want to know that so-called normal people actually do these things.

4. Julia Heiman, personal e-mail to author, fall 2005.

5. From memo written by Judy Guerin, Executive Director, National Coalition for Sexual Freedom, December 6, 2001, 2.

6. Robert Peters, "The Link between Pornography and Violent Sex Crimes," *Morality in Media*, 2004, http://www.moralityinmedia.org/index.htm?pornsEffects/Porn-Crime-Link-RWP.htm.

7. Marty Klein, "Oprah and Dr. Phil: Sex for the Simpleminded," *Playboy*, January 2003, 33–34; Also available at http://sexed.org/archive/article18.html..

8. National Coalition for Sexual Freedom, "Violence and Discrimination Survey," *National Coalition for Sexual Freedom*, 1999, http://www.ncsfreedom.org/library/viodiscrimsurvey.htm.

9. Joseph Marzucco, "Healthcare Attitudes of Individuals in the Alternative Sexual Lifestyle; Bondage and Discipline, Sadism and Masochism," unpublished study, 2005.

10. The Planned Parenthood Federation of America, "For the Record: Lesbian, Gay, Bisexual, Transgender, Questioning (LGBTQ)," *Planned Parenthood*, 2006, http://www.plannedparenthood.org/pp2/portal/files/portal/webzine/ontherecord/otr-archive-lgbtq.xml.

11. Friendship Express, "What Is Swinging?" 1994, http://friendshipexpress.com/SWINGING.HTM. Data gathered by private swing clubs indicate that 90 percent of swingers identify a religious preference and 47 percent regularly attend religious services (Friendship Express, 1994; Miller, 1994; also Gould, 1999).

12. See, Terry Gould, *The Lifestyle: A Look at the Erotic Rites of Swingers* (Toronto, Ontario: Random House, 1999), 392. This is confirmed in various survey data.

13. I am indebted to Terry Gould for bringing this investigation and other details to public attention in *The Lifestyle* (see note 12 above).

14. Robert McGinley, phone call with author, February 20, 2006.

15. Dave Gill and others ultimately lost their jobs for criminally overreaching their mandate. (See note 14 above.)

16. See note 11 above.

17. See note 14 above.

18. See note 12 above.

19. Actually, heterosexual swingers' demographics and lifestyle make them one of the lowest risk groups for STDs, especially HIV. See Gould, 1999; Richard J. Jenks, "Swinging: A review of the Literature," *Archives of Sexual Behavior* 27, no. 5 (1998): 507–21.

20. Milo Fencl, personal conversation with the author, November 10, 2005.

21. Nancy Fencl, personal conversation with the author, November 10, 2005.

22. David Holthouse, "Civil Libertines: The Battle over Phoenix's Groundbreaking Sex-Club Ban Moves into Federal Court," *phoenixnewtimes.com*, March 18, 1999, http://www.phoenixnewtimes.com/issues/1999–03–18/feature2.html.

23. Sex Blog, "US Judge Orders Sex Club to Shut Down," *Salon.com*, May 28, 2005, http://blogs.salon.com/0003915/2005/05/29.html.

24. National Coalition for Sexual Freedom, "History of the NCSF: Hard at Work to Defend Your Rights," *National Coalition for Sexual Freedom*, May 2003, http://www.ncsfreedom.org/history.htm.

25. Sam Janus and Cynthia L. Janus, *The Janus Report on Sexual Behavior* (New York: Wiley, 1993): xiii, 430.

26. Marty Klein and Charles Moser, "S/M (Sadomasochistic) Interests as an Issue in a Child Custody Proceeding," *Journal of Homosexuality* 51, no. 3 (2006): 233–42. Note that participants' names are changed to protect anonymity.

27. Ibid.

28. Ibid.

29. Ibid, p. 240

30. Austin Cline, "Religious Right: AFA, Position on Homosexuality,". *About. com,* http://atheism.about.com/library/FAQs/rr/blfaq_rr_afa_homosexuality.htm.

31. "Hollywood Sinks to New, All-Time Moral Low to 'Homosexualize' America," *Straight Talk Radio,* January 17, 2006, http://www.earnedmedia.org/sbm0117.htm.

32. The amendment was written by the Alliance for Marriage, with the assistance of Judge Robert Bork and other constitutional conservatives. The organization wants to make marriage more important, and divorce more difficult to obtain.

33. According to the 2000 census, over one-quarter of all same-sex couples live with at least one child under 18—that's over a million kids. See www.hrw.com.

34. CNN Larry King Live, "Debate over Gay Marriage," *CNN.com,* January 17, 2006, http://transcripts.cnn.com/TRANSCRIPTS/0601/17/lkl.01.html.

35. For example, N. Andersen, C. Amlie, and E. A. Ytteroy, "Outcomes for Children with Lesbian or Gay Parents: A Review of Studies from 1978 to 2000," *Scandinavian Journal of Homosexuality* 43, no. 4 (2002): 335-351; S. Dundas and M. Kaufman, "The Toronto Lesbian Family Study," *Journal of Homosexuality* 40, no. 2 (2000): 65-79.

36. Timothy J. Dailey, "The Slippery Slope of Same-Sex 'Marriage'," *Family Research Council,* http://www.frc.org/get.cfm?i=BC04C02&f=WA06B27.

CHAPTER FIFTEEN

1. Citizens for Community Values, "Sexually Oriented Businesses," *CCV.org,* http://www.ccv.org/What_is_a_Sexually_Oriented_Business.htm.

2. Adam Thierer, "Of *Desperate Housewives* and Desperate Regulators," http://www.cato.org/tech/tk/050105-tk.html.

Selected Bibliography

Elias, James, et al., eds. *Porn 101: Eroticism, Pornography, and the First Amendment.* Amherst, NY: Prometheus Books, 1999.

Gould, Terry. *The Lifestyle.* Toronto, Ontario: Random House, 1999.

Harvey, Philip. *The Government vs. Erotica.* Amherst, NY: Prometheus Books, 2001.

Heins, Marjorie. *Not in Front of the Children: "Indecency," Censorship, and the Innocence of Youth.* New York: Hill and Wang, 2001.

————. *Sex, Sin, and Blasphemy.* New York: The New Press, 1998.

Horowitz, Helen Lefkowitz. *Rereading Sex.* New York: Vintage Books, 2002.

Kincaid, James. *Erotic Innocence: The Culture of Child Molesting.* Durham, NC: Duke University Press, 1998.

Kipnis, Laura. *Bound and Gagged: Pornography and the Politics of Fantasy in America.* Durham, NC: Duke University Press, 1999.

Lane, Frederick. *The Decency Wars.* New York: Prometheus, 2006.

Levine, Judith. *Harmful to Minors.* Minneapolis, MN: University of Minnesota Press, 2002.

Lynn, Barry. *Piety & Politics: The Right-Wing Assault on Religious Freedom.* New York: Harmony, 2006.

Morone, James. *Hellfire Nation.* New Haven, CT: Yale University Press, 2003.

Petersen, James and Hugh Hefner. *The Century of Sex.* New York: Grove Press, 1999.

Strossen, Nadine. *Defending Pornography.* New York: New York University Press, 2000.

Taverner, Bill and Sue Montfort. *Making Sense of Abstinence.* Morristown, NJ: Center for Family Life Education, 2005.

Taylor, Timothy. *The Prehistory of Sex.* New York: Bantam Books, 1996.

Soble, Alan. *Pornography, Sex, and Feminism.* Amherst, NY: Prometheus Books, 2002.

Williams, Linda. *Hardcore.* Berkeley, CA: University of California Press, 1989.

About the Author

Dr. Marty Klein has been a Licensed Marriage and Family Therapist and Certified Sex Therapist for 25 years (that's 30,000 sessions). His entire career has been aimed toward a single set of goals: telling the truth about sexuality, helping people feel sexually adequate and powerful, and supporting the healthy sexual expression and exploration of men and women.

Marty's five previous books have been acclaimed by everyone from *USA Today* to *The California Therapist* to the Playboy Advisor, and are available in nine languages. A tireless speaker, Marty has given over 600 keynote speeches, training programs, and popular lectures across North America and countries including Russia, Israel, Morocco, Latvia, Austria, Turkey, and Croatia (where he is affectionately known as the Father of Sex Therapy). He estimates he has trained some 75,000 marriage counselors, nurses, psychologists, and physicians in human sexuality.

Marty has been honored by both the California Association of Marriage and Family Therapists and the Society for the Scientific Study of Sexuality. He has been an expert witness or consultant in several historic federal anti-censorship trials. For six years he has written and published the electronic monthly *Sexual Intelligence* (www.SexualIntelligence.org), whose wit, passion, and research highlights the ways in which our sexual rights are being challenged.

Marty's speaking schedule, original articles, extensive Q/A, and descriptions of all his books and tapes are available on his Web site at www.SexEd.org.

Marty lives in northern California with his wife, cactus garden, and enormous collection of rock and roll albums. He can be reached at Klein@AmericasWarOnSex.com.

Index